THE
PRESCRIPTIONS
THAT
R COUNT

THE
PRESCRIPTIONS
THAT
R COUNT

Charles F. Scheide

"PREVENTATIVE MEDICATION FOR CHURCH PROBLEMS"

(From the Pastoral Epistles)
Take as Directed: Dr. Paul, Apostle

Edited by Lorna Simcox
Typeset by Kathy Thielke
Commentary Formatted by Fran Ingersoll
Cover Design by Tom Williams

Unless otherwise indicated, all Scripture
References are from THE NEW SCOFIELD
REFERENCE BIBLE, Authorized King James
Version. © 1967 Oxford University Press.

For additional information, contact:

Dr. Charles F. Scheide, Sr.
c/o Word of Life Bible Institute
13001 Word of Life Drive
Hudson, FL 34669

Printed in the USA by

3212 East Highway 30 • Kearney, NE 68847 • 1-800-650-7888

Dedication of Appreciation

To My Family

...my wife, Joanna, and my three children, Chris, Chuck, and George, whom I love dearly, and who have "hung in there" with me through these many years of ministry, sharing in the victories, and weeping in the defeats. Your constant support and love has been a continual blessing

To My People

...they are really His, but He's assigned them to me... to those faithful members of my congregations in New York, Michigan, New Jersey and now North Carolina. It has been in the "laboratories" of these four congregations that for well over a quarter of a century the principles in this book have been tested. We have experienced blessing when the biblical prescriptions outlined were applied, and suffered when they were ignored. May the joy and memory of faithful service together bring much delight as we "keep on keeping on."

To My Students

...at the Word of Life Bible Institute (from 1977 to the present) where many of the lessons taught in this book were first verbalized in "Council Hall." Your genuine interest in that which was "passed on" was a great impetus to "put it down." May it be a source of much direction and guidance in your church life in the years ahead.

Acknowledgments

Just as there are many people to be thanked in the development of one's ministry (see "Dedication of Appreciation" and "Pass It On" - Chapter 4), there are also those people to be thanked in the production of a book. Two who stand out in the production of this book are Lorna Simcox and Kathy Thielke.

Lorna was my editor, and painstakingly poured herself into her task of endeavoring to knock the rough edges off the original manuscript in order to make the final product more readable. An experienced journalist, Lorna and her husband Tom, are missionaries serving with Friends of Israel Gospel Ministry, Inc. I first met Lorna when, as a young widow, she was a student of mine at Word of Life Bible Institute. I introduced her to the Friends of Israel where, in the providence of God, she met her husband, and the rest they say is history (still in the making).

Kathy (Mrs. Keith) Thielke is a very committed member of my congregation in North Carolina. For some time now she has set in type my weekly newspaper column, FROM THE PASTOR'S STUDY. When it came time to prepare this book for publication, Kathy, with an assist from husband Keith, accepted that responsibility as well.

To both Lorna and Kathy, who accomplished their tasks exceedingly well, I extend my deepest thanks. They are partners with me in this publication. I know they both join me in praying that these studies may be used of God in helping multiplied churches of Christ avoid those diseases that could cripple their ministries, and to help churches already suffering from such maladies to overcome them.

A Note of Apology. As you read through THE PRESCRIPTIONS THAT COUNT you will find a handful of unattributed quotations. For these I apologize. Omission of the endnotes was not intentional, but simply the result of a failure on my part to take note of where I originally secured the material. Your understanding is most appreciated.

COVER DESIGN: *Tom Williams*

CONTENTS

ADDITIONAL COMMENTARY

Foreword

As its title suggests, *Prescriptions That Count* assumes that many, if not most, churches in our contemporary age possess symptoms that are crying for spiritual diagnosis and remedy. Although this patient, the local church, is the product of a miraculous birth by its creator and sustainer, Jesus Christ, there are occasions in which a local assembly of the Body of Christ must step, as a patient, into God's "waiting room" and seek special medicinal assistance for the struggles and challenges that come from within the church itself, from the world or from Satan.

The author appropriately focuses attention on the only true source and assistance available for church problems -- God's Word -- especially as it is revealed in the Pastoral Epistles. For over a decade Charles Scheide, Sr., has taught Paul's letters to Timothy and Titus to Bible college students and to local church congregations. In addition, he has made an intensive personal study of this trilogy of New Testament books as they apply to the care and growth of local churches.

Because of this book's emphasis on "preventative medication," every pastor and church leader would be well advised to read and absorb Scheide's spiritual insights long before the next church crisis appears. *Prescriptions That Count* is at times a "medical case history" of a successful and effective servant of God who has personally encountered the opportunities, disappointments, and victories that commonly affect those who have received God's high calling for pastoral ministry. After having observed Chuck's life and ministry for two decades, I can attest that his medication is sound and it really does work!

W. Sherrill Babb, Ph.D.
President, Philadelphia Biblical University

9

Introduction

It has been my privilege to serve my Lord as a pastor for more than a quarter of a century. To be sure, we have tasted God's very rich blessings, but we have not been immune to occasional defeat. As I reflect on those years, I am convinced that nearly all the problems we faced, we brought upon ourselves. If there is anything at all that I have learned while in the ministry, it is this: Jesus Christ is the Great Physician -- not only for what ails man physically, but also for those things that ail His church as it attempts to carry out the Great Commission with which it has been charged. By failing to follow His advice as spelled out in His Word, our ministry was forced on occasion to suffer through the "illnesses" that preventative medication would have helped us to avoid.

This book rests on the premise that the Local Church is God-ordained and God-designed. Since He knows the beginning from the end, since He knows what makes the church tick and how it functions, and because He wants it to be successful, then it is logical to presume that somewhere in His Word He would divulge the formula for that success. In a general way He does that throughout Scripture; in a specific way He delineates it on the pages of three little books we know today as The Pastoral Epistles: 1 Timothy, 2 Timothy and Titus. Together, they total just 13 chapters in length. Yet those 13 chapters address a substantial share of the problems that confront the local church.

This book attempts to identify those problems and to share the

Biblical formulas...prescriptions, if you will...that will carry God's church to victory. Someone once said, "To be forewarned is to be forearmed." If you know in advance that the enemy is coming, you are wise to be prepared to meet him. The pastoral epistles forewarn us. Following God's prescription forearms us.

This book examines the problems that confronted Timothy and Titus as they endeavored to shepherd their churches in Ephesus and Crete, respectively. After identifying a potential problem, we share the preventative medication. I firmly believe that if the prescriptions designated by the Great Physician -- the ultimate author of Scripture -- are followed faithfully, many debilitating sicknesses could be avoided entirely.

So I begin this book with a plea to all those in church work. Take the prescriptions that count, and be freed from the arduous chore of performing lengthy corrective procedures, or enduring costly spiritual hospitalizations. To that end this book has been written. May God use it for His honor and His glory, to assist His people in accomplishing the task to which He has called us. May it prove to be a helpful resource to all those churches of Jesus Christ that are desirous of doing God's work, God's way.

Background of
the Pastoral Epistles

The title itself, <u>The Pastoral Epistles</u>, indicates in large measure what these books are about. They are epistles (letters) written to pastors to instruct them in the carrying out of their duties in the ministry. In this case, God inspired the elder Apostle Paul , probably in his 60's by now, to write to two younger men named Timothy and Titus. Paul wished he could be with these men as they struggled in their pastoral ministries. But since that was not possible, dispatching a letter was the next best thing. He sums up the emphasis of all three epistles when he writes to Timothy (1 Tim. 3:14-15):

> These things write I unto thee, hoping to come
> unto thee shortly; but if I tarry long, that thou
> mayest know how thou oughtest to behave thyself
> in the house of God, which is the church of the
> living God, the pillar and ground of the truth.

Titus and Timothy, probably in their 30's, had been greatly influenced by Paul and had entered the Lord's service at his urging. There is little doubt that they both came to know Christ through Paul's ministry. He addressed each of them as his "own son" in the faith, using the Greek word <u>teknon</u>, which means "a born one," rather than <u>huis</u>, which means "an adult son." Paul also attaches the qualifier "in the faith" in his address to Timothy, and "after the common faith" to Titus, leading to the conclusion that he is their spiritual father.

Timothy was born of mixed parentage. His father was Greek, his mother Jewish (Acts 16:1). In the absence of his father, who may have died, Timothy's mother Eunice and grandmother Lois schooled him as a child in the Holy Scriptures and prepared him for Paul's ministry in Timothy's hometown of Lystra. There, under Paul's preaching, Timothy apparently came to trust Christ as his Savior. It appears he grew rapidly in the faith and had been endowed with spiritual gifts that equipped him for a public ministry. Soon he was ministering at Paul's side in such places as Philippi, Thessalonica, Berea, Corinth and Ephesus. It was at Ephesus where Timothy was left on his own, becoming the "senior pastor" of the Ephesian Church.

In reading the letters to Timothy, it becomes obvious that this young man with the apparently fragile psyche was very special to the apostle. One scholar, perceiving their close, father-son relationship, has speculated that Timothy may have taken the place in Paul's heart of a son Paul lost at childbirth, at which time he may have also lost his wife. This speculation was based, in part, upon Paul's membership in the Sanhedrin, which required its members to be married, at least in later years. Although extensive research still has not proven these theories, it has provided ample evidence that the relationship these two men enjoyed, although they were a generation apart, was very special. Of all Paul's letters, none is more personal than 2 Timothy. In it, the apostle implored his young protege to hang in there... "to keep on keeping on." Restated in the words of a 20th century saint, Dr. V. Raymond Edman, the late president of Wheaton College, "It's always too soon to quit!"

Titus' background was quite different. He was a Greek believer who was converted from heathenism. Unlike Timothy, he is not mentioned in the book of Acts, though it is clear from a reference in 2 Corinthians that he belonged to Paul's ministering team. Some speculate that Titus may have been Luke's younger brother, and to avoid charges of nepotism Luke failed to mention him when he penned Acts. Once again, no such proof exists, but that may be the case nevertheless.

Both these young men had at least one important thing in common: they were left to minister in exceedingly difficult locations. In Ephesus stood the famed Temple of Diana or Artemis (the god/goddess who changed sexes), where all sorts of vile acts took place in the name of worship. It was a city famous for sorcery, superstition and sexual debauchery. Paul had ministered there personally for three years and the ministry had borne fruit. Yet, he warned that after his departure, "grievous wolves would enter in... not sparing the flock" (Acts 20:29). It is to this work and to this condition that Timothy was called.

Titus fared no better. His assignment: Crete. The people there, by their own admission, were "liars, evil beasts, lazy gluttons" (Titus 1:12). Epimenides, a legendary Cretan poet who lived some 600 years prior to Paul, originally coined that description and Paul affirmed it as still being true six centuries later. It is no wonder that Paul advised Titus as he did. When confronted by those who would cause trouble in the churches of Crete -- for the trouble-makers were professing Christians (Titus 1:16) -- Titus was to "stop their mouths" and to "rebuke them sharply" (Titus 1:11,13).

As for Paul himself, little needs to be said. This is the great champion of the Christian faith, who at one time was a "blasphemer, and a persecutor" of those who claimed the name of Christ (1 Tim. 1:13). But on the road to Damascus (Acts 9) he became a believer and the change in his life became a pattern for others to follow (1 Tim. 1:16).

It is important to note that all three pastoral epistles were letters addressed to individuals, yet Paul identifies himself as "an apostle of Christ Jesus." Surely neither Timothy nor Titus needed such substantiation. What they did need, however, was the weight of Paul's title behind them as they discharged their duties. On their own merit they could have been challenged. So Paul gives them a hammer -- the hammer of his apostleship. In those days, prior to the completion of the canon of Scripture, this substantiation gave these young men the authority they would not otherwise have had.

Formed from two Greek words apo and stello, the word apostle literally means "one who is sent forth," or "one who is sent off on a commission to do something as another's personal representative, with credentials furnished; an envoy, an ambassador." In origin, the word apostle is an Athenian Greek word that meant "the admiral of the fleet." He is the one recognized as being in charge; the senior flag officer of the fleet. What he said could not be overruled. He was, in effect, the possessor of dictatorial power. And so, an apostle was "a spiritual dictator." What he said or wrote as directed by the Spirit of God, was final. The believer had no choice but to respond affirmatively, for defying the apostle would be defying God.

The Books Themselves

1 Timothy 3:15 reveals the common thread that runs through all three of these letters: "that thou mayest know how thou oughtest to behave thyself in the house of God." Here is how the local church is to function, to behave. Herein is found divine direction for both pastor and people, "prescriptions" that will protect God's church from crippling and sometimes fatal disease.

At least three themes recur repeatedly in all three epistles, but each epistle emphasizes a different one. They are:

Church Organization
Sound Doctrine
Consistent Christian Living

It should be noted that these epistles do not appear in the order in which they were written. 1 Timothy and Titus were written about the same time following Paul's release from house arrest. 2 Timothy was written several years later from a prison cell. Thus, the chronological order is 1 Timothy, Titus, 2 Timothy. Yet their sequential order in the Bible is logical, practical and invaluable in helping us understand the flow and the purpose behind the writings:

1 Timothy = CHURCH ORGANIZATION
2 Timothy = SOUND DOCTRINE
Titus   = CONSISTENT CHRISTIAN LIVING

First you organize, so (2) you may teach, so (3) lives may be changed. That identical, practical progression is commonly used in many avenues of life. For example: churches (1) organize their program and identify the starting times of services, so (2) when the Word of God is taught people can attend. When people attend and hear the Word, (3) God can work in their lives.

Charles Erdman, in his commentary on these three dynamic little books, writes: "Church government is not an end in itself; it is of value only as it secures sound doctrine: and doctrine is of value only as it issues in life."[1] The local church must be organized so teaching may take place, because from that teaching emanates the ultimate goal of the Christian life: conformity to the person of the Lord Jesus Christ (Rom. 8:29).

So it was that these written instructions to two young undershepherds from their father in the faith gave the ministries of Timothy and Titus stability and credibility. Through Paul's direction, these pastors knew what God wanted. Today these epistles are no less important. They address areas critical to the functioning of the local church. Unlike Timothy and Titus, those of us in Christian work now have God's completed revelation to us -- the Bible. It is imperative that we use it wisely, but it is even more imperative that we USE IT. "For unto whomsoever much is given, of him shall much be required" (Luke 12:48).

ENDNOTE

1. Charles R. Erdman, *The Pastoral Epistles of Paul* (Philadelphia: Westminister Press, 1925), p. 10.

1

The Supreme Standard

It has been my privilege in recent years to conduct local church seminars dealing with church leadership. I deal with questions such as: Who is the head of the church? What are the biblically assigned responsibilities of pastors and deacons? How do these two local church offices work together? What form of church government is most biblical?

For the most part, those who attend are already involved in leadership positions. At the conclusion of one day-long seminar, a man serving as a deacon asked me if the things I had been sharing about local church leadership were all in the Bible. How he missed that I don't know, for I had been teaching for six hours. I assured him that, "Yes, the principles we have looked at today are all in the Scriptures," to which he replied, "Well, if that's true, then that's where me and the Bible disagree." I did my best to suppress my surprise and moved on to the next question, but in the back of my mind, I thought, "I hope he's the exception on that board, not the rule, or that church is in for major problems in the days ahead."

Well, he wasn't the exception. He was the rule. He was a member of a church that paid lip-service to the importance of the Word of God, its inerrancy, infallibility and authority -- but a church that was able to ignore it rather easily when the Word conflicted with the church's ideas, traditions and practices. Sure enough, within six months, a pastor committed to the Word of God and to implementing its directives was out of work, and the church was in the throes of a major split. Now, a number of years later, the church is still "hospitalized," a full recovery appears far off and that church's testimony for Christ has been severely damaged.

This grave illness could have been avoided with preventative medication. The prescription? UNDERSTAND THE IMPORTANCE OF THE SCRIPTURES and be committed to the Word of God in practice, not just in theory. Everything we believe must emanate from the Book; everything we do must hinge upon its principles.

The historic New Hampshire Confession of Faith reads:

> We believe that the Holy Bible was written by men divinely inspired, and is a perfect treasure of heavenly instruction; that it has God for its author, salvation for its end, and truth without any mixture of error for its matter; that it reveals the principles by which God will judge us; and therefore is, and shall remain to the end of the world, the true centre of Christian union, and the supreme standard by which all human conduct, creeds and opinions should be tried. (2 Tim. 3:16,17; 2 Pet. 1:19). [1]

One local church has stated its position on the Scriptures as follows:

> We believe in the Scriptures of the Old and New Testaments as verbally inspired of God, and inerrant in the original writings, and that they are of supreme and final authority in faith and life. [2]

If these two statements are genuinely believed and practiced, particularly the sections I have underlined, then every action undertaken will come under the all-penetrating eye of the Scripture.

In his two letters to Timothy, Paul clearly underscored the importance of the Word of God at five major junctures.

I.   Scripture is inspired of God -- 2 Tim. 3:16
II. Scripture is authoritative -- 1 Tim. 5:18
III. Scripture can make one wise -- 2 Tim. 3:15
IV. Scripture can furnish for service -- 2 Tim. 3:17
V.   Scripture is to be studied -- 2 Tim. 2:15

I. Scripture Is Inspired of God

R_x:

Understand the importance of the Scriptures.

2 Timothy 3:16   All Scripture is given by inspiration of God, and is profitable for doctrine, for reproof, for correction, for instruction in righteousness.

By **INSPIRATION** we mean that God has superintended the writing of Scripture or protected it from error. The Greek word used is theopneustos, which means "God-breathed." The Scofield Reference Bible states that:

> Without impairing the intelligence, and individuality, literary style, or personal feelings of the human authors, God supernaturally directed the writing of Scripture so that they recorded in perfect accuracy His comprehensive and infallible revelation to man. [3]

The Scofield note goes on to include this extremely significant statement: "If God Himself had done the writing, the written Word would be no more accurate and authoritative than it is" (note on 2 Tim. 3:16).

21

Numerous theories try to explain inspiration, but most of them are inadequate and deprive the Bible of its divine authority. Dr. Charles Ryrie, in his <u>Concise Guide to the Bible</u>, lists them:

> **The Inspired Writer Theory**: The writers of the Bible were men of great genius who either needed no supernatural help in writing the Bible, or had the help of the Holy Spirit just as any believer can have today.
>
> **The Partial Inspiration Theory:** Parts of the Bible are inspired and other parts are not. For example, the doctrinal portions are inspired, but the historical sections are not.
>
> **Karl Barth's Theory:** The Bible is a witness to the Word of God (which is Christ), but a fallible witness. This view is called neoorthodoxy.
>
> **The Inspired Concept Theory:** The concepts are inspired, but the words are not.
>
> **The Existential Theory:** The Bible becomes God's Word to me when I feel it speaking to me. It is not God's Word until I have a personal encounter with it.[4]

While these theories are interesting, they overlook the fact that Paul wrote Timothy that "ALL Scripture is given by inspiration of God." All means all -- every bit until there is no more. Only one view of inspiration reflects 2 Timothy 3:16. It is called VERBAL AND PLENARY INSPIRATION.

<u>**VERBAL**</u> emphasizes that inspiration penetrates to the very

words of Scripture. Verbal inspiration maintains that the Bible, in its original words from first to last, is the exact record of the mind and will of God as He intended it to be.

PLENARY emphasizes that the entire text in all of its parts is equally from God. History, science, genealogy, etc., are all subjects of inspiration. There is, therefore, no portion of the Word of God that is not inspired. It is <u>all</u> God-breathed.

REVELATION is the act of God revealing Himself to man and revealing truth to man which man could not otherwise know (Deut. 29:29). That revelation has taken place in two ways:

(1) <u>Natural Revelation</u>
 The universe (Ps. 19:1; Rom. 1:19-20)

Just as a watch tells us something about the watchmaker, so the universe tells us something about God. It reveals, among other things, wisdom, order, power, law. This natural revelation is limited, however, for it stops short of telling mankind of forgiveness and immortality. It offers no way of salvation, no escape from guilt, no hope, no glimpse of the future, nor can it impart even the slightest bit of holiness.

(2) <u>Special Revelation</u>
 His Word, written and living (Heb. 1:1; John 1:1)

The <u>Written Word</u> we call the Bible; the <u>Living Word</u> is His Son, the Lord Jesus Christ. It is only through special revelation that man is able to know God personally; to receive forgiveness of sin and eternal life; to understand God's plan through the ages; and to learn how to live a life pleasing to Him.

The great doctrines of the creation, the attributes and decrees of God, the nature of man, etc., are all God-revealed through

Scripture. Of all the ancient nations of the world, only Israel came to monotheism, and her knowledge was the result of direct revelation. Again, the Scofield Bible elaborates:

> 1 Corinthians 2:9-14 gives the process by which a truth passes from the mind of God to the minds of His people. (a) The unseen things of God are undiscoverable by the natural man (v. 9). (b) These unseen things God has revealed to chosen men (vv. 10-12). (c) The revealed things are communicated in Spirit-taught words (v.13). This implies neither mechanical dictation nor the effacement of the writer's personality, but only that the Spirit infallibly guides in the choice of words from the writer's own vocabulary (v.13). And (d) these Spirit-taught words, in which the revelation has been expressed, are discerned, as to their full spiritual content, only by the spiritual among believers (1Cor. 2: 15-16).[5]

Illumination is the presence and ministry of the Holy Spirit in each believer, enabling him to understand the Word of God (1 Cor. 2:10-16). This ministry was foretold by the Lord Jesus (Jn. 14:26; 16:13-15).

The Bible is often referred to as the "canon" of Scripture. Canon means "rule" -- the measuring rod used to determine which books were determined to be scriptural (or canonical) and which were not. The Old Testament canon was closed about the 5th century BC. It was accepted by the Jewish people and was confirmed by Christ in Luke 24:44-45. The early church accepted it, as does the church today. The New Testament canon was closed sometime in the 4th century AD. The criteria for determining what was included in the canon focused on the writings themselves. There were rigid tests, which included:

-- the test of <u>GENUINENESS</u> -- the writing was not a forgery. There were many spurious works.

-- the test of <u>AUTHENTICITY</u> -- the writing itself bore witness of inspiration and divine authority.

-- the test of <u>CONSISTENCY</u> -- the writing agreed with all other Scripture. There could be no conflict, even though revelation was progressive.

Although much more could be said, the point here is not to teach the Doctrine of Bibliology, but rather to underscore the fact that the Bible, all 66 books, is inspired -- God-breathed. It is the Word of God, not of men (1 Thes. 2:13), and as such, its importance can never be overestimated. When it speaks to a subject, any subject, no other voice should be permitted to drown it out.

II. Scripture Is Authoritative

1 Timothy 5:18 -- "For the Scripture saith ... "

Because the Bible is God's inspired revelation to man, it is profitable "for doctrine, for reproof, for correction, for instruction in righteousness" (1 Tim. 3:16). An extremely valuable verse speaks to this matter.

<u>Isaiah 8:20</u> -- To the law and to the testimony; if they speak not according to this word, it is because there is no light in them.

Hence, to give support to what he is about to teach, the great apostle Paul directs young Timothy to the authority of Scripture. Paul was not alone in making such an appeal. Our Lord Himself did so. In His temptation in the wilderness, He rebuffed Satan's attacks with, "It is written, 'Man shall not live by bread alone, but by every word that proceeds out of the mouth of God'" (Matt. 4:4).

For the true Christian, the Word of God must be the supreme authority in faith and practice. Unregenerate man may look for authority in other places -- the state, an infallible (?) church, individuals, reason, tradition, feelings ("I felt led"), experience (cp. Job's "comforters"), etc. But for a follower of Jesus Christ there is only one final authority -- the Word of God.

III. Scripture Can Make One Wise

> 2 Timothy 3:15 -- And that from a child thou hast known the Holy Scriptures, which are able to make thee wise unto salvation through faith which is in Christ Jesus.

While the Scriptures certainly can make one wise in many areas, at issue here is salvation. The Word of God can do what no other writing can -- take a human being who is dead in trespasses and sins and lead him to new life in Christ (Eph. 2:1). As it is written, "faith cometh by hearing, and hearing by the word of God" (Rom. 10:17).

Timothy came to know Christ through the ministry of Paul, but he was prepared beforehand by his training in the Old Testament. That instruction made him "wise unto salvation." We now extend Paul's admonition to include the New Testament as well. One writer, Thomas D. Bernard, comments:

> The significance of the Old Testament is not that it contains an account of the creation of man or the history of the fortunes of Israel; its aim is not knowledge, whether scientific or historical, but wisdom, and that unto salvation. Salvation, the salvation of man, is the final purpose of the whole Bible. [6]

IV. Scripture Can Furnish for Service

2 Timothy 3:17 -- That the man of God may be perfect, thoroughly furnished unto all good works.

While verse 16 tells us that God's Word "is profitable for doctrine, for reproof, for correction, for instruction in righteousness," verse 17 tells us to what end: to be furnished for service.

I can remember when my wife and I and our daughter (the first of three children the Lord blessed us with) moved into our first parsonage. The house was more than adequate for our needs, considering we moved from a one-bedroom apartment to a three-bedroom home. We now had a living room, kitchen, dining room, etc. It took a number of years before we fully furnished all those rooms. The same is true of our theological or ministerial house. It takes time, but the man of God can be furnished, equipped, prepared for successful service in that portion of the vineyard where he has been placed, providing he diligently studies God's Word. It is all well and good to be knowledgeable in many areas, but the one area that dare not be overlooked is knowledge of the Holy Scriptures.

V. Scripture Is To Be Studied

2 Timothy 2:15 -- Study to show thyself approved unto God, a workman that needeth not to be ashamed, rightly dividing the word of truth.

The Greek word translated "study" has a much broader connotation than we attribute to it in English. It implies to "be eager, be zealous, make every effort, to do your utmost." It really could be translated "be diligent," and is translated that way in 2 Timothy 4:9, 21 and Titus 3:12. Paul was encouraging Timothy to do his utmost to "show" himself "approved unto God" in the work to which he had been called. For Timothy, that work was to build the Ephesian church. To shepherd his church properly, Paul told him, he must be a diligent student of Scripture. He must "rightly divide (handle correctly) the word of truth," so God's desired end would be accomplished.

The same holds true today. To receive God's approval we must understand our roles as "workmen in the Word." We must diligently study the Bible or our understanding of it will be faulty, the ministry to which we have been called will fall far short of God's expectations, and our work will never merit His approval. I often tell couples in pre-marital counseling that they are not the architects of marriage. They are simply the builders. God is the architect. They are to study the blueprints and build their home as drawn. Similarly, we in church work must understand that our job is to help build the church, but in doing so we must faithfully follow the blueprints of God the architect.

As more and more churches today pay lip-service to the Word of God but falter in genuine commitment to its directives, Paul's admonition to Timothy becomes even more crucial. The farther a church moves from the Supreme Standard, the surer it is to suffer the blight of non-direction and to contract crippling, perhaps even fatal, disease. Indeed, it is not even enough that the undershepherd be dedicated to the Word, the flock must be as well. If both accept the Bible as the final authority in faith and practice, and order their lives along Scriptural principles, that church will succeed in accomplishing God's ordained goals.

UNDERSTANDING THE IMPORTANCE OF THE SCRIPTURES is one of God's most important prescriptions for a healthy and effective local church. In the God-breathed words of the great prophet Isaiah: "The grass withereth, the flower fadeth: but the word of our God shall stand forever" (Is. 40:8).

ENDNOTES

1. Edward T. Hiscox, *The New Directory for Baptist Churches* (Valley Forge, PA: Judson Press, 1894, 1962) p. 543.

2. George H. Slavin, *Basic Bible Studies* (Southfield, MI: Highland Park Baptist Church, n.d.) p. 1.

3. C. I. Scofield (E. S. English, rev.) *The New Scofield Reference Bible* (New York: Oxford University Press, 1967) p. 1304.

4. Charles C. Ryrie, *Ryrie's Concise Guide to the Bible* (San Bernadine, CA: Here's Life Pub., 1983) p. 27-29.

5. C.I. Scofield, ibid, p. 1234.

6. Thomas D. Bernard (see acknowledgment note).

2

Healthy Teaching

I once came across an excellent statement concerning the importance of reading: "He who knows how to read, but fails to do so, is no better off than he who cannot read." In the New Testament book that bears his name, James wrote something similar: "Be ye doers of the Word and not hearers only" (Ja. 1:22). It does you no good to have medicine that will prevent disease if you fail to take it. In the same vein, it does the church no good to have the Word of God if it fails to use it. Unless the teaching is biblical, it has no significant spiritual worth. Prescription #2: PREACH AND TEACH SOUND DOCTRINE.

What is sound doctrine? The word <u>sound</u> means "healthy," or "health giving." It comes from the Greek word <u>hugiainouse</u>, which is the equivalent of our English word <u>hygiene</u>. The word <u>doctrine</u> means "teaching." Together, <u>sound doctrine</u> means "healthy teaching." Incidentally, the word <u>sound</u> occurs often in the Pastoral Epistles, but nowhere else.

1 Timothy 1:10 contains the first mention of the phrase. Paul states that the law was not made for the righteous, but for the lawless. After listing many vile types of lawbreakers, he includes in that category "any other thing that is contrary to sound doctrine." Timothy and Titus were dealing with many individuals who were teaching contrary to the Word of God. Paul considered it no small matter to combat their error. How does one do that? By providing healthy teaching -- <u>sound doctrine</u>.

There are instances when these two words stand alone and instances when they are linked together. Following is a locational review with emphasis on the word <u>sound</u> as found in the King James Version.

1 Timothy 1:10	sound doctrine
1 Timothy 6:3	wholesome (same as sound) words
2 Timothy 1:13	sound words
Titus 1:9	sound doctrine
Titus 1:13	sound in the faith
Titus 2:1	sound doctrine
Titus 2:2	sound in the faith
Titus 2:8	sound speech

The word <u>doctrine</u> is used 16 times:

1 Timothy 1:3	teach no other doctrine
1:10	sound doctrine
4:6	nourished up in ...good doctrine
4:13	give attendance...to doctrine
4:16	take heed...unto the doctrine
5:17	labor in the word and doctrine
6:1	that the name of God and his doctrine be not blasphemed
6:3	to the doctrine which is according to godliness
2 Timothy 3:10	thou has fully known my doctrine
3:16	scripture...is profitable for doctrine
4:2	exhort with...doctrine
4:3	they will not endure sound doctrine
Titus 1:9	by sound doctrine...exhort
2:1	speak...sound doctrine
2:7	in doctrine showing uncorruptness
2:10	adorn the doctrine of God

Paul obviously believed that pastors must be committed to the teaching and preaching of sound doctrine. For example, it is not enough to dwell on the fact that "God is love" to the exclusion of "God is a consuming fire" (Heb. 12:29). It is not enough to exhort people to bring all their cares to Jesus without teaching them who Jesus really is. In fact, Paul warns us that failure to preach and teach sound doctrine will produce a negative condition (2 Tim. 2:15-17):

R_x:

Preach and Teach Sound Doctrine.

vs. 15 -- (POSITIVE) Study to show thyself approved unto God, a workman that needeth not to be ashamed, rightly dividing the word of truth.

vs. 16 -- (NEGATIVE) But shun profane and vain babblings; for they will increase unto more ungodliness.

vs. 17 -- And their word will eat as doth a canker. (If we fail to do the positive, we will suffer the negative consequences.)

The word translated "canker" in the King James Version is the Greek word gangraina, and would better have been translated "gangrene." In Paul's day it was a medical term used to describe a malignant sore that ate away healthy tissue. False teaching -- "profane and vain babbling" -- generates "ungodliness" that will grow like gangrene and infect the healthy members of the body of Christ. To tolerate such teaching diseases the church. If this malignancy cannot be arrested, the only recourse is to sever it from the body. Paul prescribes such action:

1 Tim. 1:3   Charge some that they teach no other doctrine
      1:4   Neither give heed to fables and endless
               genealogies, which minister questions
               rather than godly edifying.

33

4:7	refuse profane and old wives' fables
6:3-5	If any man...consent not to wholesome words...and to the doctrine which is according to godliness...from such withdraw thyself.
2 Tim. 2:16	...shun profane and vain babblings; for they will increase unto more ungodliness.
2:23	...foolish and unlearned questions avoid, knowing that they breed strifes.
2:24-25	And the servant of the Lord must not strive, but be gentle unto all men, apt to teach, patient, in meekness instructing those that oppose him...
Titus 1:9-13	...by sound doctrine...convince (refute) the gainsayers (opposers)...there are many unruly and vain talkers and deceivers...whose mouths must be stopped ...rebuke them sharply...
2:15	These things speak, and exhort, and rebuke them with all authority
3:9	...avoid foolish questions...genealogies... contentions...strivings...they are unprofitable and vain.
3:10-11	A man that is an heretic, after the first and second admonition, reject, knowing that he that is such is subverted (warped, turned inside out), and sinneth, being condemned of himself.

The dictum is clear. False teaching must not be tolerated. It must be dealt with firmly even to the point of amputation. Although serious and painful, amputation has saved the lives of many people who otherwise would have died due to uncontrollable infection. Losing a limb is tragic, but not as tragic as losing a life. People with a misguided concept of love may consider it extreme to deal with false teachers by removing them from fellowship. But sound teaching must prevail. The amputation saves the remainder of the body, and that, of course, is the desired result.

The False Teachers

It is important to understand why Paul places such stress upon the preaching and teaching of sound doctrine. It stems from a conference he held for the pastors of the Ephesian churches while he was at Miletus (Acts 20:17-38) en route to Jerusalem. Paul and Ephesus had a long history. Christianity probably first came to Ephesus when Paul stopped there briefly on his second missionary journey (Acts 18:18-19). On his third journey he stayed approximately three years, pouring into believers there the Word of God (Acts 20:31).

Now, sometime later, he calls the Ephesian church leaders together, reminds them of his earlier on-site ministry with them, and closes with these words:

For I have not shunned to declare unto you all the counsel of God (Acts 20:27).

Then he gives them an exhortation and a prophetic warning:

The Exhortation:

Take heed, therefore, unto yourselves, and to all the flock, over which the Holy Spirit hath made you overseers, to feed the church of God, which he hath purchased with his own blood (Acts 20:28).

35

The Warning:

> For I know this, that after my departing shall griev-
> ous wolves enter in among you, not sparing the
> flock. Also of your own selves shall men arise,
> speaking perverse things, to draw away disciples
> after them. Therefore watch, and remember, that
> by the space of three years I ceased not to warn
> every one night and day with tears (Acts 20:29-
> 31).

Paul was telling the Ephesian pastors to FEED their people
sound doctrine/healthy teaching, for the day was coming when
"grievous wolves" teaching heresy would descend upon the Christians to devastate them unless they were steadfast in their beliefs.
Indeed, as Paul was writing, his prophesy was already coming to
pass. The false teachers had arrived and were creating problems
for the church. No doubt there were believers who were being
"tossed to and fro, and carried about with every wind of doctrine"
(Eph. 4:14). These false teachers needed to be confronted. There
were two major types: the Judaizers and the Apostasizers.

I. The Judaizers

No false teachers were more persistent than a group of legalistic Jewish men called Judaizers. Although they believed that
salvation was a result of the death and resurrection of Jesus Christ,
they taught that man's good works also were an integral part of
the process. This teaching contradicted Paul's message of salvation by God's grace alone. The Judaizers were returning to the
bondage of the Jewish observances of days, months, years, etc.,
as well as to such acts as circumcision. Paul, through inspiration
of the Holy Spirit, declared these practices a total violation of the
grace of God. In fact, he told the Galatian believers that the

Judaizers were perverting the Gospel of Christ (Gal. 1:6-7) and making it of no effect (Gal. 2:17).

In Galatians, Paul labels such an admixture of law and grace "another gospel, which is not another" (Gal. 1:6-7). In Romans, he shows how the two principles conflict. He writes: " If it is by grace, it is no more of works; otherwise grace is no more grace" (Rom. 11:6). To the believers in Ephesus he writes: "For by grace are ye saved through faith, and that not of yourselves, it is the gift of God - Not of works, lest any man should boast" (Eph. 2:8-9). The heresy of the Judaizers was perverting the doctrine of pure grace.

Grace is most popularly defined as "unmerited favor," but it really is far more. Grace is "favor extended where wrath is deserved." When measured against God's holy standard, all members of the human race deserve nothing less than total condemnation, "for all have sinned and come short of the glory of God" (Rom. 3:23). But the marvelous truth of the grace of God is that God lifts that penalty and bestows eternal life upon an undeserving sinner when he comes to Christ. "There is, therefore, now no condemnation to them who are in Christ Jesus" (Rom. 8:1). Hence, through faith, totally apart from works (good deeds), a sinner becomes the recipient of God's "so-great salvation." Favor was extended where wrath was deserved.

Paul deals with the false teaching concerning the doctrine of grace in three significant passages:

1 Timothy 1:3-11 -- Men of a Judaistic background were attempting to be teachers of the law, but did not understand the law themselves. They did not really deny the essentials of the faith, but attempted to add to the message of pure grace. In verses 8 through 10, Paul explains to Timothy the significance of the law. "God never gave the law to save people," he points out, "but to show people how much they need to be saved." Then in verses 9 through 10, Paul lists the sinners who are convicted and condemned by the law. This listing includes nearly all the sins covered by the

10 Commandments of Exodus Chapter 20. In verse 11, Paul makes it clear that what had been entrusted to them (Paul and Timothy, and by extension, to us) was a glorious gospel, not a system of laws.

1 Timothy 4:1-8 -- Again, here is another "works" effort to please God. In this case, verse three describes the work of an ascetic abstention: of forbidding to marry and commanding to abstain from certain foods. As the passage progresses, bodily exercise, apparently beyond the point of real wisdom, becomes an issue. The Judaizers apparently believed that physical deprivation would find much favor in God's sight.

This error comes from the false conception that our physical bodies are evil just because they are physical. Consequently, these false teachers considered it quite praiseworthy to deny the body's normal appetites. However, it is both illogical and unscriptural to ascribe anything meritorious to these ascetic abstentions. In fact, Paul even calls them demonic (1 Tim. 4:1).

This subject is touched upon again in 1 Timothy 5:23 where Paul prescribes wine as a medicine for Timothy's stomach problems. Paul's rebuke of the teaching of ascetic abstentions is summarized in 1 Timothy 4:4-5:

> For every creature of God is good, and nothing is
> to be refused, if it is received with thanksgiving;
> for it is sanctified by the word of God and prayer.

Titus 1:9-16 -- Here Paul deals with Titus' ministry on the Island of Crete. Not all of Titus' problems were similar to Timothy's, but one they had in common involved the Judaizers. Paul instructs Titus:

> ...rebuke them sharply, that they may be sound in
> the faith, Not giving heed to Jewish fables and
> commandments of men, that turn from the truth
> (vs. 13-14).

After describing what awful sort of men these false teachers were (vs. 10-13), Paul describes their practice. They carried lies from house to house and even destroyed the faith of some. Whole families succumbed to their unhealthy teaching. They promoted Jewish legalism ("they of the circumcision" Titus 1:10, 3:9), which Paul rejected outright. They also taught "Jewish fables" (1:14), which probably included fanciful stories about Old Testament saints and imaginative interpretations of Old Testament genealogies (1 Tim. 1:4).

II. The Apostasizers

These constitute the second group of "grievous wolves" that will, in the last days, descend upon the church with doctrine that could devastate the church's effort to carry out the Great Commission. The key passage of identification is 2 Timothy 3:1-17. "This know, also, that in the last days perilous times shall come." Paul is referring to what we know today as apostasy, or "falling away." The New Scofield Reference Bible notes 2 Timothy 3:1 with the following: "Apostasy is the act of professed Christians who deliberately reject revealed truth."[1] The note identifies the major areas of rejected truth as (1) the Deity of Jesus Christ, and (2) redemption through His atoning and redeeming sacrifice (1 John 4:1-3; Phil. 3:18; 2 Pet. 2:1).

The note then explains the difference between apostasy, error and heresy. While apostasy is a deliberate rejection of revealed truth, error may be the result of ignorance (Acts 19:1-6), and heresy may be due to the snare of Satan (2 Tim. 2:25-26). Both error and heresy may exist with true faith. Apostasy does not.

The Apostle Paul very clearly points out the apostates to Timothy, describing them in the letter's next and final chapter.

> 2 Timothy 4:3-4 -- For the time will come when they will not endure sound doctrine but, after their

own lusts, shall they heap to themselves teachers,
having itching ears; And they shall <u>turn away</u> their
ears <u>from the truth</u>, and shall be turned unto fables.

Apostates "turn away...from the truth;" they depart from the faith.
Unfortunately, like wolves in sheep's clothing, they do not depart
from their outward profession of Christianity.

> <u>2 Timothy 3:5</u> -- Having a form of godliness, but
> denying the power of it...

Apostate teachers are described in 2 Timothy 4:3; 2 Peter 2:1-
19; Jude 4, 8 11-13, 16. The Scofield note concludes by saying:
"Apostasy in the church, as in Israel (Isa. 1:5-6; 5:5-7), is irreme-
diable and awaits judgement" (2 Thes. 2:10-12; 2 Pet.2:17, 21;
Jude 11-15; Rev. 3:14-16).[2]

How do you withstand the evil forces? Homer Kent, in his
book <u>The Pastoral Epistles</u>, outlines the method:

1. <u>Endure Persecution.</u>

> But you followed closely my teaching, my con-
> duct, my purpose, my faith, my longsuffering, my
> love, my patience, my persecutions, my sufferings,
> such as came to me in Antioch, in Iconium, in
> Lystra; such persecutions as I bore, and out of all
> the Lord delivered me. But also all who wish to
> live godly in Christ Jesus shall be persecuted. And
> evil men and imposters shall progress to the worse,
> deceiving and being deceived (2 Tim. 3:10-13,
> Kent).[3]

2. <u>Abide in the Word.</u>

> But you, keep remaining in the things which you

> have learned and were assured of, knowing from
> whom you learned, and that from a babe you know
> sacred letters (KJV - The Holy Scriptures), which
> are able to make you wise unto salvation through
> faith which is in Christ Jesus (2 Tim. 3:14-15),
> Kent).[4]

Timothy, as noted earlier, was trained from childhood in the Word
of God by his mother Eunice and grandmother Lois. They were
bound to him by love and their teaching evidently was supported
by an observable lifestyle. He too was to abide in the Word.

3. <u>Employ the Word.</u> Scripture is a powerful weapon against
apostasy.

> All Scripture is God-breathed and profitable for
> teaching, for refutation, for correction, for educa-
> tion which is in righteousness, in order that the
> man of God may be equipped, for every good work
> fully equipped (2 Tim. 3:16-17, Kent). [5]

As Paul outlines it, Scripture has four functions:

a. <u>It is profitable for teaching.</u> -- It contains all man needs to
know to be saved. Doctrines not found in Scripture have no substantial spiritual significance.

b. <u>It is useful in refutation.</u> -- It can be employed to counteract
religious falsehood and to rebuke those who are in sin.

c. <u>It functions in correction.</u> -- It can raise up those who have
fallen and provide the means for restoration.

d. <u>It is profitable for education.</u> -- It not only reveals fault and
restores to a path of righteousness, it also helps believers to walk

in that path.

I've heard it said, "I don't like doctrine. Doctrine is divisive." Evidently the Lord tells us just the opposite. Through the inspired pen of the Apostle Paul, He teaches us that sound doctrine is critical to maintain a unified, strong and healthy church. Prescription # 2: PREACH AND TEACH SOUND DOCTRINE. Do not tolerate false teaching or it will spread like gangrene and sicken the body. All teaching must be based upon "thus saith the Lord, " so local churches can be Bible teaching centers where the doctrines of God's Word, from Bibliology through Eschatology and everything in between, are clearly taught. If they are, then our churches will be well equipped for whatever enemies of destruction they will inevitably face, and emerge victorious.

ENDNOTES

1. C. I. Scofield (E.S. English, rev.) *The New Scofield Reference Bible* (New York: Oxford University Press, 1967) p. 1304.

2. C.I. Scofield, ibid, p. 1304.

3. Homer A. Kent, Jr. *The Pastoral Epistles* (Chicago IL: Moody Press, 1958, 1982) p. 278.

4. Homer A. Kent, ibid, p. 279.

5. Homer A. Kent, ibid, p. 281.

3

The Pillar and
Ground of Truth

One apocryphal wag was once asked: "What is it that has kept your church from becoming all the church it could be for Christ: ignorance or apathy?" His reply: "I don't know and I don't care." Unfortunately, behind the humor lurks a tragic reality. Far too many believers simply do not know or understand the importance of the local church. Even worse, far too many do not care.

Nowadays a popular ecclesiastical equation goes like this: "Cut your morning service attendance in half and you will have your evening attendance; cut the evening service in half and you will have your prayer meeting attendance." I praise the Lord that the churches I've pastored over the years generally fared better. However, far too many do not and the leadership and membership fail to comprehend just how crippling a problem they have.

Erwin Lutzer, senior pastor of the famed Moody Memorial Church in Chicago, addressed this issue when he spoke to pastors on the subject of "Christian Loafers."

> Faithfulness. You preached on it; so have I. But
> have our sermons done much good? At a recent

pastor's conference, several men shared with me their frustration about the casual attitude some believers have in serving the church. Every congregation can boast of a few dependable, joyful volunteers. Unfortunately, they are sometimes the exception rather than the rule.[1]

He illustrated his comments by identifying some of the "loafers," and then said:

So we continue with latecomers, promise-breakers, and procrastinators. And our volunteer army limps along. Many of us can appreciate this parody of the hymn, Onward Christian Soldiers:

'Like a mighty turtle, Moves the church of God: Brothers, we are treading, where we've always trod.'[2]

Prescription #3: UNDERSTAND THE IMPORTANCE OF THE LOCAL CHURCH. It is, as A.W. Tozer said, "the highest expression of the will of God in this age." In a brief article entitled "The Vital Place of the Church" in his book God Tells the Man Who Cares, Tozer wrote:

The highest expression of the will of God in this age is the church which He purchased with His own blood. To be scripturally valid any religious activity must be part of the church. Let it be clearly stated that there can be no service to God in this age that does not center in and spring out of the church. Bible schools, tract societies, Christian businessmen's committees, seminaries, and many independent groups working at one or another phase of religion need to check themselves reverently and courageously, for they have no true spiritual significance outside of or apart from the church.[3]

Tozer clearly was referring to the <u>local</u> church not the <u>universal</u> church, since he continues, "Whoever scorns the local church scorns the Body of Christ."

In Greek, the word for church is <u>ekklesia</u> and it occurs 115 times in the New Testament according to <u>Young's Analytical Concordance</u>. It comes from two other Greek words, <u>ek</u> meaning "out of" and <u>kaleo</u> meaning "to call." Thus, a church is an organized assembly whose members have been properly called out.

R_x:
Understand the
Importance of the
Local Church

That "calling out" covers two major categories: (1) The local church, a church with some specific geographical location, and (2) the universal church, a reference to all believers from Pentecost to the Rapture -- some now alive, some now in heaven, some yet to be called out, and some not yet born. Of these 115 references, four have no direct application and only 16 can be considered applicable to the universal church. That leaves 95 unquestionable references to local churches.

It is impossible to misconstrue where the stress of the New Testament lies. It lies upon the local church. Any subject important enough to merit 95 references certainly merits the careful attention of every believer and church leader. I think Paul would agree, based upon three rather pointed descriptions of the local church in 1 Timothy 3:15-16:

...that thou mayest know how thou oughtest to behave thyself in the house of God, the pillar and ground of truth. And without controversy great is the mystery of godliness: God was manifest in the flesh, justified in the Spirit, seen of angels, preached unto the nations, believed on in the world, received up into glory.

Warren Wiersbe, in his <u>Expository Outlines on the New Testament</u> (Calvary Baptist Church Book Room, Covington, KY) and then later in his commentary on the pastoral epistles, <u>Be Faithful</u>, addressed all three descriptions.

> (1) **The House of God** (vs. 15) That is the family of God on earth. All believers are sons of God, and the church is His family, His household (See Gal. 6:10 and Eph. 2:19). Paul is writing this letter to teach men how to behave in God's family. If the church is God's family, then certainly it is more important than any other organization on earth.[4]

If we all acted as though we believed that statement, the grim ecclesiastical equation used earlier would be false.

> (2) **The Pillar and Ground of Truth** (vs. 15) This is architectural language. Paul is teaching that the church is what holds up God's truth in this world. The word "ground" means bulwark or foundation; one translator renders it "basement." As the local church is faithful to preserve, preach, and practice the truth, God's work prospers on earth. The unfaithful Christian is wrecking the very foundation of God's truth in the world![5]

Unfortunately a lot of "wrecking" is going on today. Many churches are afflicted with an unbelievably high percentage of unfaithful members who manifest little or no interest in the mission of the church. They meander merrily on their way, ignorant and insouciant of the spiritual damage they leave in their wake.

(3) **The Body of Christ** (vs. 16) Verse 16 is perhaps an early Christian hymn, memorized by the saints for their worship services. "The Mystery of Godliness" is God's hidden program to bring godliness into the world. Of course, Christ is God's great mystery, and this song exalts him: His birth (manifest in the flesh); His death and resurrection (justified in the Spirit, see Rom. 1:4 and 3:4); His earthly ministry (seen of angels, or witnesses, for it is the same word; preached ...received up). This is a summary of the Person and Work of Christ, and the idea is that the local church now continues the work He began. The church on earth is the Body of Christ on earth (see 1 Cor. 12:12 where he is speaking of a <u>local</u> church, not the church <u>universal</u>). It is time Christians started believing in the importance of the local church and started supporting this 'pillar and ground of truth' with their time, talents and tithes.[6]

I could not agree more. Here are comments on the same subject from other servants of the Lord:

> **D.B. Eastep** -- I believe the Kingdom of Christ on earth has suffered severely because individual men as well as denominations have failed to recognize THE IMPORTANCE OF THE LOCAL CHURCH, and the fact that the church is the working unit of the Kingdom of God on earth at this present time.[7]

> **Lewis Sperry Chafer** -- In fact, all should be saved before they join a church; and if saved, it is <u>normal</u>

for the individual to choose the fellowship of the people of God in one form or another. [8]

Richard W. DeHaan -- The growing <u>importance</u> of the local church is evident as we survey the book of Acts. [9]

Gene Getz -- The local church must be kept in focus as the <u>primary means</u> by which edification is to take place [10]

Paul R. Jackson -- Note in the New Testament that from the beginning of the ministry of the apostles local churches were established and were the <u>centers</u> of all activity in the Lord's work. [11]

Harold L. Fickett -- In our day unfortunately there are many who take great pride in claiming membership in the church universal while at the same time they deprecate the importance of the local church. They don't seem to realize that it is the local church not the universal church that builds buildings, conducts Sunday School, engages in evangelistic campaigns, and sends missionaries around the world. <u>The work of Jesus Christ in our day humanly speaking is dependent upon the effectiveness of the ministry carried on by local churches.</u> Every true believer, thankful for his membership in the church universal, should be affiliated with a local church seeking to work with his fellow believers in implementing the Great Commission. [12]

Bible teacher after Bible teacher have come to the same con-

clusion: THE LOCAL CHURCH IS OF PREEMINENT IM-
PORTANCE in the program of God. That fact is emphasized in
Scripture through use of the word ekklesia, and is confirmed by
the very nature of the following four tasks that clearly belong to
this "working unit of the kingdom of God."

1. The Local Church Is Ordained of God to Fulfill the Great Commission.

Under direct mandate by the Lord to go into all the world and
preach the gospel (Mt. 28: 16-20; Acts 1:2,8), the apostles organized the first local church. In doing so they established a pattern
(Acts 2:41-42; 6:1-70) that led to the planting of other local assemblies under the direction of the Holy Spirit (Acts 8:1-17; 9:31;
11:19-26). Paul was sent out as a missionary by a local church
(Acts 13:1,2) and his work was that of local church planting (Acts
14:23-28). Later, he wrote many of his letters to those churches
and their leaders. Our Lord's last words were addressed not to
Christendom in general but to local churches (Rev. 1:11; chapters
2-3).

Clearly the local New Testament church is a divine institution.
When Paul wrote his first letter to believers in Corinth he addressed it to "the Church of God which is at Corinth" (1 Cor.
1:2). He referred not only to its geographical location ("at
Corinth") but also to its divine origin ("of God"). Correlating
passages are: Acts 20:28; 1 Cor. 10:32; 11:16; 15:9; 2 Cor. 1:1;
Rom. 16:16; Gal. 1:13.

2. The Local Church is the Pillar and Ground of Truth.

In 1 Timothy 3:15 Paul explains that the leadership and membership of the local church shoulder the great responsibility of
upholding the truth. The analogy is to a building: the pillars hold
up the structure; the ground or support constitute the foundation

upon which it rests. Thus, the local church is both a <u>pillar</u> and <u>foundation</u> for the truth of God's Word in a world that needs it so desperately.

3. The Local Church Is a Light in a Dark World.

In Revelation 1:20 the seven literal, local churches in Asia Minor (Rev. 2-3) are likened to seven candlesticks or lampstands, instruments designed to shed light. Such is the function of the church. We live in a sin-darkened world and it is the church's responsibility to radiate the light of God's Word upon those for whom Christ died.

Perhaps that is why Christ Himself voiced such great concern for the seven churches in Revelation Chapters two and three. Using the Apostle John to communicate His message, He articulated a type of last will and testament. Far from telling believers to forsake their local assemblies, He instructed them to do everything they could to strengthen them.

4. The Local Church Is the Umbrella Under Which Service to God Is Carried Out.

Stephen, the man who delivered the official message from God to Israel (Acts 7), began his ministry as a deacon in the local church at Jerusalem (Acts 6:5). Philip, the great evangelist, had a similar start. The Apostle Paul first ministered as a teacher in the local church at Antioch (Acts 11:25,26; 13:1,2).

The Book of Acts abounds with information concerning the beliefs and practices of the local church. The Jerusalem church had a benevolent ministry (Acts 6:1-8). The church at Antioch gave financial assistance to its needy brothers and sisters in Jerusalem and officially sent Paul and Barnabas on their first missionary journey (Acts 11:26-30; 13:1-5). Believers met at the church for instruction in "the apostles doctrine and fellowship, and in breaking of bread, and in prayers" (Acts 2:41-42). Indeed, after Paul preached in various locations he "ordained elders in every church" (Acts 14:23). The apostles clearly demonstrated that their missionary outreach at a given location was incomplete until a local assembly was formed and functioning.

If these men of God so highly valued the local church and expended such great energy in service to it, certainly believers today should do no less. It is the Biblical vehicle established by God to convey His eternal truth to the world, and as such it should be the center of activity for the Lord's work and the primary place where believers are to be nurtured and edified. After years of observation I am convinced that the believer who does not enter wholeheartedly into the local church program seriously restricts his ability to serve the Lord.

What About Para-Church Organizations?

These organizations usually focus on a narrow, specialized aspect of ministry, which sometimes enables them to minister more effectively in their areas of expertise than the local church. Para-church organizations include Christian educational institutions, mission boards, youth ministries, counseling services, etc. Obviously there are individuals who love the Lord, want to serve Him, and do so through these organizations. I myself am a member of a youth ministry council and serve on the board of trustees of a Bible college and of a mission agency. I even helped found a Christian counseling service and was the founding pastor of a Christian day school.

However, service in para-church organizations to the exclusion of service in a local church is an unacceptable practice and should be discouraged. Kenneth Good spoke well on this subject:

In our experience we have known some of God's

> people who were quite concerned about their membership in a mission society ...school ...broadcasting agency, or ...some evangelical association or committee, but who were relatively very little concerned about membership in a local church. One such brother said to the writer some years ago, 'Why should I be concerned about membership in a local church, am I not an active member of the _____ Mission?' Yet churches are ordained of God with Biblical authority, but the New Testament knows nothing of these other organizations, and its pages will be searched in vain to find a requirement for their existence. [13]

As for the organizations themselves, I wholeheartedly support those that operate within the proper framework. In particular, they must clearly understand that they in no way replace the local church but are resources or tools to aid it in evangelizing the lost and edifying the saved.

Unfortunately too many such groups today suffer from an identity crisis. They fail to understand their roles in life and end up in conflict with the Word of God by usurping prerogatives that belong exclusively to the assemblies. Rather than helping the church, they actually attempt to supplant it.

Evangelist James Gent, in a self-published booklet that addresses the subject, wrote:

> Many church-related organizations would do well to realize the truth of 1 Tim. 3:15. Recently, while looking over a certain follow-up manual by a well-known Christian organization I noticed that they [sic] devoted just 5 of the 499 pages of this manual to the subject of the local church. In those 5 pages, the subject of the local church was cov-

ered in a very light and general way. How sad in the light of 1 Tim. 3:15.

When functioning properly, para-church organizations can greatly assist the church. However, I recommend steering clear of those that wander off "to do their own thing" with little or no accountability to the local assembly. God's Word teaches that the local church is the prime force in His plan for this age and no other program should side-step it. Lutzer, in the conclusion to his book <u>Pastor to Pastor</u>, writes:

> The church is God's number one priority in the world. It displays His wisdom, both now and in the ages to come "in order that the manifold wisdom of God might now be made known through the church to the rulers and authorities in heavenly places. This was in accordance with the eternal purpose which He carried out in Jesus Christ our Lord" (Eph. 3:10-11).[14] NASB

Prescription #3: UNDERSTAND THE IMPORTANCE OF THE LOCAL CHURCH. Emphasize its importance to your people and teach them to guard against ignorance and apathy, which infiltrate the body to drain the lifeblood, dull the vision and divert the people of God from serving Him through the divine institution of the local assembly. If the church avails itself of this preventative medication, even the gates of hell will not prevail against it (Matt. 16:18). And if that is not a blessed thought, I do not know what is.

ENDNOTES

1. Erwin W. Lutzer, *Pastor to Pastor* (Chicago, Il: Moody Press, 1987) p. 43.

2. Erwin W. Lutzer, ibid, p. 44.

3. A. W. Tozer, *The Best of A.W. Tozer* (from: God Tells the Man Who Cares) (Grand Rapids, MI: Baker Book House, 1978) p. 64-65.

4. Warren W. Wiersbe, *Whole Bible Study Course - Orig. by D.P. Eastep* (Covington, KY: Calvary Baptist Church Book Room, n.d.) Notes on 1 Tim. 3.

5. Wiersbe, ibid (1 Tim. 3).

6. Wiersbe, ibid (1 Tim. 3).

7. D. P. Eastep, *Highway Robbery from the Scriptural Standpoint* (Covington, KY: Calvary Baptist Church Book Room, n.d.)

8. Lewis Sperry Chafer, *Major Bible Themes, Walvoord rev.* (Grand Rapids, MI: Zondervan, 1926, 1953, 1974) p. 240.

9. Richard W. DeHaan, *Your Church and You* (Grand Rapids, MI: Radio Bible Class, 1975) p. 10.

10. Gene A. Getz, *Sharpening the Focus of the Church* (Chicago, IL: Moody Press, 1974) p.83.

11. Paul R. Jackson, *The Doctrine and Administration of the Church* (Des Plaines, IL: Regular Baptist Press, 1968) p. 27.

12. Harold L. Fickett, Jr., *A Layman's Guide to Baptist Beliefs* (Grand Rapids, MI: Zondervan, 1965) p. 60-61.

13. Kenneth H. Good, *Why Every Christian Should Be a Member of a Local New Testament Church* (Elyria, OH: Baptist Mission of North America, rev. 1987) p. 3-4.

14. Erwin W. Lutzer, op. cit., p. 139.

Prescriptions That Count

56

4

Pass It On

Jack Wyrtzen, the founder and director of Word of Life International, had just filled the pulpit for me as a guest speaker and we were on our way home. I was driving, Jack rode in the passenger seat and my wife Joanna sat between us. "Chuck," said Jack, "That week that you are going to be with us at camp this summer is going to be a week of prophecy conference. So get some messages together on prophecy."

Now, most of us in the pastorate do not consider our greatest expertise to lie in the realm of prophecy. But it was only November and I wasn't scheduled to be at Word of Life in Schroon Lake, New York until July. Surely, I thought, in eight months I could put together a half dozen good prophetic messages without distinguishing myself as a total novice in the area.

Then I made my mistake. Knowing that Word of Life always has more than one speaker, I asked Jack who the others would be. He replied, very matter-of-factly, "Charles Ryrie and John Whitcomb." Suddenly I went numb. My wife elbowed me in the ribs and in somewhat stunned silence I managed to get us home.

Here I was, the pastor of a local church, about to share a platform with two men esteemed the world over as Biblical scholars, theologians and authors. In fact, Dr. Ryrie had been president of

Philadelphia College of Bible when I was an undergraduate there. With tongue in cheek, I often refer to that week of ministry as the time I shared a platform with the man who wrote the Bible (the Ryrie Study Bible) and the reporter who covered the flood for CNN (Dr. Whitcomb, with Henry Morris, wrote <u>The Genesis Flood</u>).

Needless to say, I made it through the conference and remember it as one of the thrills of my ministry. I am grateful to Jack for having given me such a wonderful opportunity. (I even saved the advertising brochure to show my future grandchildren!)

It has been a number of years now since that conference, and my perspective, tempered by hindsight, has been somewhat altered and/or adjusted. That doesn't mean that the awe of being on the same schedule with those two men has changed, for it hasn't. But what I now see is this: the day will come, all things being equal, when Charles Ryrie and John Whitcomb will no longer be on the scene, but Chuck Scheide will be. That's because they are both close to a generation older than I. And the awareness that such a realization drove home to this pastor's heart is this: every generation of believers must see to it that whatever knowledge God has shared with them is passed on to the generation that follows in the same faithfulness demonstrated by Drs. Ryrie and Whitcomb.

That concept is the heartbeat of this chapter. It is a concept that Jack Wyrtzen put into practice with me. Jack, with a schedule that has always been unbelievably hectic and of major importance, has always had time for me. My first church was located in upstate New York about 85 miles from Word of Life. It wasn't long before Jack enlisted me to teach at conferences and at the Bible Institute, nurturing my gifts and helping me to mature in my service to the Lord. His counsel has enriched me and I have benefited immeasurably from his wisdom and experience.

In other words, he passed on to me what had been passed on to him. It is this principle that Paul addressed when he wrote to

The things that thou hast heard from me ...the same
commit thou to faithful men, who shall be able to
teach others also (2 Tim. 2:2).

If we neglect to prepare leaders for the generations that follow, our churches will deteriorate from within. They will crumble
from lack of strong, godly direction and will be rendered incap-
able of making any significant impact for Christ. Prescription #4:
PLAN FOR THE FUTURE. Be diligent in "passing it on."

R_x:

**Plan for
the Future.**

This sense of a relay is con-
veyed in 1 Timothy by Paul's use
of the key word <u>charge</u>, sometimes translated "commandment"
(1:3,5,18; 4:11; 5:7; 6:13,17). It
is a military term in keeping with
Paul's charge (or command) to
Timothy to "war a good warfare."

By definition <u>charge</u> means "to give strict orders from a superior
officer" -- orders that are to be passed down the line. The relay is
as follows:

Step One: God commits the truth of His word to Paul.
> <u>1 Timothy 1:11</u> -- "According to the glorious gospel
> of the blessed God, which was committed to
> my trust."

Step Two: Paul passes it along to Timothy.
> <u>1 Timothy 1:18</u> -- "This charge I commit unto thee,
> son Timothy..."
> <u>1 Timothy 6:20</u> -- "O Timothy, keep that which is
> committed to thy trust..."

Step Three: Timothy is "charged" to guard it.
> 2 Timothy 1: 13-14 -- "Hold fast the form of sound words
> ... That good thing which was committed unto thee keep
> by the Holy Spirit, who dwelleth in us."

Step Four: Timothy is instructed to pass it along to faithful men.
> 2 Timothy 2:2 -- "... the things that thou hast heard
> from me... the same commit thou to faithful men..."

Step Five: The faithful men are then to pass it along to others.
> 2 Timothy 2:2 -- "...the things that thou hast heard from
> me ...the same commit thou to faithful men, who shall be
> able to teach others also."

Thus, "the glorious gospel of the blessed God" traveled this path:

> (1) God, to
> (2) Paul, to
> (3) Timothy, to
> (4) Faithful men, to
> (5) Others also.

Today believers in the local church comprise the "others also," and the charge that went first to Paul now comes to us. We are "to keep that which has been committed to our trust" and then to pass it on to "others also."

Unfortunately, as in football, not every pass will be completed. Many Christians will fumble, either by failing to mature in their walk with the Lord or by neglecting to pass on what they know to someone else. Yet we must "keep on keeping on." The Apostle Paul "fought a good fight," "finished his course" and "kept the faith," but even he still lost some. He records for us some of his uncompleted passes:

1 Timothy 1:6	"some have turned aside"
1:19	"some have made shipwreck"
5:15	"some have turned aside after Satan"
6:10	"some have been led astray"
6:21	"some have erred"
2 Timothy 1:15	"all are turned away from me"
4:16	"all forsook me"

It is important to remember that the Lord does not command us to be successful. He commands us to be faithful. Like Paul, Timothy and the other saints who went before us, we must pass on the tenets of Christianity by faithfully proclaiming God's Word, challenging God's flock and holding fast to God's program. Our congregations must constantly be encouraged to remain doctrinally pure and conscientiously faithful. They must be thoroughly inculcated in the Holy Scriptures, which are able to "make one wise unto salvation" and to "furnish" for effective service those who have been saved.

More specifically, however, Christians in leadership positions must conscientiously seek out young Timothys and train them as did Paul, who called Timothy his "beloved son, and faithful in the Lord" (1 Cor. 4:17). Sad to say, some pastors and church leaders are so insecure they deliberately squelch young preachers and teachers. Instead of providing opportunities for service, they withhold them. Not only are they failing to prepare their church for future growth, but they are guaranteeing there will not even be a future.

Paul was not so shortsighted. Timothy no doubt came to Christ as a result of Paul's ministry during the apostle's first missionary journey in Timothy's hometown of Lystra. It was during that visit, while Timothy was yet an impressionable boy, that people first tried to worship the apostle then tried to kill him. Timothy not only heard Paul preach the gospel but saw him heal a cripple, appeal to the multitude, then rise up, reenter the city and continue with his journey after he was stoned and left for dead (Acts 14:1-20).

When Paul returned to Lystra on his second missionary journey, he enlisted Timothy to help him carry the gospel to Phillipi, Thessalonica and Berea (Acts 16: 1-17:14). Timothy helped edify the church in Thessalonica where he served in a pastoral capacity and he assisted Paul in founding the church in Corinth (Acts 18:5). It was Paul's careful provision of "hands-on" experience that eventually prepared this new convert for his role as "senior pastor" in Ephesus, the position he held when he received the letters of 1 and 2 Timothy.

"Thou hast fully known my doctrine," Paul wrote, "manner of life, purpose, faith, long-suffering, love, patience, persecutions, afflictions which came unto me ... what persecution I endured... " (2 Tim. 3:10-11). As death approached, Paul encouraged his young protege to do for others what Paul had done for him and to continue serving the Lord faithfully, even as he himself was doing --- to the very end.

As he had exhorted the Christian believers earlier, "be ye followers of me, even as I also am of Christ" (1 Cor. 11:1), now he exhorts Timothy: "Follow me ... follow the pattern that I have laid down. Just as I have encouraged you, and discipled you, and encouraged you, you do the same for others."

> For I am now ready to be offered, and the time of my departure is at hand. I have fought a good fight, I have finished my course, I have kept the faith; Henceforth there is laid up for me a crown of righteousness, which the Lord, the righteous judge, shall give me at that day; and not to me only, but unto all them also that love his appearing. (2 Tim. 4:6-8.)

The remarkable growth of the early church would lead us to believe that Paul's nurturing of Timothy was not wasted. Timothy committed to others what Paul had committed to him.

Every young man who desires to serve the Lord could use a Paul. Mine was Dr. George H. Slavin -- my father-in-law. Nearly four decades of pastoring gave him wisdom that was a continual source of blessing to me. His last two assignments, at Faith Community Church in Roslyn, Pennsylvania (22 years) and Highland Park Baptist Church in Southfield, Michigan (8 years) were the examples of superior pastoring that any man would do well to emulate. Never one to push himself or his ideas on me, he was, however, always ready to answer any question I had. He went home to be with the Lord in 1979 and he is sorely missed. I inherited his library, his personal notes, more than 250 message tapes and the precious insights that my wife has given me as a result of having been his daughter. In Hebrews 11:4 it is written of Abel that "he being dead yet speaketh." The same can be said of George Slavin.

And of course there is my friend Jack Wyrtzen. Even after the Lord carries him home someday, the very memory of him will remind us that we are "on the victory side" and will exhort us as did Paul, to "preach the word" (2 Tim. 4:2). Prescription #4: PLAN FOR THE FUTURE. George Slavin and Jack Wyrtzen have proven where the future of the local church lies. It does not lie in the construction of buildings, or in 5-year and 10-year plans. The future lies in preparing people who will be committed to proclaiming the glorious gospel message that God gave to Paul, who gave it to Timothy, who gave it to faithful men, who gave it to others also. The future lies in "passing it on."

Author's Note: Others (apart from George H. Slavin and Jack Wyrtzen) who have played a significant role in my development as a pastor, and who "passed on" to me insight and encouragement that has proven to be invaluable, include: Dr. Douglas B. MacCorkle, Dr. Charles C. Ryrie, and Dr. W. Sherrill Babb, past and present presidents of Philadelphia College of Bible; Dr. Harry Bollback and Dr. George Theis, Word of Life Fellowship Directors; as well as a host of good friends in the ministry: Dr. Charles W. Anderson (deceased), Paul Bubar, Jimmy DeYoung, Don Lough, Dr. John F. McGahey (deceased), Dr. Clarence E. Mason, Jr. (deceased), Dr. John Master, Col. Jack McGuckin, Dr. Gordan McMinn, Dr. Elwood McQuaid, Stuart Page, Dr. Gilbert A. Peterson, Dr. Renald Showers, Dr. Elmer Towns, Dave Virkler, Dr. John White and Dr. Spiros Zodhiates. Thank you all, as well as to unnamed scores of individuals who, because of space limitations cannot be listed, who have assisted me and counseled me in my ministry.

Author's Note: Since the original publication of this book in 1996 a major change has taken place in my life. Following over 34 years of pastoring, the Lord in 1999 moved me into a new phase of ministry, that of helping to prepare the next generation to lead the church when my generation passes on. That, in effect is the major emphasis of this fourth chapter. I am deeply indebted to Dr. Joe Jordan, the Executive Director of Word of Life Fellowship, for the confidence he has placed in me in assigning me the task of serving as Associate Executive Dean of Word of Life Bible Institute (Florida Campus), and as his Administrative Consultant. To serve at the side of this visionary man of God is indeed a supreme honor. And to serve alongside my fellow workers in this new position...Dr. Stu Page, Wayne Lewis, Dr. Tom Davis, Marshall Wickes, Gary Ingersoll and Tom Phillips...is a genuine privilege. (March, 2001)

5

Getting Back to Basics

It is interesting to note that the three pastoral epistles, which contain the majority of the Lord's instructions concerning church organization, total only 13 chapters. In my favorite study Bible, that constitutes a mere 13 pages. Yet, I have seen church constitutions that run more than 40 pages in length and cover almost everything from how to change a lightbulb to how to dispose of communion cups. (That last, of course, would apply only to churches that have successfully circumnavigated the meetings involved in securing approval for switching from glass to plastic.)

Granted, I am being a bit facetious, but some church constitutions are so expansive, so burdened down with rules, regulations and procedures that any resemblance they bear to the Scriptures is purely accidental. One church I know wanted to raise its summer camp registration fee by $1.50. The change had to go through nine committees and/or subcommittees for approval. When the approval was finally secured, summer camp was history. The fee adjustment had to wait a full year for implementation. Perhaps this is why so many pastors own wall plaques bearing the immortal words: "God so loved the world that He didn't send a committee."

For a church to be healthy, it must get back to basics: Prescription #5: UNDERSTAND THE SIMPLICITY OF CHURCH

GOVERNMENT and stick to the scriptural model.

G. Campbell Morgan, often referred to as the "Prince of Expositors," came to America from England in 1900 to carry on the preaching ministry of Dwight L. Moody. In analyzing the early church of the New Testament, Morgan called its organizational structure "spiritual, simple, and sufficient." He then pointed out that by contrast, many of our modern day churches have devolved into organizations that are "carnal, complex and corrupt." When it comes to church government, more is not better and much more is not even biblical.

Admittedly, there is not a lot of specificity in the Scriptures regarding the governmental structure of the church. Yet the Bible obviously contains everything the Lord wanted us to know. It reveals the format the Lord wanted us to follow. If more had been necessary, He would have provided it. In his book The Church: God's People, Bruce Shelley approaches the Bible's brevity on the subject this way:

> At first glance... the New Testament seems disturbingly indecisive about the specific kind of government God had in mind for His church... it seems that the Spirit of God has allowed a certain flexibility... that helps to explain the persistent differences among Christian denominations. [1]

Some differences in church governments and ministry structure are not worth arguing about: how often should business meetings be held; what percentage of a vote constitutes approval; should provisions for absentee ballots be provided; should Sunday School precede or follow the preaching service; must the doxology be sung at the beginning of all worship services; should the Lord's Supper be held weekly, monthly or quarterly, etc., etc., etc. All these, for the most part, fall into the category of preference, not conviction, and sanctified common sense should be permitted to prevail. But when the form of government strays from the biblical model, the church begins to head down a road God never intended, and that road could lead to serious illness. Since the Word of God constitutes the supreme and final authority in faith and practice, the model it sets forth should be the one we emulate.

Forms of Church Government

Historically, there are four basic types of church government:
I. <u>PAPAL or AUTHORITARIAN</u> (<u>Rule by Roman Pope</u>)

R_x:
Understand the Simplicity of Church Government.

Here the pope has total authority over the church and all the individuals in it. This Roman Catholic system is predicated upon the belief that Peter was chief among the apostles and that the pope is the successor to Peter. He is thus regarded as the vicar of Christ in the world and the supreme head of the church on earth. Consequently, the church of Rome is akin to an absolute monarchy with the pope the absolute monarch. This structure is found nowhere in the Word of God and is an entirely non-biblical form of church government.

II. <u>EPISCOPALIAN</u> (<u>Rule by Bishops</u>)
This too is an authoritarian form, but the authority rests with bishops instead of a pope. This system contends that Christ gave His authority to His apostles, who passed it on to others, who passed it on to others, etc. Episcopalians believe that Christ's authority now rests with bishops who alone can ordain people into the priesthood and confirm them into church membership. The congregation has no voice in such governments, which include the Anglican, Protestant Episcopal, Methodist, Orthodox

and some Lutheran churches. As with papal government, this form too is totally unscriptural.

III. PRESBYTERIAL (Rule by Presbytery)

Here a presbytery has jurisdiction over a geographical grouping of pastors and churches. The presbytery is composed of the pastor and one elder from each of the area churches. Though elected by the churches, the elders are viewed as having received their authority from God and consequently are not answerable to their local congregations. This form of government does provide a relative degree of local church autonomy, and is more biblical than either the papal or episcopalian forms. However, its major flaw is that it does not go far enough.

IV. CONGREGATIONAL (Rule by the Congregation)

As the name suggests, the authority here rests exclusively with the congregation. The local assembly is sovereign in itself and answerable to Christ alone. Individuals or committees may be appointed to perform certain duties, but they are directly accountable to the church and to the Lord, who is the sole Head of the church. No other power or authority is recognized. The major practitioners of this form of government are the Baptist churches, the United Church of Christ, and most independent churches. This structure conforms to the Word of God and is, therefore, the biblical standard we are to follow.

Many portions of Scripture besides the pastoral epistles, make this standard abundantly clear. John C. Whitcomb, in his revision of Alva J. McClain's syllabus The Kingdom and the Church, writes the following:

Local church government is congregational in form. Each local church has supreme authority in its affairs.

(1) The local church has authority to judge its own mem-

bership (1 Cor. 5:13).

Even an apostle does not assume to excommunicate a member, but calls upon the local church to do it.

(2) The local church has authority to elect its own officers (Acts 6:1-6).

Not even the apostles assume to choose the officers of a local church, but call upon the church to do it.

(3) The local church has authority to guard and observe the ordinances (1 Cor. 11:23 -- "I delivered unto you").

Not to the clergy, the elders or bishops. This means that no church can be deprived of the sacred rites, as the hierarchy of Rome assumes. Even if all ministers should be withdrawn, the local church could elect officers to lead its services.

(4) The local church has authority to settle its own internal difficulties (1 Cor. 6:1-5).

Paul does not appoint a committee, but directs the Church to look after the matter. We find an interesting suggestion in verse 5 -- sometimes it is best for the church to designate a person of wisdom to decide rather than air a difficulty before the whole congregation. But, the church is responsible.

(5) The local church has authority in matters involving the relations of different local churches (Acts 15:1-2, 22, 23, 25, 30).

This was not a conference of ecclesiastical overlords, but of two local churches, each sovereign in its own affairs. One protests through chosen delegates. Even the apostles do not assume exclusive authority in the matter.

(6) All "Church Government in the New Testament applies only to the local bodies." E.J. Forrester, "Church Government" ISBE, I, 653 ff).

(7) The authority of the local church is final as far as its own affairs are concerned (See Matt. 18:17).[2]

There is no higher court.

Personnel of the Local Church

Paul no doubt assumed that both Timothy and Titus understood church government and he concentrated the pastoral epistles primarily upon qualifications for office rather than upon church organization. These offices are often misunderstood, with churches often opting to follow traditional patterns as opposed to the clear biblical model. The entire personnel makeup of the New Testament church can be summed up in Philippians 1:1:

> Paul and Timothy, the servants of Jesus Christ, to all the saints in Christ Jesus who are at Philippi, with the bishops and deacons.

The breakdown is as follows:

(1) The SAINTS in Christ Jesus at Philippi, with
(2) The BISHOPS and
(3) The DEACONS

The Scofield Reference Bible succinctly defines the local church and its personnel:

> Churches (local), Summary: A local church is an assembly of professed believers in the Lord Jesus Christ, living for the most part in one locality, who meet together in His name for baptism, the Lord's Supper, worship, praise, prayer, fellowship, testimony, the ministry of the Word, discipline, and the futherance of the Gospel (Acts 13:1-4; 20:7; 1 Cor. 5:4-5; 14:26; Phil. 4:14-18; 1 Thes, 1:8; Heb. 10:25). Every such local church has Christ as its center, is a temple of God, and is indwelt by the Holy Spirit (1 Cor. 3: 16-17). In organization a local church is here stated (v.1) to be composed of "saints, with the bishops (elders, see 1 Tim. 3:1-13; Ti. 1:5) and deacons."[3]
> [emphasis added]

THE SAINTS

As a result of a salvation experience, an individual becomes a member of the Body of Christ, the Church of God. It is to these saved individuals living in Philippi that Paul wrote Philippians, addressing them as saints (cp. 1 Cor. 1:2; Rom. 6:3, 4; 8:1; Eph. 1:3, etc.). The term comes from two Greek words, hagios and hagiazo. Hagios is translated "saint" and means holy, set apart, sanctified, consecrated. Hagiazo is translated "sanctify" and means to render holy, to separate. Both explain exactly what God has done for persons who have become born again. He has made them holy and has separated them unto Himself by placing them in the Body of Christ.

THE BISHOPS

This Greek word, episkopos, is used interchangeably with the words for elder, presbuteros, and pastor, poimen (1 Pet. 5:1-2).

All three terms refer to the same individual -- the pastor of the church -- but each has its own shade of meaning. Together, these terms form a complete picture of the duties involved in holding this important office.

Episkopos is an administrative term that means overseer, or someone in charge of an estate. It refers to someone who superintends or oversees the ministry. Paul uses presbuteroi (plural of presbuteros) in Acts 20:17 when he calls the leaders in the church at Ephesus to join him in Miletus:

> And from Miletus he sent to Ephesus, and called
> the elders (presbuteroi) of the church.

The word simply means "old man." While sometimes a reference to age, here it refers to leadership and emphasizes not age, but authority and rank. It refers to the president of a deliberative assembly -- in this case a local church -- particularly in the aspect of conducting its business (1 Tim. 5:17; Acts 11:30).

These Ephesian elders (presbuteroi) now receive Paul's instructions, which outline their major duties:

> Take heed (you elders), therefore unto yourselves,
> and to all the flock, over which the Holy Spirit
> hath made you overseers (episcopoi - bishops), to
> feed (to shepherd, the Greek word we often trans-
> late "pastor") the church of God (Acts 20:28).

In the study Bible bearing his name, Dr. W. A. Criswell, long-time pastor of the First Baptist Church of Dallas, Texas, clarifies this beautifully:

> Three descriptive terms were employed in the New
> Testament to depict the role of the pastor. All three
> are used in this passage, though here two are used
> in verb form: (1) Elders (presbuteros, Gr.) is a term

generically referring to a fully mature man. The respect accorded to an elderly man is transferred to the office of the pastor. The use of the word 'elder' indicates profound respect and esteem for the office. (2) 'Feed' the flock of God employs the Greek verb <u>poimaino</u>, which means 'to shepherd.' The nominal form of the word is poimen, which is rendered 'pastor' or 'shepherd.' The word describes the spiritual ministries of the leader of the church. As pastor or shepherd, he is to feed, protect, guide and pray for the flock of God. (3) 'Taking the oversight' is a translation of the Greek episkopountes, meaning 'to oversee.' The noun form episkopos is usually translated 'bishop.' The emphasis is upon the administrative responsibilities of the chief officer of the church. These terms are all synonymous in that they refer to the same office. They differ only in the emphasis... The term 'bishop' indicates strong leadership but not dictatorship.[4]

Thus, it is the pastors who are the elders, the "old men," the esteemed ranking authorities in local congregations. As such they have two major responsibilities: (1) Administratively, they are to oversee (bishop) the business affairs of the church, and (2) spiritually, they are to feed, nurture and guide (pastor) the congregation.

THE DEACONS

This is an office that most likely came into being with the appointment of seven men to serve tables in Acts 6:1-6. Their ministry to the widows in the Jerusalem church was a practical service designed to free the apostles so they could preach the Word and pray. In Philippians 1:1, Paul mentions both bishops and deacons and thanks them for a recent collection on his behalf. As

Criswell writes:

> Paul's distinction here between bishops and dea-
> cons reflects this division of labor. The deacons
> were responsible for ministering to the physical and
> material needs of the congregation; whereas the
> bishops or elders provided spiritual leadership.
> Obviously both pastors and deacons worked
> closely together in the work of the church (Acts
> 6;8). [5]

The term "deacon" comes from the Greek word diakonos
meaning "servant." Diakonos and its corresponding verb, diakoneo
("to serve") and noun, diakonia ("service") are used throughout
the New Testament to denote service of various kinds. For example, Jesus used this word in describing His ministry in Matthew
28:20. Paul used it in describing himself in Colossians 1:25. In
Philippians 1:1 and in passages such as 1 Timothy 3:8-13, it is
used more technically to denote a local church office.

A deacon in today's church should be a man who possesses
that priceless treasure called a servant's heart. His desire to serve
the Lord should be paramount, and his willingness to serve the
congregation should be evident to all. But in a very special way,
those who are deacons have been placed there by God to help the
pastor bear the load. Charles Erdman, in dealing with the office
of deacon, makes this observation in his book The Pastoral Epistles
of Paul:

> It would seem wise, and in accordance with the
> practice of the primitive church, to have in every
> congregation the service of such authorized offic-
> ers to aid the pastor in his work, and to relieve him
> from the burden of many duties, particularly in the
> care of the more needy members of the flock. [6]

Guy King, in his commentary on 1 Timothy entitled <u>A Leader Led</u>, refers to the office of deacon as the "minor," subordinate office and to that of pastor as the "major" office.[7] Unfortunately, some church goers needlessly take offense at this distinction. No one disputes the equality of deacons and pastors concerning their position in Christ. It is only their responsibilities that are different. These differences are biblical and necessary to stave off chaos and make the local church organized and efficient. As Paul writes to Titus:

> For this cause left I thee in Crete, that thou shouldest set in order the things that are wanting, and ordain elders in every city, as I had appointed thee (Titus 1:5).

A properly written constitution can be of enormous benefit to the congregation and can maximize the church's effectiveness. One local church, understanding the proper relationship of its constitution to the Word of God, includes the following preamble to its constitution:

> By the Grace of God, our Saviour, and our faith in Him, we the members of _____ _____ Church of _____, _____, do ordain and establish the following articles, to which we voluntarily submit ourselves. We do so recognizing that in the case of a local New Testament Church a constitution is simply a tool to be used to aid said church in the implementation of its goals, not an end in itself. While we will not tolerate any adjustments in the Biblical and doctrinal portions of this document, minor adjustments in the mechanical portions can be made from time to time, without disturbing its integrity. <u>In essence, the</u>

Bible is the final authority in all faith and practice; this constitution is simply a means to an end (emphasis added). While it should be adhered to under normal circumstances, and on most occasions, it is not to be administered legalistically.

Apart from discussing the offices of pastor and deacon, I have said very little about church mechanics. The reason? Apart from these two church offices, the Bible says very little. Why then do we have churches whose mechanisms are so stopped up with committees, subcommittees, rules and regulations that every move the church tries to make becomes clogged up in committee or weighted down with regulation? That style of government is, pardon the phrase, more "constipational" than it is constitutional. Very little ever gets accomplished. The result? The church whimpers to a halt in its attempt to carry out its Great Commission responsibilities. For a church to be healthy, it must get back to the basics. Prescription #5: UNDERSTAND THE SIMPLICITY OF CHURCH GOVERNMENT and stick to the scriptural model. Avoid the disease of constitutional constipation. It is far more pleasant to take the preventative medication beforehand than it is to take the laxative afterward.

ENDNOTES

1. Bruce L. Shelley, *The Church: God's People* (Wheaton, IL: Victor Books, 1978) p. 103.

2. John C. Whitcomb, *The Kingdom and the Church* (Winona Lake, IN: Grace Theological Seminary, n.d.) p. 100-101.

3. C.I. Scofield (E.S. English, rev.) *The New Scofield Reference Bible* (New York: Oxford University Press, 1967) p. 1280.

4. W. A. Criswell, *The Criswell Study Bible* (Nashville, TN: Thomas Nelson Pub., 1979) p. 1456.

5. W. A. Criswell, ibid, p. 1414-1415.

6. Charles R. Erdman, *The Pastoral Epistles of Paul* (Philadelphia, PA: Westminister Press, 1925) p. 42.

7. Guy H. King, *A Leader Led* (London: Marshall, Morgan & Scott, 1951) p. 57,63.

Prescriptions That Count

6

The Importance of Leadership

My father was a wonderful man. He loved the Lord and wanted to serve the church of Jesus Christ. So when he was asked to become a deacon, he accepted willingly. Years later I became a pastor and undertook a major study on the biblical office of deacon. As I shared with him the responsibilities of that office, my father asked incredulously, "A deacon is supposed to do all that?"

"Yeah, dad," I answered.

"I had no idea," he said. "If that's what a deacon is supposed to do, I'm not so sure I should have ever become one. No one ever explained all of that to me."

I imagine a lot of deacons would say the same thing if they were ever truly confronted with an accurate biblical explanation of the role of a deacon. Unfortunately, many think their sole purpose is to keep the pastor in line and tell him what to do. In some cases, they either view themselves as the Board of Directors and the pastor as the Chief Executive Officer, or they see themselves as a type of Congress whose function is to check and balance the pastor. Although these forms of management are fine for business and government respectively, they in no way resemble the biblical function of a deacon board.

Deacons exist to lighten the pastor's load by caring for the needs of the people (Acts 6) and to model godliness and servanthood in the church of Jesus Christ (1 Tim. 4:12). If they do the job right, deacons are used of God to produce harmony and unity within the assembly. If they fail to do the job, however, distrust and dissension can break out like a rash and spread throughout the body of Christ.

The church I currently pastor in Hickory, North Carolina has an exceptional deacon care ministry. Each deacon is responsible for 12 to 15 families. He prays for them, visits them, telephones them and communicates to them all non-confidential business transacted at deacons' meetings. By taking the time to really know these people, the deacons have learned their needs.

In a former church, Faith Bible in Vineland, New Jersey, our deacons got to know their flock so well that our Deacon's Fund was able to assist needy members of the congregation by purchasing used cars and refrigerators and by paying rent, fuel, heating and insurance bills. The result? Our members felt cared for and our fund grew from very little to multiplied thousands of dollars. The harmony and unity that resulted produced significant growth both spiritually and numerically.

The job of deacon is not easy. Yet it is critical and can be extremely rewarding for the right men. Prescription #6: CHOOSE YOUR LEADERS WISELY. Many churches have crippled themselves by putting the wrong men, or men with a faulty perception of their role, in important positions.

Leaders should be like Christ, who came not to be served, but to serve. By modeling godliness and servanthood, good pastors and deacons can lead the family of God into the kind of peace and harmony that even the outside world cannot ignore. Poor leadership, on the other hand, can cripple it.

1. Leaders Must Lead

God has established only two positions within the church:

pastor and deacon. The pastor is the shepherd and overseer of the flock. The deacons are placed under him to help lighten the load and care for the flock. Together they form a team. For a local church to be effective, each member must exercise the leadership responsibilities appropriate to his office. The deacon is not to play the obstructionist, nor is the pastor to play the dictator.

In football, it takes 11 men to form an offensive team. Yet there is only one quarterback and he calls the play. The others must support that call or the play is "busted" and yardage is lost. In the church, the pastor is the quarterback. Without proper support, much of which must come from the deacons, the church becomes fragmented, people start quarreling and bickering and the main goal of glorifying God and spreading the Gospel is lost.

R$_x$:

Choose
Your Leaders
Wisely

Obviously no deacon should support non-biblical quarterbacking. But as long as the pastor pursues a biblical course and faithfully preaches the Word of God, he has every right to expect the full support and cooperation of the men who serve under him. Deacon support then leads to congregational support which leads to unity in the church.

In the body of Christ, a leader is not supposed to be a cowboy who drives the cattle from behind. He must be like a shepherd who leads the sheep by going before them. Ted Engstrom, in his book The Making of a Christian Leader, has several excellent definitions.

> A leader is one who guides and develops the activities of others and seeks to provide continual training and direction.[1]

> Leadership is an act or behavior required by a group
> to meet its goals. It is an act by either word or
> deed to influence behavior toward a desired end.[2]

Another good definition of leadership comes from Kenneth Gangel's Leadership for Church Education. Gangel writes:

> Leadership is the exercise by a member of a group
> of certain qualities, character and ability which at
> any given time will result in the direction of mutu-
> ally acceptable goals.[3]

A leader must ask himself the questions: "Where are we heading? What is our ultimate goal?" And then he must be able to develop a structure to achieve that goal. A leader must understand that his job is to lead because the outreach of a church depends substantially upon the ability of its leadership.

2. Leaders Must Be Qualified

My years in the pastorate have convinced me that if a man is qualified, he will find a way to get the job done.

Although it may be possible for morally and spiritually unqualified men to know all the ins and outs of pastoring and deaconing and to generate a modicum of visual success, that "success" will not please God and will constitute only a fraction of what God would have done had the men been fit for office. The Lord has far more to say about job qualifications than He does job descriptions. No church leader will be profitable to God without possessing the qualifications that God Himself deems indispensable.

The Biblical Qualifications for a Pastor

Two key passages in Paul's letters, 1 Timothy 3:1-7 and Titus 1:5-9, form a most comprehensive review of pastoral qualifications. They are incorporated into an outline of Warren Wiersbe's which I have used for years. The passage addressed is 1 Timothy 3.[4]

The Pastor's Personal Qualifications

1. <u>Blameless</u> (vs. 2) -- not sinless, but without reproach. There is nothing in his life that the enemy can lay hold of to hinder the work or ruin the witness.

2. <u>Husband of one wife</u> (vs. 2) -- better translation: a one-woman man. To counteract the moral laxness of the day, there must be no question as to marriage standards. The emphasis here is on the positive... this is what he is.

3. <u>Temperate</u> (vs. 2) -- King James Version says "vigilant," a reference to sober judgment and action.

4. <u>Sober-minded</u> (vs. 2) -- seriousness of purpose, free from excess, well-balanced, self-controlled.

5. <u>Good behavior</u> (vs. 2) -- a reference to conduct that is orderly, respectable, honorable... a real gentleman.

6. <u>Hospitality</u> (vs. 2) -- he should like people and enjoy having them in his home.

7. <u>Apt to teach</u> (vs. 2) -- skillful, able, good at teaching. In Ephesians 4:11 he is called a pastor-teacher. A high degree of competency and aptitude are assumed.

8. <u>Not given to wine</u> (vs. 3) -- literally reads "not beside wine." He should not be a constant drinker (Titus 1:7). Paul deals with this issue later when he tells Timothy to "use a little wine for thy stomach's sake" (1 Tim. 5:23). In the culture of that day, wine was an acceptable bever-

age. As the alcoholic content of the wine increased, it was watered down to decrease its intoxicating effects. A pastor must have no affinity for wine, regardless of its age or intoxicating effects. In our contemporary culture infatuated with alcoholic beverages, it would be wise and proper for a pastor to practice the Nazarite vow of never drinking wine as an act of dedication to God. (Num. 6:3). Futhermore, with the vast amount of non-alcoholic beverages now available, and with the advances made in water purification, the need for such a beverage and its medicinal value no longer exists.

9. Not violent (vs. 3) -- King James Version says "no striker"; means not belligerent nor quarrelsome; doesn't use physical force to get his way.

10. Not greedy of filthy lucre (vs. 3) -- not a lover of money, not money hungry.

11. Patient (vs. 3) -- a positive trait. Its basic meaning is gentle, peaceable. It is a reminder that he is dealing with sheep.

12. Not a brawler (vs. 3) -- one who is "disinclined to fight," not contentious or argumentative.

13. Not covetous (vs. 3) -- literally means "not a lover of silver." The pastor must be a lover of the Master, not of money (see 1 Tim. 6:10). He puts Christ and His church first in his life.

The Pastor's Family Qualifications

14. The head of his household (vs. 4-5). The pastor, not his wife, should be the head of the household, and his chil-

dren should be under control. This does not mean that the pastor's children will be perfect. After all, they are still children. It does mean, however, that they respect the Lord and their parents and are growing to be examples as all Christians should. A pastor deals with all types of people, many of whom are looking for direction in family living. The pastor's family, at least to a degree, provides a model for other church families to emulate.

The Pastor's Church Qualifications

15. <u>Not a novice</u> (vs 6) -- The Greek word for "novice" is the root of the modern term "neophyte," or "new plant." "Lifted up with pride," which is a real danger when one assumes a position of responsibility before he is ready, literally means "to wrap up in smoke." That cloud of smoke obscures one's spiritual sight so that a man does not see himself for what he is. Filled with pride, he is then vulnerable to a second danger. He may fall, as did Satan when pride got in the way (see Ez. 28 and Isa. 14).

16. <u>Good report</u> (vs. 7) -- He should have a good testimony among the unsaved, "a good report of them who are outside" or his bad reputation could damage the testimony of the church. What he knows to be true about himself, what the church sees and what the unsaved report, should all agree.

Pastoral leadership is not something to be taken lightly. It is serious business. On the other hand, no one should expect a pastor to be perfect. As long as we are human, our human frailties will strain our efforts to be all God wants us to be. Certainly if a man fails to meet certain of the 16 pastoral qualifications, he is automatically disqualified from serving in the pastorate. Failing to meet others, however, may limit him but not necessarily disqualify him unless these failings are habitual. No godly pastor ever feels that he is all he ought to be. He needs the constant prayers of his people, and he must commit himself to a program of spiritual development (1 Tim. 4:16). Serving as a pastor/elder/bishop is not easy, but it surely is much easier if one's character meets the standards set by God.

The Biblical Qualifications for a Deacon

Two key passages address the issue of a deacon's qualifications. One is in Acts Chapter 6 and the other in 1 Timothy Chapter 3. In Acts 6 we see the position of deacon established in its historical context. The church was trying to rectify a problem. Some of the widows were not being cared for. This caused unrest within the congregation. Since the apostles themselves were unable to meet the needs, they instructed the congregation to choose from among themselves a group of men who could be trusted with the responsibility. These men were to be (1) honest, (2) full of the Holy Spirit, (3) full of wisdom and (4) full of faith. That done, the apostles could then turn their full attention to "prayer, and to the ministry of the Word" (Acts 6:4).

Replace "apostles" with "pastors" and Acts Chapter 6 reveals the function of deacons and their relationship to the pastor. By accepting their ministry of servanthood, the deacons:

> 1. Lightened the pastor's load because they:
> 2. Cared for the needs of the people (Acts 6 deals with the physical need, though it could be spiritual), which in turn
> 3. Created harmony in the body of Christ while providing latitude for the pastor to carry out his duties.

When deacons understand that such is the purpose for their existence, and they handle their responsibilities to the best of their ability, then their local church will be well on its way to accomplishing God's perfect will.

A good summary of a deacon's qualifications is outlined by Charles F. Treadway (in some cases expanded by this author):[5]

1. <u>A man of honest</u> (good) <u>report</u> (Acts 6:3) --a good reputation among those in the church as well as those outside the church.

2. <u>Full of the Holy Spirit</u> (Acts 6:3) -- bigness of character, in spiritual outlook and personal dedication, controlled and guided by the indwelling Holy Spirit.

3. <u>Full of wisdom</u> (Acts 6:3) -- an ability to discern right and wrong and to stand for his convictions; a man of sanctified common sense.

4. <u>Full of faith</u> (Acts 6:5) -- like Stephen's faith, a deacon's faith requires him to risk himself and his possessions; he is fully aware that without faith it is impossible to please God (Heb. 11:6).

Dr. David Hocking comments on these four Acts 6 qualities:

These men were to be full of the Holy Spirit, wisdom and faith. It doesn't mean they were perfect. It means they manifested these qualities as habits of life. There should be a period of time in which the good seed of God's Word can bring forth recognizable fruit. Leaders need wisdom and faith, and that comes through experience and maturity. Without faith, there will be little growth, vision or outreach. Without wisdom, many wrong decisions will be made. Placing new converts into leadership is not wise. Their leadership traits as believers have not had enough time to develop and become obvious to others.[6]

5. Grave (1 Tim. 3:8) -- possesses Christian purpose, who has great reverence for spiritual matters, and whose word carries weight.

6. Not double-tongued (1 Tim. 3:8) -- dependable and honest in relating to all persons, publicly and privately.

7. Not given to much wine (1 Tim. 3:8) -- temperate in living, steward of good influence, doing all to the glory of God.

8. Not greedy of filthy lucre (1 Tim. 3:8) -- a right attitude toward material possessions, never exploiting others for his own gain.

9. A holder of the faith (1 Tim. 3:9) -- gives strength to the church fellowship and possesses spiritual integrity beyond reproach.

10. Tested and proved (1 Tim. 3:10) -- demonstrates his commitment to ministry before being elected to serve as a deacon.

11. Blameless (1 Tim. 3:10) -- a person against whom no charge of wrongdoing can be brought with success.

12. Christian family life (1 Tim. 3:11-12) -- a person whose family is well cared for, whose family relationships are healthy and growing.

13. <u>Husband of one wife</u> (1 Tim. 3:12) -- a model of faithful devotion to one spouse, committed to the sanctity of the marriage bond.

14. <u>Ruling his children and his own house well</u> (1 Tim. 3:12) -- loved and respected by all family members, caring for them as Jesus cared for others.

15. <u>Bold in faith</u> (1 Tim 3:13) --holds to what he believes, taking every opportunity for ministry.

It does not take long to realize that many of the qualifications for deacon are the same as those for pastor. The only major difference is that the deacon need not be "apt to teach" (qualification #7 for a pastor) since preaching and teaching fall to the pastor. He certainly may have this ability, but it is not a necessity in the carrying out of his duties. For a pastor, however, it is a must.

God has set high standards for both pastors and deacons. A leader cannot remove himself from bearing the extra degree of responsibility that comes with his office. In Christian service, ministry and qualification cannot be separated. One without the other is functionally impractical and any attempt to minister without adequate credentials will not only weaken one's personal influence, but will eventually weaken the entire church. On the other hand, men with the character and credentials to do the job will enjoy a ministry deeply pleasing to our Lord.

3. Leaders Must Be Carefully and Slowly Chosen

We have seen that a pastor is not to be a novice (qualification #15) and a deacon is to be tested and proved (qualification #10). Both positions require an extremely high level of spiritual maturity and it is foolhardy to place into leadership anyone who is not ready. Bruce Thelamin, the chaplain of Grove City College in Pennsylvania, suggests:

There is no special honor in being called to the
preaching ministry, there is only special pain. The
pulpit calls those anointed to it as the sea calls its
sailors; and like the sea, it batters and bruises, and
does not rest. To preach, to really preach, is to
die, naked, a little at a time... and to know each
time you do it that you must do it again. [7]

Maturity, however, is not necessarily synonymous with age.
Some men mature faster than others and some never mature at
all. I have known churches that have placed a man in office hoping he would grow into it and when he did not, the results were
devastating. Warren Wiersbe writes: "An untested Christian is an
unprepared Christian. He will probably do more harm than good
if you give him an office in the church."[8] Wiersbe is right.

Spiritual leaders are not born. They are carefully cultivated
over time. Local assemblies should place in leadership only those
whose visible maturity, understanding and experience have already
born good fruit. It is far better to leave a position vacant than to
fill it with the wrong person.

4. Leaders Must Provide a Proper Example

Let no man despise thy youth, but be thou an example of the believers, in word, in conduct, in love,
in spirit, in faith, in purity (1 Tim. 4:12).

Timothy is relatively young when Paul writes this letter and
many members of his congregation are older than he. It can be a
difficult calling to minister successfully to those who are older
than you. Paul's suggestion: give those who are older nothing to
despise but be a positive example of godliness that will inspire
proper emulation. Paul tells Timothy to lead a life worth imitat-
ing, as well as one that brings honor to the cause of Christ.

Indeed, Paul was not giving any advice he did not try to follow himself. When he writes to Timothy a second time he says:

> ...thou hast fully known my doctrine, manner of
> life, purpose, faith, long-suffering, love, patience,
> persecutions, afflictions, which came unto me at
> Antioch, at Iconium, at Lystra, what persecutions
> I endured; but out of all of them the Lord deliv-
> ered me (2 Tim. 3:10-11).

Second Timothy is the most personal of all Paul's letters. It is a father-to-son plea to "hang in there," to "keep on keeping on." And he says to his young protege, "If you want to know how to accomplish that task, just follow the pattern I've lived out in front of you."

This is not the only time that Paul has clearly pointed out the great responsibility of setting the pace, of being the example for others to follow.

> <u>1 Thessalonians 3:7-9</u> -- For ye yourselves know
> how ye ought to follow us; for we behaved not
> ourselves disorderly among you. Neither did we
> eat any man's bread for nothing, but wrought with
> labor and travail night and day, that we might not
> be chargeable to any of you; Not because we have
> not power, but **to make ourselves an example
> unto you to follow us.**

> <u>1 Corinthians 4:16</u> -- Wherefore, I beseech you,
> **be ye followers of me.**

> <u>1 Corinthians 11:1</u> -- Those things, which ye have
> both learned, and received, and heard, **and seen
> in me**, do, and the God of peace shall be with you.

What a fantastic example Paul has set for us. He was fully aware that Christian leadership carries with it the high price of setting an example that is worthy to be followed. If it is a price that you are unwilling or unable to pay, then leadership in the church is not the place for you. Everything rises or falls upon the quality of leadership. And if the leadership falls, so might the church. Unfortunately, people can follow a bad example as well as a good one. If the men in office fail to live godly in Christ Jesus there is no reason to believe that the congregation will either. That particular assembly will likely become just one more casualty in the war against the Enemy.

5. Leaders in Sin Must Be Rebuked

Leadership is not exempt from sin, nor from its consequences. Yet sin cannot be permitted in the church or it will kill that body's credibility and effectiveness while stripping it of the blessings of God. Paul deals with this issue in 1 Timothy 5:19-21:

vs. 19 -- Against an elder receive not an accusation but before two or three witnesses.

vs. 20 -- Them that sin rebuke before all, that others also may fear.

vs. 21 -- I charge thee before God, and the Lord Jesus Christ, and the elect angels, that thou observe these things without preferring one before another, doing nothing by partiality.

The world may tolerate iniquity, but even the world expects the church to be above reproach in this regard. The Jim Bakker and Jimmy Swaggert episodes of the late 1980s make that clear. Non-Christians do not differentiate between theologies. The world paints everyone who names the name of Christ with the same brush and when Bakker and Swaggert were caught in sin for all the world to see, the entire body of Christ, regardless of denomination or association, suffered.

Paul knew well that sin within leadership taints the entire body. Thus he instructs us to deal with sin in the leadership this way:

> 1. <u>Get the facts</u> (vs 19) -- any accusation must be supported by two or three witnesses.

> 2. <u>Give the matter honest appraisal</u> (vs. 21) -- no favoritism should be shown to leaders simply because they are leaders. Their position does not give them an exemption.

> 3. <u>Rebuke them in public if they are guilty</u> (vs 20) -- the context here suggests that the offender has confessed his sin and has asked for forgiveness.

Public sin demands public rebuke. If two or three witnesses can be found, no doubt there are more. Sin cannot be swept under the rug because the testimony of the church is at stake. I know of a good, fundamental Bible-believing church in a rural area whose testimony was all but destroyed because a pastor was having an affair with a woman in the community. The whole town knew about it. Who knows how many unbelievers scoffed at Christianity because of the sin they saw in that church. Yes, God will deal with it. But that does not remove the church's obligation to obey His instruction.

In his introduction to a message entitled "Requirements for Leadership," my late father-in-law, Dr. George H. Slavin, wrote:

> God uses men rather than methods. This is the divine plan through all the ages. It is men like Abraham, Moses, Joshua, and David who stand out in God's plan. Such men were leaders, and it

is the character of things to stand or fall depending upon the type of leadership involved. This is true of movements, of schools, of homes, of nations, and certainly of churches. [9]

To the church that is serious about accomplishing its mission to reach the lost, I offer this advice: Be biblical. Place in positions of leadership only those who measure up to the standards God has laid down in the pages of His Word. Take Prescription # 6: CHOOSE YOUR LEADERS WISELY. And to those who serve in those positions, I offer this advice: You have been assigned a strategic position in the on-going work of the church of Jesus Christ. Don't take that assignment lightly. Leadership is not for everyone. The demands are great and the pressure can be intense. You are responsible to God for the manner in which you discharge your duties. Serve in a manner that will enable you to stand before your Lord and Master and one day hear Him say: "well done, thou good and faithful servant... enter thou into the joy of thy Lord" (Matt. 25:21, 23).

ENDNOTES

1. Ted Engstrom, *The Making of a Christian Leader* (Grand Rapids, MI: Zondervan Pub. House, 1976) p. 16.

2. Ted Engstrom, ibid, p. 20.

3. Kenneth O. Gangel, *Leadership for Church Education* (Chicago, IL: Moody Press) 1970, p.12.

4. Warren W. Wiersbe, *Whole Bible Study Course* - Orig. by D. B. Eastep (Covington, KY: Calvary Baptist Church Book Room, n.d.) Notes on I Tim. 3.

5. Howard B. Foshee, *Now That You're a Deacon* (Nashville, TN: Broadman Press, 1975) p. 43-44.

6. David L. Hocking, *The Seven Laws of Christian Leadership* (Ventura, CA: Regal Books, 1991)) p. 21.

7. Kenneth O. Gangel, *1 & 2 Timothy and Titus* (Wheaton, IL: Victor Books, 1987) p.31.

8. Warren W. Wiersbe, *Be Faithful* (Wheaton, IL: Victor Books) p. 48.

9. George H. Slavin, *Requirements for Leadership* (Personal Sermon notes, n.d., #1462).

Prescriptions That Count

7

Avoiding a Stroke

Joe is a faithful member of his local church and would gladly do anything to serve the Lord. For the past three years he has spent every Saturday morning mowing the church lawn and pruning the shrubbery. He doesn't enjoy the job and would much rather spend the time talking about the Bible. In fact, he is so good at explaining God's Word that people often call him with questions. But yard work also calls. An unkept, overgrown lawn would be a terrible testimony in the community, and if he were to quit, who would take over? So Joe presses on.

Henry is a faithful member of the same church. He teaches math at the local high school and loves the Lord with all his heart. When the adult Sunday School needed a teacher, Henry was immediately pressed into service because of his many years at the high school. For some reason, however, his Sunday School class has steadily diminished in size. He really doesn't enjoy teaching it either. He spends so much time indoors that he would much rather do something outdoors. But Henry truly wants to help and if he were to quit, who would take over? So Henry presses on.

Joe and Henry are, of course, fictional Christians. But the scenario is all too real. In many churches today believers assume necessary but inappropriate jobs because (a) they do not know their spiritual gifts and/or (b) they are being used where they are not gifted. Worse still, some believers are not being used at all. Consequently, the body of Christ cannot function according to design. Rather than marching stalwartly forward to carry out the Great Commission, the afflicted church limps along like a man who has suffered a stroke, the functioning members of the body dragging along the dysfunctional ones.

Beloved, it ought not to be. Prescription #7: UNDERSTAND THE IMPORTANCE OF SPIRITUAL GIFTS AND MAKE THE MOST OF THEM. Use the tools that God has provided to accomplish the work that He has prepared. It is a spiritual work and it requires spiritual tools.

If I were to ask you to dig a ditch, you could expect me to give you a shovel. God has commanded us to evangelize the world and make disciples. Certainly He has given us the equipment necessary to do so.

In each of Paul's letters to Timothy, Paul refers to the provision that our Lord made available to the apostle's young protegé to help him carry out his God-given responsibilities. So too has He provided for all of us. Our mission involves danger (it is a warfare, 2 Tim. 2:34), discipline (study to show yourself approved unto God, 2 Tim. 2:15), diligence (in season, out of season, 2 Tim. 4:2), durability (endure afflictions, 2 Tim. 4:5), and determination.

Surely we cannot expect to accomplish all this through human strength. Success depends entirely upon the working of God. "Without me, " said the Lord, "ye can do nothing" (John 15:5). Even the great Rabbi Gamaliel understood that fact. In Acts 5:38-39, Luke quoted Gamaliel's warning to the men who opposed the apostles in the early days of the church: "If this...work be of man, it will come to nothing, but if it be of God, ye cannot overthrow it." Hence Paul was able to write later in Philippians 4:13, "I can do all things through Christ who strengthens me." As Dr. Ryrie once said, "That verse kicks all excuses right in the seat of the can'ts."

God has given every Christian a function in the body of Christ, and has supernaturally equipped him to perform that function. Not only are we equipped, Paul reminds us, but we are obligated to use what we have received to the glory of God:

> Neglect not the gift that is in thee...
> Tim. 4:14

> stir up the gift of God...
> 2 Tim. 1:6

R_x:
Understand the Importance of Spiritual Gifts and Make the Most of Them.

How has He equipped us? With the spiritual gifts we read about in God's Word. And just as they were critical for Timothy's success in the ministry, so are they critical for us. Unfortunately, far too many believers fail to understand their importance. For that reason Paul addressed the church at Corinth with these words:

> Now concerning spiritual gifts, brethren, I would not have you ignorant...there are diversities of gifts...the manifestation of the Spirit is given to every man to profit...all these (gifts) worketh that one and the selfsame Spirit, dividing to every man severally as he will...that there should be no schism in the body, but that the members should have the same care one for another.
> Selected verses, 1 Corinthians 12

Ignorance of spiritual gifts should not be a problem today. There is a proliferation of material on the subject. That was not true during the first half of our century. In his forward to Kenneth

Gangel's book You and Your Spiritual Gifts, Ray Stedman writes:

> The whole subject of spiritual gifts is the lost trea-
> sure of nineteenth and twentieth century Christian-
> ity. The church has been impoverished beyond
> belief by the prevailing ignorance of the existence
> of these spiritual riches. But now the long-buried
> truth is coming to light again. Widespread excite-
> ment has possessed the churches, and the tide of
> interest in the subject is running at full flow. [1]

How I hope that Dr. Stedman's analysis is correct. But in the church where it is not, a stroke lurks just around the corner. The church that fails to understand the importance of spiritual gifts will fail to use them. And since our battle is spiritual, failure to use the equipment issued will result in heavy damage to the cause of Christ.

Every local church must avail itself of the material written on spiritual gifts. Read it. Digest it. Use it.

More than 20 years ago Dr. Earl D. Radmacher, former long-time president of Western Conservative Baptist Seminary, challenged pastors to preach on the gifts. In an article entitled The Jack of All Trades Syndrome, he wrote:

> Every pastor ought to have a goal of helping each
> member to identify his gift and then to find the
> place where his gift fits into the total work of the
> church. It is a rare pastor who has preached a
> series of messages covering each of the spiritual
> gifts. I ask pastors I meet, 'Why don't you take
> 15 weeks and preach on one gift of the Spirit each
> week and then ask for decisions from your people?'
> Ask them, 'What are your gifts? How are you
> using them?' And really dig in deep because, as I

understand it, shaping up the saints in large part means enabling them to find out what their gifts are and where they can use them.[2]

John Stott has passed on this bit of doggerel composed by an anonymous clergyman's family.

> The Rector is late,
> He's forgotten the date,
> So what can the faithful do now,
> Poor things?
> They'll sit in a pew
> With nothing to do
> And sing a selection of hymns
> Poor things![3]

One way to solve that problem is to take Dr. Radmacher's advice. Open the Word of God, identify the gifts and challenge God's people to see which one(s) they possess. Then exercise them.

In today's church age, a believer serves God as he carries out the will of God through the ministry of the Holy Spirit, i.e. "walking in the Spirit" (Gal. 5:16). His service for the Lord can be divided into two parts:

> General Service -- for all believers.
> This is what all children of God are expected to give.

> Specific Service -- specific work, revealed by the Holy Spirit, for the edification of the body, the enjoyment of the individual believer, and the glory of God (as His purpose is accomplished).

The General Service of the Saints

Although the Old Testament and New Testament economies differ, they are strikingly similar regarding the service of God.

1. Old Testament service of God was in the hands of the priests. The same is true in the New Testament (Rev. 1:6; 1 Pet. 2:5-9).

2. Both Old (Ex. 28:1) and New Testament (John 1:12) priests are born into that office.

3. Both Old (Ex. 29:4) and New Testament (Titus 3:5, 1 Cor. 6:11) priests required cleansing at the beginning of their ministry.

4. In both economies the priesthood involves:

    (a) Sacrifice
        O.T. -- Exodus 29:38-44
        N.T. -- Romans 12:1, Hebrews 13:15-16.

    (b) Worship
        O.T. -- Exodus 30
        N.T. -- 1 Peter 2:5, 9.

    (c) Intercession
        O.T. -- Exodus 30:10
        N.T. -- 1 Timothy 2:1, Colossians 4:12.

[Note: The perfect illustrations of the ministry of intercession are the Lord Jesus and the Holy Spirit (Rom. 8:34, Heb. 4:14-16, 7:25, Rom. 8:26-27).]

At the very minimum every Christian should render general service to God in his capacity as a believer-priest. For the local church to be vibrant and healthy, however, he also must render specific service.

The Specific Service of the Saints
(Romans 12, 1 Corinthians 12-14, Ephesians 4)

God gives each believer a specific task, then uniquely equips him to perform it by endowing him at the point of salvation with a special "tool" known as a spiritual gift. Some definitions of spiritual gifts are:

-- divine endowment of special abilities for service given to a member of the body of Christ.

-- divinely ordained spiritual abilities through which Christ enables His church to execute its task on earth.

-- extraordinary endowments bestowed by the Holy Spirit sovereignly and undeservedly on believers as instruments for Christian service and church edification.

As we can see:

* Their source is the special grace of the Holy Spirit.
* Their nature is spiritual ability, endowment, power.
* Their purpose is for service, or ministry to edify saints.

Thus, they are not ordinary talents, but Spirit-given abilities for Christian service. Our friend Henry may be a great math teacher, but as we saw at the beginning of this chapter, God in His wisdom endowed him with the gift of helps, not teaching. Beware of the trap of assuming that because someone does something for a living, God has spiritually gifted him in that area. The Lord is not limited in what He can do, nor is He that limiting in what He allows us to do.

It follows naturally that because the gifts vary, the specific service rendered will vary too. In fact, Scripture teaches there are three diversities.

1. Diversities of gifts -- 1 Corinthians 12:4, Romans 12:6.

2. Diversities of ministrations (administrations) --
    1 Corinthians 12:5.

3. Diversities of operations...1 Corinthians 12:6.

All Believers Are Gifted

Scripture teaches that God leaves no one out (1 Cor. 12:7, 11; Eph. 4:7; Rom. 12:5-6) and bestows upon every child of His one (or more) of these special abilities (1 Cor. 12:8-10). The ascended Lord gives the gifts, but the Spirit of God divides them (Eph. 4:7-11; cp. 1 Cor. 12:11).

These gifts can make the servant of God profitable (1 Cor. 12:7). Of course, the converse of this truth implies that service rendered in the energy of the flesh is not profitable. God's work must be done God's way.

Listing the Gifts

Romans 12, 1 Corinthians 12 and Ephesians 4 list the gifts, with some variation and repetition. In 1 Corinthians 12 some are mentioned more than once. Only two gifts, prophecy and teaching appear in all three places. Apostleship, ministrations (helps) and government (ruling) are found in two locations. Thirteen of the gifts are mentioned only once. In all, 18 different gifts (not all-inclusive no doubt) are listed. A nineteenth gift is found in 1 Peter 4. (A good book on this subject is 19 Gifts of the Spirit by Leslie Flynn.)

Romans 12:3   Prophecy
         Ministering (helps)
         Teaching
         Exhorting
         Giving
         Government (Ruling)
         Showing Mercy

1 Corinthians 12:8-10, 28-30
         Word of Wisdom
         Word of Knowledge
         Faith
         Healing [mentioned three times (3X)]
         Miracles (3X)
         Prophecy (3X)
         Discernment
         Tongues (3X)
         Interpretation (2X)
         Apostleship (2X)
         Teaching (2X)
         Ministration (Helps)
         Government (Ruling)
Ephesians 4:11   Apostleship
         Prophecy
         Evangelism
         Pastoring
         Teaching [4]

Classifying the Gifts

"Whoever <u>SPEAKS</u>, let him speak as if it were utterances of God; whoever <u>SERVES</u>, let him do so as by the strength which God supplies." This passage of 1 Peter 4:11 (NASV) alludes to

two classifications of gifts: speaking and serving. A third classi-
fication encompasses the four <u>SIGN</u> gifts, two of which are listed
under speaking gifts and two under serving gifts.

Speaking
1. Apostleship
2. Prophecy
3. Evangelism
4. Pastoring
5. Teaching
6. Exhorting
7. Knowledge
8. Word of Wisdom
* Tongues
* Interpretation of Tongues

Serving
9. Helps (ministration)
10. Hospitality (from 1 Pet. 4:9-10)
11. Giving
12. Government (Ruling)
13. Showing Mercy
14. Faith
15. Discernment
* Miracles
* Healing

Signifying
16. Miracles *
17. Healing *
18. Tongues *
19. Interpretation of Tongues *5

[* Since the signifying, or "SIGN" gifts are no longer necessary
or operational today, they are omitted in the gift analyzation that
follows. Material supporting this comment is voluminous.]

ANALYZING THE GIFTS

<u>Speaking Gifts</u>

APOSTLESHIP...Ephesians 4:11

Technically, the gift of apostleship does not exist today.
However, a portion of the apostle's ministry continues
through what some term the "missionary gift." Although
a missionary lacks the credentials (sign gifts) of an apostle,
he <u>is</u> one sent to minister transculturally with church-plant-
ing goals.

PROPHECY...Ephesians 4:11

There are no prophets today in the purest sense of the word. The true prophet foretold the future and foretold God's message, which often was one of warning. The forthtelling aspect alone remains today as the Spirit-given ability to persuasively explain the Word and wisdom of God.

EVANGELISM...Ephesians 4:11

Unlike the missionary gift, the gift of evangelism does not involve crossing cultural lines. Unlike the prophetic gift, it does not thunder judgment, but majors in the loving and gentle grace of God. It is the gift of proclaiming the good news of salvation in a way that stirs people's hearts to respond.

PASTORING (Shepherding)...Ephesians 4:11

The word itself means "one who pastures the sheep," and refers to the gift of being able to care for a congregation (sheep). Although everyone divinely called to the office of pastor will have received this gift, God has not reserved it exclusively for pastors or for men. This gift involves guiding, guarding and feeding the sheep. Believers so gifted could appropriately serve as deans in schools, as youth advisors, etc.

TEACHING...1 Corinthians 12:29; Romans 12:7

This is the supernatural ability to explain clearly and effectively the truth of the Word of God. A person with the gift of teaching can systematically construct the complete ladder of a doctrine and apply it incisively and diligently to life.

EXHORTATION...Romans 12:8

This is the God-given ability to draw alongside people to insightfully comfort them, encourage, rebuke and inspire them toward action.

KNOWLEDGE...1 Corinthians 12:8; 13:2

This God-given ability enables a believer to arrange facts of Scripture, to categorize them into principles and to apply them to repeated or familiar situations.

WISDOM...1 Corinthians 12:8; 13:2

This is the God-given ability to locate formerly unknown principles as well as to combine known principles of God's Word and to communicate them to fresh situations.

Serving Gifts

HELPS...1 Corinthians 12:28

The ability to see tasks and to do them for or with someone in order to lift external burdens.

HOSPITALITY...1 Peter 4:9-11

The supernatural ability to provide open house and warm welcome to those in need of food and lodging.

GIVING...Romans 12:8; 1 Corinthians 13:2

The God-given ability to make and to give things most liberally and beyond all human expectation.

GOVERNMENT...Romans 12:8; 1 Corinthians 12:28

The executive ability to lead people aggressively but carefully, and the legislative ability to collect data, set policy and to skillfully and wisely set a course of action.

SHOWING MERCY...Romans 12:8

The ability to be sensitive or empathetic to people suffering affliction and misery and to lift internal burdens with cheerfulness.

FAITH...1 Corinthians 12:9; 13:2

The visionary ability to see past mountainous problems to Jesus, The Ultimate Resource. A person with this gift can rely absolutely on both God's ability and His willingness to provide in whatever the particular circumstance may be.

DISCERNING SPIRITS...1 Corinthians 12:10

The supernatural ability to distinguish between true and false sources of supernatural, oral revelation. This gift was essential before the written Word was completed because many false prophets claimed to be delivering revelation from God. Today the gifts of knowledge and wisdom, properly used, should be sufficient.

As previously noted, any church that sincerely desires to develop the spiritual gifts of its members can delve into a wealth of material. A great source of help for me came from studies done under Dr. Gordon McMinn, formerly of Western Conservative Baptist Seminary. Dr. McMinn regularly conducts workshops around the country on the subject.

Timothy was fortunate enough to have the Apostle Paul as his teacher. "Neglect not the gift," wrote Paul, and "stir up the gift." The Spirit of God gave Timothy special tools to accomplish his ministry. Like Timothy, we also have a ministry and we also have received special tools. They are vital and must all work together at full capacity if we are to make an impact for Christ in the world. Flynn has a wonderful little parable to illustrate this point.

Someone once imagined the carpenter's tools holding a conference. Brother HAMMER presided. Several suggested he leave the meeting because he was too noisy. Replied the HAMMER, "If I have to leave this shop, Brother SCREW must go also. You have to turn him around again and again to accomplish anything." Brother SCREW then spoke up. "If you wish, I'll leave. But Brother PLANE must leave too. All his work is on the surface, his efforts have no depth."

To this Brother PLANE responded, "Brother RULE will also have to withdraw, for he is always measuring folks as though he were the only one who is right." Brother RULE then complained against Brother SANDPAPER. "You ought to leave because you're so rough and are always rubbing people the wrong way."

In the midst of all this discussion, in walked THE CARPENTER OF NAZARETH. He had arrived to start His day's work. Putting on His apron, He went to the bench to make a pulpit from which to proclaim the Gospel. He employed the hammer, screw, plane, rule, sandpaper and all the other tools. After the day's work when the pulpit was finished, Brother SAW arose and remarked, "Brethren, I observe that all of us are workers together with the Lord."[6]

The church of Jesus Christ is to proclaim God's redeeming grace, the "good news" that one can place his faith in the finished work of Christ on the cross of Calvary and receive everlasting life. But for the church to be effective, every "tool" in the shop must be operational. Each was designed with a purpose and each must do what it was designed for. So we must all ask ourselves the questions: Am I doing the job for which I have been designed? Am I utilizing the "tools" that God has given me?

God intends for His local assemblies to be robust and fully functioning. It must grieve Him terribly to see His gifts squandered. The body does not function properly when the healthy members are forced to drag along those who are not.

To avoid such stroke-like symptoms, the local church must take regular doses of Prescription #7: UNDERSTAND THE IMPORTANCE OF SPIRITUAL GIFTS AND MAKE THE MOST OF THEM. That way Joe will not be mowing the lawn when he should be teaching Sunday School; Henry will not be teaching Sunday School when God would be pleased to have him mow the lawn; and George will not be warming the pew every Sunday and doing absolutely nothing more in the body of Christ.

ENDNOTES

1. Kenneth O. Gangel, *You and Your Spiritual Gifts* (Chicago, IL: Moody Press, 1975) p. 5.

2. Earl D. Radmacher, *"The Jack-of-All Trades Syndrome"* - article (Chicago, IL: Moody Monthly, March 1971).

3. Leslie B. Flynn, *19 Gifts of the Spirit* (Wheaton, IL: Victor Books, 1974) p. 10.

4. Leslie B. Flynn, ibid, p. 29.

5. Leslie B. Flynn, ibid, p. 32.

6. Leslie B. Flynn, ibid, p. 28.

8

Women in the Church

"While on vacation recently," wrote Dr. Ryrie in a 1977 issue of <u>Moody Monthly</u>, "I glanced at the Saturday church page of a large metropolitan newspaper. Among the 20 or so display ads for services the next day were three churches pastored by women. Two could be called mainline churches; one was a cult. Typical? Probably. Even evangelical churches, on whose staffs women have long served in various capacities, are now ordaining or discussing ordaining women as pastors."[1]

Certainly one of the changes in our modern society is the rise to prominence of women. This fact has forced the church to ask, "What is the woman's role within the local church, especially with regard to leadership?" Where men are concerned, the Scripture is clear. But what about where women are concerned?

Fortunately, God has not left us directionless. But the issue is highly volatile in some circles and can sorely test one's personal view of the inspiration of Scripture. The Bible teaches that women are gifted; women can teach other women and children, but women cannot pastor or exercise authority over men.

It is at this juncture where many take umbrage with the Word of God. They don't like it. They call it "sexist." They argue with it or attempt to ignore it. For anyone who believes, as I do, that the Bible is inspired, God-breathed, verbally and plenarally, word

113

for word to the fullest extent, this is one area where the rubber meets the road. The Lord does not care about political correctness. He cares about truth and gave it to us in His Word. "Heaven and earth shall pass away," He tells us in Matthew 24:35, "but my words shall not pass away."

With that in mind, churches must get out their yardsticks (the truth of the Word of God) and begin measuring their practices. If the practices do not measure up, we reject them, not the Scriptures. In Leadership Is Male, J. David Pawson writes: "Truth must not be based on cultural consensus but on the revealed mind of God."[2] For some, it may be a difficult pill, but we must swallow Prescription #8 and consider it preventative medicine from the Great Physician who knows much more than we: UNDERSTAND GENDER ROLES IN THE CHURCH AND UPHOLD THE BIBLICAL STANDARD. Contrary to what the world may think, women can and should play a vital role in the church, but it is not the identical role as men.

Certainly the women of the early church were good examples of how God uses women in the ministry.

1. Like all believers, women in the early church spread the gospel as evidenced by Priscilla in Acts 18:26 and the Samaritan woman at the well in John 4:28 and 39-42.

2. They supported Paul's ministry as evidenced by Phoebe in Romans 16:1 and Lydia in Acts 16:15.

3. They received spiritual gifts as do all believers (1 Cor. 12:4-11).

4. They taught. Paul tells us that older women are to teach younger women (Titus 2:4-5).

5. They provided hospitality. In 1 Timothy 5:10 widows per-

formed certain church-authorized and church-related functions that involved hospitality and possibly visitation.

In "Caught in the Middle" (<u>Kindred Spirit</u>, Summer 1989) H. Wayne House writes of the first century believing women:

> Women are fellow-laborers with men in the vineyard of God and in the world in general. They are equal image-bearers. Only in functioning in spiritual authority, similar to that expressed by the husband or an elder in the church, they are restricted. Elders, based upon the authority of the Word of God were to reprove, rebuke, correct, and instruct in righteousness. This was the sense of teaching in the first century church and world at large. Teachers expected their students to learn and obey their teaching; this is how Paul develops the idea of teaching in the letters I and II Timothy and Titus. Though certain women may have this ministry over other women, Scripture clearly restricts women from exercising this type of authority -- or functioning as elders -- over men.[3]

R$_x$:

Understand Gender Roles in the Church and Uphold the Biblical Standard

Paul addresses the role of women in the church in four major passages: Galatians 3:28, 1 Corinthians 11:2-16, 1 Corinthians 14:33b-35 and 1 Timothy 2:9-15. The principles to be extracted from these and other New Testament passages include:

A. Men and women are positionally equal in the body of Christ.

There are no second-class citizens. That is what Paul meant when he wrote:

> There is neither Jew nor Greek, there is neither
> bond nor free, there is neither male nor female; for
> ye are all one in Christ Jesus (Gal. 3:28).

The Jewish people had always considered the Gentiles to be second class; slave owners had always considered their slaves to be less than second class; and everyone considered women to be second class. There was only one place where everyone was positionally equal and that was within the Body of Christ. Galatians 3:28 does not mean that these distinctions are eliminated. Becoming a Christian does not alter one's race, one's station in life or one's sex. But it does guarantee us all the same gift of eternal life and the same spiritual blessings.

Identical status within the body, however, does not translate into identical responsibility or opportunity. There are different ministries based upon spiritual gifts. These diversities strengthen the body, enabling it to function properly. Paul's analogy of the human body (1 Cor. 12:12 ff) demonstrates that though the members are different they are all necessary. The same truth applies here.

B. Local church leadership in the New Testament is assigned to men and not to women.

The only two categories of leadership in the New Testament church, pastor and deacon, are both composed of men exclusively. This is rather obvious since one of the qualifications for both is to be the husband of one wife, i.e., a "one-woman man" (1 Tim. 3:2, 12).

C. Women are not to teach publicly in the church.

1 Timothy and 1 Corinthians make this clear. When the church is gathered for public services, men and women worship together. For a woman to assume a teaching position when dealing with spiritual truth places her over the God-assigned leadership authority and constitutes a direct violation of Scripture because leadership in the church is male.

This does not mean a woman cannot teach. If she has the necessary spiritual gifts it would be a sin if she did not teach. In Titus 2:4-5 she is commanded to teach. Her audience, however, is restricted. In Titus the command is for the older women to teach the younger women. There also are no biblical restrictions forbidding her to teach minor children because they are not included in the church leadership structure.

Of all the passages that address the issue of male-female roles, one is outstanding for its practicality. It is 1 Timothy 2:9-15. Here Paul virtually lists the characteristics that should be observable in spiritually mature women.

1. Modesty

> In like manner, also, that women adorn themselves
> in modest apparel, with Godly fear and sobriety,
> not with braided hair, or gold, or pearls or costly
> array (1 Tim. 2:9).

The contrast here is between the artificiality of the world and the true beauty of a godly life that radiates from within. Paul is not telling women to ignore their appearance, but rather to concentrate on the internals which are far more important. The externals will someday become self-defeating.

2. Godliness

> But which becometh women professing godliness
> (1 Timothy 2:10a).

She "professes godliness." She demonstrates purity. "Godli-ness" is a word that Paul uses 11 times in the pastoral epistles and is a shortened form of "god-likeness."

3. Good Works

> ...with good works (1 Tim. 2:10b).

She practices good works. They are a natural, on-going part of her life. If she happens to have an unsaved husband who has been unmoved by the Word, her industrious attitude toward her responsibilities may draw him toward Christ.

4. Humility

> Let the women learn in silence with all subjection.
> But I permit not a woman to teach, nor to usurp
> authority over the man, but to be in silence.

This command is amplified in 1 Corinthians 14:34-40. Here Paul gives instruction regarding public worship. He makes it clear that a woman must sit in humble silence and listen prayerfully when the local church meets in assembly. If she has any questions she is to ask her husband at home.

Paul gives two important reasons for this requirement of pub-lic humility.

1. The Doctrinal Reason

There is a principle of headship which runs throughout the

Pauline epistles (i.e. Eph. 5:22 ff, 1 Cor. 11:1-16). As elementary as it may sound, the head must always be over the body. To reverse the situation by placing the body over the head is simply upside-down, and things do not work well that way.

Headship touches three major areas;
- (1)   The headship of **Christ** over the **Body** (Col. 1:18).
- (2)   The headship of the **Pastor** over the **Flock** (Acts 20:28).
- (3)   The headship of the **Man** over the **Woman** (1 Cor. 11:1-16; 1 Tim. 2:12).[4]

When the church rejects the headship of the pastor and the woman rejects the headship of the man, there is an implicit rejection of the headship of Jesus Christ. That is treading on dangerous territory.

The Bible teaches that headship is even written into the very course of nature.

> For Adam was first formed, then Eve (1 Tim. 2:13).

Adam was created first and had precedence over Eve. Paul addressed this when he wrote to the church at Corinth:

> For the man is not of the woman, but the woman of the man. Neither was the man created for the woman, but the woman for the man (1 Cor. 11:8-9).

When a church violates this headship principle, chaos ultimately results as it did in the Corinthian church which suffered from confusion and carnality partly because the men and women had exchanged roles. God has specific roles for both. Christianity, like no other religious faith, has elevated the position of women.

Paul's writings have done more to emancipate women and to secure their social, civil and political rights than the writings of any other author in the history of the human race. Studies have shown that women enjoy the highest degree of happiness in countries where this biblical principle forms an intimate part of the country's ethic.

2. The Practical and Observational Reason

> And Adam was not deceived, but the woman, being deceived, was in the transgression (2 Tim. 2:14).

This is not to be construed as a commentary on the mental prowess of women or as a suggestion that they lack the intellectual acumen of men. In fact, my observations have often led me to believe just the opposite. However, Paul does teach here and elsewhere (2 Cor. 11:3) that women are more gullible than men and Satan finds it easier to deceive them. Because of her trusting nature, a woman, says the Word of God, is more easily led into false beliefs than is a man. In the right roles, this quality can change from a weakness into a strength. Women, for example, are more apt to listen to their children with tenderness and compassion than are men.

Nor can the church ignore passages such as 1 Peter 3:7, where God calls the wife the weaker vessel in the marital relationship. "Weaker" does not mean less valuable. It simply means different. God has equipped women to carry out the roles for which they were created. While this may pose limitations in some areas, it produces great blessing in others.

All of this brings us to 1 Timothy 2:15. Many commentators feel this is the most difficult verse to understand in all the pastoral epistles.

> Notwithstanding, she shall be saved in childbearing, if they continue in faith and love and holiness with sobriety.

Several questions arise here. How is Paul using the word "saved"? Who is the "she"? Does becoming a mother save a woman?

First of all, the salvation spoken of does not refer to the salvation of one's soul. It is not a reference to a woman placing her faith in Christ and being born-again. The Greek word "to save" (so-zo) has a number of different uses. For instance, one may be saved from illness and death (Mark 5:34); from shipwreck (Acts 27:20); or from indoctrination into false teaching (1 Tim. 4:16). Certainly we all know women who have born children but who are not born-again. If childbearing saved souls, salvation would be of works and giving birth would be like buying a ticket to Heaven -- a heretical teaching if ever I heard one.

Another interpretation says that godly women will always be delivered in dangerous childbirth. The problem here is that many godly women have died bearing children. This interpretation forces the conclusion that these women were somehow to blame for their own deaths because of some deficiency "in faith and love and holiness with sobriety." There is no basis for that assumption.

Some see the woman in 1 Timothy 2:15 as Mother Eve. Her "deliverance" came through the pain of childbirth (Gen. 3:15, 16) because eventually the "seed of the woman" came to bring salvation. Still others see "she shall be saved in childbearing" as a reference to the One who is the Savior.

I do not hold any of these views as being correct. To understand the meaning we have to look at the context, which, in this case, goes back to the garden of Eden.

Genesis contains the record of man's creation. God placed Adam and his wife Eve in the perfect condition of innocence in the Garden (Gen. 1-2). Man fell from that perfect condition through sin (Gen. 3:1-13) and his fellowship with God was interrupted. Now he deserves to be punished for his sin. God spells out the consequences for both the man and the woman (Gen. 3:16-19, 22-24) and metes out judgment.

The Curse on the Woman:
Unto the woman He said, I will greatly multiply
thy sorrow and thy conception; in sorrow thou shalt
bring forth children; and thy desire shall be to thy
husband, and he shall rule over thee [more literally, "your desire shall be to rule over your husband, but he shall rule over you"] (Gen. 3:16).

Because of her sin, the woman's original place of subordination -- she was made for man, not vice-versa (Gen. 2:18) -- now
became a place of subjection. She would have to submit her desires to the desires of her husband. She also would face great
sorrow, danger and agony in bringing children into the world.

The Curse on the Man:
And unto Adam He said... Cursed is the ground
for thy sake; in sorrow shalt thou eat of it all the
days of thy life; Thorns and thistles shall it bring
forth to thee; and thou shalt eat of the herb of the
field; In the sweat of thy face shalt thou eat bread,
till thou return unto the ground (Gen. 3:17-19).

Every part of the physical world in which we live has been
affected by the curse. All the earth is afflicted by waste, desola-
tion, ruin, death and corruption. The Bible states this clearly in
Romans 8:22, where we read, "For we know that the whole creation groaneth and travaileth in pain together." Man was originally given dominion over nature and nature could not resist him.
The fall altered that structure. Now nature resists man's will.
God's assignment to Adam to subdue the earth -- originally a pleasant task -- became a back-breaking one. In effect, Adam was
sentenced to a life of hard labor.
Most of us who live in America have little idea of the truth of
Genesis 3:17-19. Extreme poverty, misery, difficult and discour-

aging work and frequent famine are the norms of life for large segments of the globe. Millions of people around the world toil unceasingly all their lives, and without an understanding of Genesis Chapter 3, they have no idea why.

For the woman the fall produced subjection to her husband and pain and sorrow in childbirth. **For the man** the fall produced hard work, sweat and toil. This is the context in which 1 Timothy 2:15 must be interpreted:

> Notwithstanding, she shall be saved in childbearing, if they continue in faith and love and holiness with sobriety.

Man fell and was cursed. However, he will be able to find "salvation" in his circumstances if he accepts the consequences of the curse, goes to work and overcomes the obstacles blocking his way. By doing so, the "curse" becomes a blessing. By accepting those consequences and recognizing them as responsibilities, a man is able to provide for the family which God has called him to head. In doing so, he receives "societal salvation." Note that, for the most part, the man's work is carried on **outside** the home.

The woman also finds her "salvation" when she accepts the consequences of the fall. Her penalty involved conception... children are involved... as well as subjection to her husband. Her work -- caring for her children and her husband -- is for the most part carried out **within** the home. As she carries out those responsibilities, she experiences a "societal salvation" that the woman who rejects her after-the-fall role does not. Her "curse" too then becomes a blessing.

Kenneth S. Wuest writes:

> Just as hard labor is the man's salvation in a set of circumstances and surroundings that without it, would cause him to deteriorate instead of make progress in character, so the pains of childbirth become the salvation of the woman, and in the same

sense and for the same purpose, that of enabling
the woman to adjust herself in her circumstances
and surroundings so that she too will do the same.[5]

The Expositor's Greek Testament says the same thing:

> The penalty for transgression, so far as woman is
> concerned, was expressed in the words, "I will
> greatly multiply thy sorrow and thy conception; in
> sorrow thou shalt bring forth children" (Gen. 3:16).
> But just as in the case of man, the world being as it
> is, the sentence has proved a blessing, so it is in
> the case of woman. "In the sweat of thy face shalt
> thou eat bread" expresses man's necessity, duty,
> privilege, dignity. If the necessity of work be a
> stumbling block, man can "make it a stepping-
> stone" (Browning, The Ring and the Book, The
> Pope, 413). Nay, it is the only stepping-stone avail-
> able to him. If St. Paul's argument had led him to
> emphasize the man's part in the first transgression,
> he might have said, "He shall be saved in his toil,"
> his overcoming the obstacles of nature.
>
> So, St. Paul taking the common-sense view that
> child-bearing, rather than public teaching or the
> direction of affairs, is woman's primary function,
> duty, privilege, and dignity, reminds Timothy and
> his readers that there was another aspect of the
> story in Genesis besides that of the woman's tak-
> ing initiative in transgression: the pains of child-
> birth were her sentence, yet in undergoing these,
> she finds her salvation. She shall be saved in
> childbearing. That is her normal and natural duty;
> and in the discharge of our normal and natural
> duties we all, men and women alike, as far as our

individual efforts can contribute to it, "work out our own salvation." [6]

We live in a society ailing with galloping welfareism... where man expects to be supported by the state. In many ways, that mindset has affected all of us. Taxes go up, inner cities deteriorate and crime increases. The old philosophy (which, by the way, is biblical) "no work, no pay," has, in many places gone by the boards.

Compounding the problem of the man who refuses to go out and work for a living is the woman who refuses to stay home. In these cases the curses have not turned to blessings because man has been unwilling to conform to the regulations which God has laid down. Divorce, broken homes, alienation among family members have all skyrocketed. And is it any wonder? When a society wanders out from the protection of a God-authored structure, the result can only be chaos.

Unfortunately, that chaos is not limited to the non-Christian world. Much the same has taken place in the church. We have become appallingly infected by our culture.

Ultimately, the real issue of women in the church revolves around who will teach the Word of God. A Bible-believing church must take great care that no one who can easily be led astray instructs the local congregation. As Warren Wiersbe writes:

> Just as Satan got a foot in Eden through Eve, so he often gets a footing in the local church through some sincere, misguided woman. It is significant that women have played a big role in the false cults (Adventists, Christian Science, Theosophy, I Am Cult, etc.) as well as in the Pentecostal movement.[7]

We are in the world, but not of the world. Is that not what Christ said in His great high priestly prayer in John 17:16: "They are not of the world, even as I am not of the world." Neither are we to be conformed to the world, Paul tells us in Romans 12:2.

How do we accomplish this in the structure of the local church? One way is to take heavy doses of Prescription #8: UNDER-STAND GENDER ROLES IN THE CHURCH AND UPHOLD THE BIBLICAL STANDARD. What is right in God's eyes is not always popular in man's eyes. When a church strays from God's blueprint it encounters problems God never intended.

It is critical that men accept the roles of leading and teaching. If they do, the women who will fight for control of these responsibilities will be few and far between and certainly the fighters will not be those who "practice godliness."

All these points duly noted, however, there exists a great tragedy within the 20th Century church. Many women today have assumed male roles simply by default. Either there were no men available to fill positions or none of the available men were willing to accept their responsibilities. In these cases, I do not know how anyone can fault the women. After all, if the men are wearing the skirts, somebody will have to put on the pants.

ENDNOTES

1. Charles C. Ryrie, *"Is There Really a Reason for Not Ordaining Women"* - article (Chicago, IL: Moody Monthly, December 1977).

2. J. David Dawson, *Leadership Is Male* (Nashville, TN: Oliver Nelson Books, 1988) p. 17 (and on book jacket).

3. H. Wayne House, *"Caught in the Middle"* - article (Dallas, TX: Kindred Spirit, Dallas Theological Seminary, Summer 1989), p. 13.

4. Warren W. Wiersbe, *Whole Bible Study Course* - Orig. by D. B. Eastep (Covington, KY: Calvary Baptist Church Book Room, n.d.) Notes on 1 Tim. 2.

5. Kenneth S. Wuest, *The Pastoral Epistles in the Greek New Testament* (Grand Rapids, MI: Wm. B. Eerdmaus Pub. Co. 1952) p. 50-51.

6. Robertson Nicoll, ed., *The Expositor's Greek Testament* (Grand Rapids, MI: Wm. B. Eerdmaus Pub Co. 1970, orig. 1909) p. 110-111.

7. Warren W. Wiersbe, op. cit. - notes on 1 Tim. 2.

9

The Family of God

One of the most common names used to describe the church of Jesus Christ is "the family of God." Every human being comes into this world belonging to the family of Adam...dead in trespasses and sins and condemned by God. Only by faith can a person receive forgiveness of sin, be made alive in Christ and be born into the family of God.

For a local church to grow, it must operate like the family that God intends it to be. Believers must bear each other's burdens, share each other's joys, pray for each other and love each other through thick and thin, good times and bad. Where hearts are knit together for His honor and His glory there are no limits to what He can do. An excellent preventative medication to avoid dissention and strife is Prescription #9: DEVELOP A FAMILY MENTALITY WITHIN THE CHURCH. This is the biblical approach to unity within the Body of Christ as evidenced by many passages of Scripture.

> **Romans 8:15** -- For ye have not received the spirit
> of bondage again to fear; but ye have received the
> Spirit of **adoption**, whereby we cry, Abba, Father.

The word "adoption" refers to becoming a member of a family, with all the commensurate rights and privileges. For the Christian, installation into the family of God occurs at the time of salvation.

> **Galatians 3:20** -- For ye are all the children of God by faith in Jesus Christ.

> **Galatians 4:5-7** -- But when the fullness of the time was come, God sent forth His Son, made of a woman, made under the law, that we might receive the adoption of sons. And because ye are sons, God hath sent forth the Spirit of His Son into your hearts, crying, Abba, Father. Wherefore, thou art no more a servant, but a son; and if a son, then an heir of God through Christ.

> **Ephesians 3:14-15** -- For this cause I bow my knees unto the Father of our Lord Jesus Christ, of whom the whole family in heaven and earth are named.

The designation of God as the "Father" of the believer is far more common to the New Testament than to the Old. Asked by His disciples to teach them to pray, the Lord Jesus said they should begin by saying, "Our Father..." (Luke 11:1-2). Not only is God a Father to the saved, but Jesus is a brother to the saved, a designation He Himself used in a post-resurrection appearance to Mary Magdalene (John 20:17) when He gave her instruction for His "brethren," referring then to the disciples and now to all who are born again. If you are a Bible-believing Christian you are more than His servant, more than His friend (see John 15:7). God Himself, the Creator of the Universe, is your Father and His only begotten Son, the Redeemer of the Universe, is your elder brother, the "first-born among many brethren" (Rom. 8:29).

Perhaps no single verse spells out the father-child relationship that believers enjoy better than John 1:12-13 where the Bible describes the actual birthing into God's family.

> But as many as received Him, to them gave He
> power to become the children of God, even to them
> that believe on His name; Who were born, not of
> blood, nor of the will of the flesh, nor of the will of
> man, but of God.

This familial relationship should be readily apparent within a church and should govern the behavior and attitudes of its members. When the human family functions properly everyone feels secure, accepted and loved. The same principle applies within the church. Sure there will be fusses from time to time and everyone will not always see eye to eye on everything, but a strong human family sticks together with a mentality that implies: "Don't poke your nose into our business or you are liable to get it broken."

R$_x$:

Develop a Family Mentality Within the Church

Harsh as that may sound, it approximates the way things ought to function within the family of God. Christians should care for one another in a manner that supersedes any purely human relationship. Unless believers feel profoundly connected by a common bond of love in Christ, they will pull apart when the tough times come instead of pull together. Paul recognized this fact and addressed it in all three pastoral epistles.

The Whole Family

"Rebuke not an elder, but exhort him as a father; and the younger men as brethren; The elder women as mothers; the younger as sisters" (1 Tim. 5:1-2).

Father-Son

"Thou, therefore, my son, be strong in the grace that is in Christ Jesus" (2 Tim. 2:2).

Mother-Daughter

"The aged women...may teach the young women...to love their husbands, to love their children, to be...keepers at home" (Titus 2:3-4).

In 1 Timothy 5:1-2 Paul delineates three concepts involved in the family mentality of a church: the social aspect, the practical aspect and the serving aspect.

The Social Aspect
of the Family of God

The church in Ephesus was rooted and grounded in the Word of God. It had been taught the whole counsel of God by Paul himself, who had spent three years there. This was a congregation well versed in the doctrines of Scripture. At the time of Paul's letter, the pastor was Timothy who enjoyed an intimate, father-son relationship with the Apostle and had learned much from him. The letter instructs believers to treat one another as members of their own family, a feat that would only be possible through the love of the Father shed abroad in their hearts.

The Older Men (1 Tim. 5:1a). "Rebuke not an elder, but exhort him as a father." You do not rebuke your father. You may exhort; you may reason; but you do not rebuke. (The term "elder" here does not refer to church leadership but to an older man.) "Rebuke" means to censure severely. Paul recommends correcting an older man by using the softer more respectful approach of exhortation. It is important to remember that many older men are wise from experience and can be greatly used of God. Rehoboam

(1 Kings 12) rejected the counsel of the older men and consequently lost his kingdom. Moses was 80 years old when God commissioned him to lead the nation of Israel. Proverbs is a book of wisdom from a father to his son.

The Younger Men (1 Tim. 5:1b). "...and the younger men, as brethren." Younger men should be treated as brothers. Churches should strive to cultivate a true brotherhood that transcends differences in temperament and personality. A family is always diverse. Even the disciples themselves were different. John and his brother, James, were known as the Sons of Thunder, though we most often think of John as the tender, loving disciple. Peter was often impetuous, acting and speaking before thinking. But he matured and the later Peter of Acts bears almost no resemblance to the Peter of the Gospels. Paul was a man of great commitment. Nothing deterred him, in contrast to Peter in John Chapter 21 who appeared ready to give everything up and return to fishing. Thomas was the doubter. "I won't believe it," he declared, "until I see it with my own eyes."

Every local assembly has its Peters and Thomases, etc. God has placed them in His family for a reason. Each has a job to do and each needs to be useful, loved, nurtured and exhorted as brethren.

The Older Women (1 Tim. 5:2a). "... the elder women, as mothers." Just as the older men are to be treated as fathers, the older women are to be exhorted "as mothers." Here is the biblical way to approach the Hannahs (1 Sam. 1-2) who have reared their sons and returned them to the Lord; the Elizabeths and Marys, highly favored women of God.

There is a disturbing tendency in our culture nowadays to treat age with contempt. But the Scriptures teach that it should be treated with reverence and honor. "Thou shalt rise up before the hoary head and honour the face of the old man, and fear thy

God: I am the LORD" (Lev. 19:32). God does not expect older people to go uncorrected, but he expects them to be corrected with honor and respect.

The Younger Women (1 Tim. 5:2b). "...the younger (women), as sisters, with all purity." Younger men are to be treated as brothers; younger women as sisters. Here Paul adds a word of caution: "with all purity." There is no mistaking that everyone in the church must avoid any hint of impropriety or intimacy when ministering to young women. Naturally it follows that a man is to treat even his fiancee as a sister until they are married.

The Practical Aspect
of the Family of God

God did not give His Word merely to pump Christians full of pithy theological insights. He gave it as a guide for an intimate daily walk with Him. The Scriptures are practical and have answers to problems that face the family of God, such as:

The Plight of the Aged (1 Tim. 5:3-4).

> Honor widows that are widows indeed. But if any widow have children or nephews, let them learn first to show piety at home, and to requite their parents; for that is good and acceptable before God.

Although this passage pertains to widows, today it could apply to widowers as well. In Biblical times it was the widow who faced more problems because the loss of her husband also meant the loss of her sole source of income. The selection of deacons (Acts 6) was for the expressed purpose of meeting the needs of widows.

The church today has a real responsibility to insure that its older saints are properly cared for when they have no family and can no longer care for themselves. It is not enough to say "The

Lord will take care of them." He will, but perhaps He intends to
do it through the church. James writes:

> Pure religion and undefiled before God and the
> Father is this: to visit the fatherless and widows in
> their affliction, and to keep oneself unspotted from
> the world (Ja. 1:27).

Paul even provides guidelines for evaluating the church's role
based upon genuine need and family responsibility.

<u>Genuine Need.</u> Determine whether these people are "widows
indeed," meaning they are in dire circumstance with no visible
means of adequate support (5:3, 5, 16).

<u>Family Responsibility.</u> Determine whether their children or
grandchildren (particularly if they are born again) have done their
duty (5:4, 16). "Nephews" actually means "descendants" and is
better translated "grandchildren." The Fifth Commandment (Deut.
20:12) makes it clear that the care of a parent or a grandparent "is
good and acceptable before God."

The Problem of the Impious Home (1 Tim. 5:4). Paul writes,
"Let them first show piety at home." Dictionaries define piety as
"fidelity to natural obligations (as to parents)." It is a word with
numerous synonyms, all with spiritual overtones.

The home is God's "First Grade" where Christians learn the
ABC's of godliness. Certainly the homes of members of the local
assembly should be characterized by piety. Unfortunately, many
are not. The Christian home should be characterized by:

Worship	A family altar at home.
Prayer	A family prayer closet.
Scripture	Daily Bible reading.
Love	If a man cannot love his wife and children, how can he love the saints in the

	assembly?
Discipline	If a man cannot get his family to obey him at home, how will they obey God?

The Problem of the Negligent Provider (1 Tim. 5:8)

> But if any provide not for his own, and specially for those of his own house, he hath denied the faith and is worse than an infidel.

God obligates His people to provide for their families. Though this verse applies primarily to the case of the widows in the Ephesian churches, the underlying principle has universal application. Christians are obligated to provide for members of the family of God. The phrase "worse than an infidel" suggests that even a pagan has a sense of family responsibility. For a Christian to neglect his or her responsibilities in this area is tantamount to having denied the faith. This is a condemning accusation.

The Serving Aspect of the Family of God

I have a friend who grew up on a street with many children. Of course, nine of those children all belonged to one family. The woman had six sons, then gave birth to twin sons, then gave birth to another son. Some ladies in the neighborhood apparently felt sorry for her, visualizing her as some frantically over-worked scullery maid toiling to care for 10 men. But that was far from the truth. She was the calmest, most serene woman on the street and probably did less housework than any of them. Why? Because each member of her family had his chores and did them. They had been taught that they had a responsibility to each other to do their work by meeting their responsibilities. Their household ran like clockwork.

The local church should run the same way. There are areas of service for everyone in the family of God and if everyone does his job the church is able to meet the needs of its members and to attract the unsaved.

The Service of the Older Women

In 1 Timothy 5:5, 9, and 10 Paul emphasizes the role of women, describing what might be termed "social work." He provides a list of "good works" which are added to the qualifications of an "official widow," one eligible for church support. These works are suitable "chores" for the older women who are members of God's family.

Social Service

Child Care "...if she hath brought up children..." (vs. 10). No doubt her own are spoken of, but today that can easily be extended. In Timothy's case, his mother Eunice and his grandmother, Lois, were both involved in child-rearing. According to historians of that period, children were frequently orphaned for a variety of reasons. Widows who took these children were showing compassion.

This is a critical area today, even in the context of a church nursery which often is desperate for workers. Many of the mothers are new believers or unbelievers who need to be in the service under the teaching of the Word. In one church I know of, the older women refuse to take the nursery and are forcing the young mothers to do it. Their reasoning: "I spent my time doing that when I was young. Now let them do it!" So those who are young in the Lord are spending their time in church diapering and feeding infants. If that is all they do in church, they may as well stay home.

Hospitality "...if she hath lodged strangers..." (vs. 10). In some cases this quality is a spiritual gift (1 Pet. 4:9), but apparently here it is a command. One does not always need to be gifted in an area to function in it. All believers are commanded to give, for example, but not all have the spiritual gift of giving.

Many people think of hospitality exclusively in terms of opening one's home for meals or lodging. That certainly constitutes hospitality, but so do other things such as sending cards, letters, notes of encouragement or even making a quick telephone call to see how someone is doing. These are some ways to show love and concern and to develop a family mentality within the church.

Humble Service "...she washed the saints' feet" (vs. 10). This refers to the literal act of foot-washing, a thankless task reserved for the household's lowest servant. Chores of humble service are usually done by a church's unsung heroes who rarely receive credit for their faithfulness and often go unnoticed. These may be the women who cook for the church, clean, set up the communion table, bring refreshments, straighten the hymnals, etc.

Benevolence "...she relieved the afflicted" (vs. 10). She was involved in helping those in distress. The church is filled with people who cannot physically care for themselves or for their homes. Women who perform this service are indeed a treasure.

Counseling Ministry

This is another crucial need in the local church. Paul instructed Titus (Titus 2:3-5) that women who counsel must be spiritually mature, "holy in behavior, not false accusers, not given to much wine." These older women should also be "teachers of good things" (vs. 2). Some of the "good things" they are to teach younger women include:

To Be Soberminded (vs. 4). Marriage is serious and should never be entered into recklessly or irreverently. Who better to advise a young bride than an older more experienced woman.

To Love Their Husbands (vs. 4). Again, a godly experienced woman would be the best teacher. A young wife without godly counsel may fail in this area, not from a lack of desire but from a lack of understanding.

To Love Their Children (vs. 4). Here too the older generation has something valuable to teach the younger. Interestingly, the word "love" in relation to children and in the previous verse when dealing with husbands, comes from "phileo" meaning "to love, have affection for, like." When such love abounds, people find great enjoyment in each other's company. Mature women also are to teach younger ones:

> "To be discreet"...sensible, self-controlled, prudent.
>
> "Chaste"...pure.
>
> "Keepers at home"...workers at home, homemakers.
>
> "Good"...kind, not hard or mean in carrying out their household duties.
>
> "Obedient to their own husbands"...acknowledging through their behavior that God has designated the husband as head of the home.

It is worth noting that Paul assigns women to counsel women and men to counsel men. He never tells Timothy or any other man in the church to counsel young women but specifically assigns that job to the aged women. This system is extremely appropriate today, particularly with young women who have marital problems. Following Paul's advice enables the men of the church to avoid potentially vulnerable or compromising situations so "that the Word of God be not blasphemed."

I rarely counsel women. I assign young women with problems to older women who can direct them and nurture them spiritually as a mother nurtures a child. A young woman whose lifestyle discredits the Word of God also wounds the testimony of the church and speaks volumes about the aged women who have failed to accept their teaching responsibilities.

The Service of the Younger Women

In Timothy 5:11-15 Paul turns his attention to the "dos and don'ts" regarding younger women.

Do Not Place Them on the Widows Roll (vs. 11-12). To do so might lead them into sin, for after having pledged their faithfulness to Christ they might develop a consuming passion to remarry and abandon their "first faith" and the commitment to serve Christ unreservedly. Their passion might even propel them into marrying an unbeliever.

Also, younger widows might lack the spiritual maturity to devote themselves to prayer and good works (mark of the mature woman) and become apathetic in their devotion to the Lord. They might "learn" to become idle busy-bodies and vicious gossips.

William Barclay comments:

> Because a woman had not enough to do, she might become one of those creatures who drift from house to house in an empty social round. It was almost inevitable that such a woman would become a **gossip**; because she had nothing important to talk about, she would tend to talk scandal, repeating tales from house to house, each time with a little more embroidery and a little more malice...She would be very apt to be over-interested and over-interfering in the affairs of others.[1]

A busy-body meddles in the affairs of others. A tattler, or talebearer, betrays another's confidence. It is important to note that one of the qualifications for a deacon's wife is that she not be a "slanderer." The Greek word used is "diabolis," a word used of the devil. The Bible is teaching that a woman can use her tongue in a way that makes her a "she-devil" (1 Tim.3:11).

Do Encourage Them to Remarry, Bear Children (see Psalm 128) **and Guide or "Rule" The House** (vs. 14-15). Occupied with things such as these she will not become a slanderer. The "adversary" who would speak reproachfully (vs. 14) probably refers to an unbeliever who would like to ruin a believer's testimony. But verse 15 warns young widows of an even more terrible adversary. Failing to heed Paul's advice opens the door to Satan himself.

The Service of the Men in the Church

Thou, therefore, my son, be strong in the grace

> that is in Christ Jesus. And the things that thou
> hast heard from me among many witnesses, the
> same commit thou to faithful men, who shall be
> able to teach others also. (2 Tim. 2:1-2)

Each generation is burdened with the responsibility of seeing that the generation that follows is prepared to carry on (see Chapter 4). That really is the essence of the pastoral epistles: preparational instruction to keep the gospel message alive in order to fulfill the Great Commission.

Rather than enumerate all the responsibilities given to men, suffice it to say that they have the leadership roles and the instructions given to them are voluminous. They are to set a proper example (1 Tim. 4:6), to provide for the physical and financial needs of their households (1 Tim. 5:8) and to train their successors in the church and at home (1 Tim. 3:4-5, 12; Titus 1:6). A good father is one who makes sure his son is prepared to someday assume responsibility as head of a home.

Obviously maturity is key to developing a church family mentality. Immature believers think only of themselves and cannot put Christ first or others ahead of themselves. Gene Getz, in his book, Building Up One Another, has an excellent outline based upon the "one another's" of Scripture and the body analogy of Romans 12. The family application is clear.

> For as we have many members in one body, and all
> members have not the same office.

Members of One Another. "So we, being many, are one body in Christ, and every one members one of another" (Rom. 12:5 NASB).

Devoted to One Another. "Be kindly affectioned one to another with brotherly love" (Rom. 12:10 NASB).

141

Honor One Another. "...in honor preferring one another" (Rom. 12:10 NIV).

Be of the Same Mind With One Another. "Now the God of patience and consolation grant you to be likeminded one toward another according to Christ Jesus: (Rom. 15:5).

Accept One Another. "Wherefore, receive ye one another, as Christ also received us to the glory of God" (Rom. 15:7).

Admonish One Another. "And I myself also am persuaded of you, my brethren, that ye also are full of goodness, filled with all knowledge, able to admonish one another" (Rom. 15:14 NASB).

Greet One Another. "Greet one another with an holy kiss" (Rom. 16:16 NIV).

Getz adds to that outline from other Scriptures.

Serve One Another. "You, my brothers, were called to be free. But do not use your freedom to indulge your sinful nature; rather, serve one another in love" (Gal. 5:13).

Bear One Another's Burdens. "Bear one another's burdens, and thus fulfill the law of Christ" (Gal. 6:2, NASB).

Bearing with One Another. "Be completely humble and gentle; be patient, bearing with one another in love" (Eph. 4:2).

Submit to One Another. "Submit to one another out of reverence for Christ" (Eph. 5:21 NIV).

Encourage One Another. "Therefore encourage one another and build each other up" (1 Thes. 5:11 NIV). [2]

Everyone has a need to feel like he "belongs." It is no different in the church. Christians refer to the local church they attend as their "home church" for a simple reason: It feels like home there. It feels like family. A family that loves, works, prays, cries and rejoices together is less likely to tear itself apart.

Being part of a family also implies responsibility. Each has a job to do and must be willing to do it as part of a team. If the jobs are not done then needs are not met and the family becomes dysfunctional. Take Prescription #9: DEVELOP A FAMILY MENTALITY WITHIN THE CHURCH to bring unity and good health to the church and to avoid the dysfunction that generates hatred and strife. The local church must develop and maintain oneness, a unity of spirit and mind that is characterized by love for one another. We would do well to paraphrase the marriage vow and abide by it:

> We take one another as family members, to have and to hold from this day forward, for better or worse, for richer for poorer, in sickness and health, to love and to cherish, till death us do part, according to God's holy ordinance; and thereto we pledge to thee our faith.

To practice such faithfulness in church life would be a giant step towards developing a family mentality that would be difficult if not impossible for Satan to tear asunder.

A CLOSING ILLUSTRATION. I bring this prescription to a close with an illustration that I am told is from Irish tradition. Following the wedding ceremony the bride and groom go on their honeymoon. Upon their return they find a length of rope lying across the doorstep. Tradition says that the husband is to pick up one end, the wife the other, and a tug-of-war is to ensue. The one who wins by pulling the other across the doorstep becomes the head of the house.

The couple of our illustration, we'll call them Michael and

Katherine, came home from their honeymoon. The rope was in place. Michael picked up his end of the rope, looked at Katherine and said, "Well, aren't you going to pick up your end?" Saying nothing she walked over to his side of the doorstep, placed her hands on the rope right next to his and said, "Michael, if this marriage is to work, we're going to have to pull together."

Irish tradition or not, it is certainly an important lesson for a family and a church to learn. If our church is going to "work," we're going to have to "pull together." That sort of family mentality is a <u>must.</u>

ENDNOTES

1. William Barclay (see acknowledgment note).

2. Gene A. Getz, *Building Up One Another* (Wheaton, IL: Victor Book, 1976) p. 7, 20, 29, 36, 43, 51, 60, 68, 78, 91, 99, 110.

10

Avoiding Ingrownitis

Have you ever heard the saying, "Us four---no more--- shut the door?" No attitude could be more contrary to the intent of the Great Commission. But believe it or not, there are churches out there with exactly that philosophy.

I know of a pastor who candidated at just such a church and was told unequivocally, "We don't want to grow. We're happy the way we are and we don't want to get any bigger." This could be rather amusing if it were not so sad. Imagine a congregation that could conceivably move to fire its pastor because the Lord blessed the church with growth!

Such a mentality has no place in the church of Jesus Christ. It is an outright disgrace to the Savior's cause. Unfortunately, the phenomenon is more common than Christians realize and is symptomatic of what we term the "ingrown" church. C. John Miller wrote an entire book on the subject entitled <u>Outgrowing the Ingrown Church.</u> It addresses the problem of congregations that turn inward and, consequently, fail to move outward for Christ. The ingrown church, says the jacket of Miller's book, "is the 'norm' for contemporary evangelical and Protestant churches. But ingrownness is a pathology. It can destroy the vital spiritual health of a church." [1]

Prescription #10: REACH OUT INTO THE COMMUNITY & THE WORLD. Do the work of an evangelist or run the risk of contracting "ingrownitis," a disease that can prevent a church from ever reaching the lost for Christ.

The preventative medication for ingrownitis is revealed in Second Timothy. The fourth chapter of this book concludes the three Pastoral Epistles and is often viewed as a kind of last will and testament from the Apostle Paul to Timothy, his son in the faith. Paul charges Timothy to accept his responsibilities and to discharge his duties. In the course of his instructions he charges his young disciple, "Do the work of an evangelist" (2 Tim. 4:5b).

The job, no doubt, was difficult for someone of Timothy's timid nature. Yet the Bible teaches that every servant of God is a steward of the gospel and must "do the work of an evangelist." God is not interested in excuses, such as, "I haven't been given the gift; I'll let someone else handle the evangelistic responsibilities; I'm a pastor-teacher, not an evangelist," etc. Second Timothy 4:5 is not a suggestion. It is a command and it pertains to everyone who is born again. It is part of the Great Commission and all four gospels address it: Matthew 28:18-20; Mark 16:15-18; Luke 24:47-48; and John 20:21-22. In the words of the Lord Jesus:

> But ye shall receive power, after the Holy Spirit is come upon you; and ye shall be witnesses unto me both in Jerusalem, and in all Judea, and in Samaria, and unto the uttermost part of the earth (Acts 1:8).

Do the work of an evangelist. The word "evangelist" is a transliteration of the Greek word euaggelistes which means, "one who brings good news." Since it is not preceded by the definite article, the stress is on the type or quality of work, not on an official position. In other words, Paul is saying: "Let your work be evangelistic in character; always announce the good news of man's redemption through Christ. Never stop reaching out to the lost souls in the ministry God has given you."

This is not an exhortation to pastors to become itinerant ministers, traveling from town to town holding evangelistic crusades and tent meetings. God has specially gifted men for that type of ministry (See Chapter 7). Paul, rather, is telling the local pastor to be evangelistic in both message and method. The undershepherd of the flock must always make every effort to reach the lost sheep, in season and out, in pulpit and out.

Unfortunately, that frequently is not the case. Rather than reaching outward, many churches only reach inward, and by doing so stunt the growth of the Body of Christ. C. Peter Wagner, an expert on church growth, notes that in spite of advances in the 1980s, the percentage of American adults attending church has remained almost the same (about 45 percent). Protestant church membership has actually declined.

R_x:

Reach Out into the Community

Wagner's mentor, Donald McGavran, sometimes referred to as the father of the modern-day church-growth movement, fervently believed that the Lord wants Christians not only to search for the lost but to FIND them.[2] He contended that the overarching concern of Christ's Commission in Matthew 28:19 was to "make disciples of all nations." Regrettably, church growth in North America does not measure up to McGavran's model. Far too often growth is due not to the addition of new believers, which is called "conversion growth," but to the movement of believers from one assembly to another, a process known as "transfer growth." In other words, sinners are not repenting; believers are just relocating. In the final analysis, that is not growth at all. It is symptomatic of an ingrown church and an ingrown membership composed of individuals who are too interested in themselves to be concerned about reaching others.

There is one other type of growth. It is called "biological." A

147

brief review of each of these three types of growth follows.[3]

BIOLOGICAL GROWTH. This is the result of already churched families growing biologically. Children are born, grow up, trust Christ as Savior and become members of the local assembly. The rate of growth in this area should at least match the growth rate in the community in which the church resides.

TRANSFER GROWTH. This takes place in a local church when Christians transfer their membership from one assembly to another. To call it "growth," however, is misleading, for while it increases attendance in one congregation, it decreases it in another. No one has been saved and no one has been added to the Body of Christ.

CONVERSION GROWTH. This is church growth of the finest degree. Souls are being saved and new blood is being infused into the local assembly. These new believers bring enthusiasm and excitement to a rundown body whose veins are flowing with tired blood. Just as a new baby excites a home, so a new babe in Christ thrills and excites a church. And since excitement breeds more excitement, conversion growth encourages and motivates the body of Christ to reach out even more to fulfill the Great Commission.

Conversion growth, however, is not accidental and it will never take place in an ingrown church. Ingrownitis is a disease that attacks the reproductive organs while overstimulating the "self-center." The result? The church ends up denying the very purpose for which it was brought into the world, even to the point of telling a pastoral candidate, "We don't want to grow. We're happy the way we are."

Like it or not, we were, as the late Dawson Trotman said, "born to reproduce." To avoid ingrownitis, a church must concentrate on two very clear Biblical directives: evangelize and edify.

EVANGELISM is the process of reaching out to the lost, exposing them to the gospel and bringing them to faith in Christ. **EDIFICATION** involves discipling and teaching believers so they mature in the faith they already possess.

Both are inter-related aspects of the Great Commission which the Lord outlined in His own words:

> Go ye, therefore, and teach all nations, baptizing them in the name of the Father, and of the Son, and of the Holy Spirit, Teaching them to observe all things whatsoever I have commanded you, and lo, I am with you always, even to the end of the age (Matt. 28:19-20).

No church will ever experience lasting growth unless it both evangelizes and edifies. An ingrown church will do neither. Donald McGavran puts it this way:

> Church growth follows where the lost are not merely found but restored to normal life in the fold -- though it may be a life they have never consciously known. Faithfulness in "folding [evangelizing] and feeding" [edifying] -- which unfortunately has come to be called by such a dry superficial term as follow-up -- is essential to lasting church expansion. When existing Christians, marching obediently under the Lord's command and filled with His compassion, fold the wanderers and feed the flock, then churches multiply; but when they indolently permit men and women who have made costly decisions for Christ to drift back into the world, then indeed churches do not grow. Faithfulness in proclamation and find is not enough. There must be faithful aftercare.[4]

149

Evangelizing and edifying are so important that no church can experience a steady, healthy growth without them. Failing to evangelize usually results in members finding themselves growing old with no one to carry on their work. Failing to edify ends up with someone available to carry on the work, but that someone is probably too unknowledgeable and immature to do so.

A preacher friend of mine named Tom Wallace very aptly described the life cycles of many churches. They begin, he said, with a wave of **red hot evangelism.** People get saved, establish a church and begin a ministry. Then a building goes up and enthusiasm continues as people begin filling it. Once the church is full, with no apparent room for expansion (without building again), everything settles down into **second-stage orthodox teaching.** The evangelism drops off and the emphasis shifts to teaching the Word. That teaching, of course, is absolutely vital. But unless it is done simultaneously with phase one -- evangelism -- it results in phase three -- **dead orthodoxy.** The result of dead orthodoxy is obvious: rigormortis sets in and unless there is a resurrection of the entire Great Commission process, it becomes only a matter of time before that church joins the graveyard of churches that once were but are no more.

A church that edifies without evangelizing ends up cold and dead. A church that evangelizes without edifying ends up weak and immature. Neither is an attractive alternative and neither is what the Lord intended.

There is another cycle, however. It is not only biblical but positive in nature. It is the one contained in the Great Commission. Phase one (evangelism) leads to phase two (edification) which leads back to phase one which leads forward to phase two, etc. Vergil Gerber develops and charts it this way:

The central imperative of the Great Commission is to MAKE DISCIPLES. This means bringing men and women to Jesus Christ so that they give

Him the all-inclusive "yes" of submission and faith. All the other action words in these verses (Matthew 28:19-20) are helping verbs. They are "going," "Baptizing" and "teaching."

It is a continuous process by which men who are converted to Jesus Christ relate themselves to each other and become responsible, reproducing church members. These disciples go out to make other disciples, baptizing, teaching, and relating them to the church also.

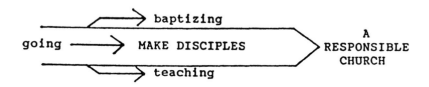

The evangelistic task, therefore, falls short of its objective unless it relates new converts to local congregations of believers.[5]

The Great Commission is the God-given responsibility of the local church. Fulfilling it involves both evangelism and edification. A church that is ingrown will be inefficient in both. Hence, one of the great challenges facing the local church today is to reach out into the community with the good news of salvation in Christ.

How can a church prevent ingrownitis?

1. It must understand the purpose of the church. It must realize that its paramount duty is to carry out the Great Commission.

2. It must commit to carrying out that purpose. It must somehow evoke a commitment from the congregation to meet its responsibility. Accomplishing this is easier said than done, but once achieved it will go a long way toward success.

3. It must design and implement a program to carry out its commitment. The leadership of the church must design and place into operation a plan to get the job done.

Unfortunately, the process is not as easy as 1-2-3. Motivating people to look beyond themselves to the task at hand (precisely what ingrown individuals do <u>not</u> do) and then getting them to commit to accomplishing that task requires leadership of the highest magnitude.

<u>Here and There</u>

Exactly how does one implement a plan to get the job done? I use what I call a "here and there" philosophy: Unsaved people are lost no matter where they are and need to be reached whether HERE in our own backyard through local evangelistic efforts, or THERE through the efforts of missionaries whom the church has sent to the regions beyond. This philosophy needs to be drummed into the hearts and minds of the members of a congregation. At one of our annual missionary conferences at my church in New Jersey, we adopted the theme "Reaching the Unreached," and added the subtitle "Both Here and There." Here is part of my written challenge to our people:

Here at Faith Bible Church missions have always been a high priority. From "Jerusalem, to Judea, to Samaria, and to the uttermost part of the earth" is the Biblical injunction. So in reality our involvement calls for a "here" and "there" commitment. The theme of this year's conference "REACHING THE UNREACHED," and its accompanying sub-theme, "BOTH HERE AND THERE" make it clear that we are aware that commitment cannot be ignored.

To accomplish it we have formed a partnership. We have enlisted missionaries to go to the ends of the earth to reach the lost that are out "there," while we immerse ourselves in an effort to reach the lost "here." In the place of God's assignment for them their tools may be medicine, linguistics, printing, camping, radio, etc. For us it may be visitation, youth evangelism, newspaper advertising, music, and so forth. But by whatever means, or by all means, and whether "here" or "there," we have got to reach the lost.

Then, after reviewing past conference challenges and enumerating the current conference's specific goals, I added:

We need to increase our support to those who have been called "there," and we need to develop new ways of carrying out our responsibilities "here." If we are to accomplish those goals it will take increased participation on the part of all who call Faith Bible Church their home, as well as unselfish willingness to back our "here and there" efforts with increased stewardship.

During this year's conference you will be challenged
to help us meet the above goals. It will involve a
deeper commitment than ever before. Let us not
be weighed in the balances and found wanting.

HERE

Every member of the congregation must have an ever-present
awareness that he or she has a responsibility to penetrate the community with the gospel. This personal effort can be accomplished
by building bridges into the lives of family, neighbors, co-workers, classmates or friends. Bruce McDonald describes the best
process I know of as "Natural Bridge Evangelism"[6]and identifies
the key bridges as RELATION, LOCATION, VOCATION, EDU-
CATION and RECREATION, all easily understood by their titles.
These bridges enable Christians to make significant contact with
lost people.

The operative phrase here is **significant contact**. Significant
contact comes in two flavors, sweet and sour; it may be positive
(Lord willing) or it may be negative (may it never be). Either way
it is significant. Unfortunately, the "significant" factor often eludes
many of the formal programs that churches use to reach the
unreached. The longer I pastor and the longer I analyze pro-
grammed-type evangelism, the less I see it as the primary way to
go. Speaking to that subject is Elwood McQuaid, a former pastor and now executive director of the Friends of Israel Gospel
Ministry, a world-wide organization dedicated to reaching Jewish
people with the gospel.

During years of ministry, a Pastor may discover
that some of his concepts of personal evangelism
are flawed. He sees his church and others sending
people into homes, armed with decision-on-de-
mand programs. These trained believers try to control thoughts, responses, and conversations leading to the coveted "yes." Secular sales techniques

become the model for "closing" the appeal with a recorded decision or commitment for Christ.[7]

McQuaid is right. Over the years I have learned that if all I do is utilize such a procedure to get someone to trust Christ, I rarely if ever see him again. The many who respond with so-called "professions of faith" seldom become incorporated into the life and ministry of the church. On the other hand, when the proper bridge is built, the percentage of incorporation escalates dramatically.

McDonald found the same thing, both by personal experience and observation. He writes:

> Recently while I was sharing concepts on Natural Bridge Evangelism, two minister friends of mine who have large, active visitation programs admitted that, though they have large numbers of decisions, the actual assimilation rate is 4 to 5 percent.[8]

In their book <u>The Master's Plan</u>, Drs. Win and Charles Arn published the results of a survey of 14,000 people who responded to the question: "How did you come to your new relationship with Christ and with your church?" The answers were astounding: A visitation program resulted in one to two percent, whereas 75 to 90 percent were led to Christ by a friend or relative.[9] Yet despite statistics like these, many churches still concentrate on programmed, structured, cold-turkey evangelism, which can be defined as "stranger one introducing himself to stranger two and asking him to take stranger three into his heart." Far too often it just won't work.

Far too often, of course, does not mean never. Some churches do not fit the statistical analysis and have dynamic, highly productive traditional visitation programs. To them I say "Praise God. Keep on keeping on!" But for the rest, perhaps it is time to rethink the church's evangelism outreach.

The HERE phase of a "here and there" philosophy requires

sweet, productive, significant contact between believers and the unsaved community. By developing these relationships over time while living a visibly loving, spirit-controlled life, Christians receive opportunities to proclaim the truths of God. According to McQuaid, the believer's lifestyle of bridge-building should incorporate three things in the following order: (1) demonstration, (2) provocation and (3) proclamation.[10] An observable demonstration of true Christianity should provoke a positive response which then produces the right to proclaim evangelistic truth.

In her excellent book Out of the Saltshaker and Into the World, Rebecca Pippert develops the concept this way:

> Most contact evangelism techniques are severely limited by the fact that nonbelievers never see the gospel fleshed out in the believer's life. One of the greatest gifts and evidences that we give (to the unbeliever) is the chance to see how Jesus lives His life through us... strangers, as long as they remain strangers, only hear a message, and never see it lived out in human relationships.[11]

Believers have the great responsibility and accompanying privilege of sharing God's plan of salvation with unsaved friends, neighbors and acquaintances. The best way to do that is by leading a spirit-filled, fruit-bearing life that earns the right to proclaim the message. Scripture after Scripture tells us so.

> Matthew 5:16 -- Let your light so shine before men, that they may see your good works, and glorify your Father who is in heaven.

> 1 Peter 2:12 -- Having your conversation [lifestyle] honest among the gentiles: that... they may by your good works, which they shall behold, glorify God.

Philippians 1:27 -- Only let your conversation [lifestyle] be as it becometh the gospel of Christ.

1 Thessalonians 4:11-12 -- And that ye study to be quiet, and to do your own business, and to work with your own hands, as we commanded you; That ye may walk honestly toward them that are without [winning their respect], and that ye have lack of nothing.

There is probably no clearer or more specific illustration of how a godly life can influence a soul for Christ than the one Peter gives concerning the saved wife's testimony before her unsaved husband. Peter writes:

Ye wives, be in subjection to your own husbands that, if any obey not the word [the spoken proclamation of the gospel], they also may be won [to Christ] by the behavior of the wives (1 Pet. 3:1).

Successful, programmed evangelistic efforts should be applauded. But churches also must recognize the huge part one's personal testimony plays in either drawing people to the Lord or driving them away. Every individual who comes into the life of a believer is put there by God. A Christian never crosses paths with anyone by accident, only by appointment. As McQuaid notes: "Every believer walking in God's will is placed in an area designed to enhance his work and witness for Christ."[12] Building bridges is one of the most effective ways for a church to use every member's walk with Christ to spread the gospel HERE -- in its own Jerusalem.

THERE

This refers primarily to a church's commitment to support home and foreign missions THERE, in its "Judea, Samaria" and "the uttermost part of the world." For a church to respond success-fully to Paul's admonition to "do the work of an evangelist," it must aggressively involve itself in a world-wide missionary out-reach -- a program that by proxy (sending others in its place) does elsewhere what it is doing in its own community: trying to reach the lost.

Dr. William Mierop, former pastor, college president and mis-sion board executive wrote a challenging article to the local church entitled <u>Make Missions an Obsessions</u>. Quite frankly, unless such takes place, ingrownitis will flourish. Creating an "obsession," however, is not easy. Here are some of my attempts when I ad-dressed our congregation during one of our missionary confer-ences.

> MISSIONS... it is the mission of the church! In fact, it is the only reason for our existence. We believe that truth, and because we do, that makes this week the most important week on our calen-dar. Your attendance at all sessions, and your per-sonal acceptance of the challenges presented will determine the success of our time together during these days of missionary conference.

> When Christ was here during His incarnation, He promised to build His church. He today is doing so, and as he does, "Body Two" [the church] has the responsibility of taking the good news of God's redeeming grace to a human race bent on destruc-tion; a world-wide community on a collision course with Hell.

> Procedurally this responsibility, known as the Great Commission, is one that begins at home and then reaches out to the four corners of the globe.

The message stressed the urgent need to commit both our manpower and our money. It detailed some of the growth and blessing the Lord had sent our way during the years in which we had made missions a major priority. It then concluded:

> It is my belief that our commitment to missions has made that possible. My prayer is that this year's congregation will be as aggressive as the congregations of the past in accepting the challenges of its hour. If that happens, the very unique blessings that have come to us from the hand of our ever gracious God will continue to be the order of the day. May it ever be so.

I am absolutely convinced that missions is the mission of the church and that Mierop's challenge to "make missions an obsession" is not optional; it is critical if a church is to fulfill its calling.

Although this book is intended to be philosophical rather than methodological, here are some of the ingredients that contribute to creating an obsession for reaching the world for Christ.

VISIBILITY. Constantly and visibly expose the congregation to the church's missionary efforts. Use maps with the locations of your missionaries noted by lights. Include their names in your weekly church bulletin.

PRAYER. Pray aloud every week for every missionary, even if just to mention their names.

INFORMATION. Print an intercessory, informational bulletin (monthly perhaps) which lists the needs of all your missionaries, as culled from recent prayer letters.

COMMUNICATION. Post all the letters from missionaries in conspicuous places so their ministries are constantly before the congregation.

UPDATES FROM THE FIELD. Invite missionaries to share

the pulpit and to report on their work on the field. One way to highlight these people is through an annual, week-long missionary conference where church members are exposed to spiritual needs around the world and learn how they can help to meet those needs.

UPDATES TO THE FIELD. Have church members write letters to the missionaries on the field. Just as the church wants to know what is happening THERE, they want to know what is happening HERE. Every missionary needs to know he or she is not forgotten.

SPECIAL PROJECTS. Organize special projects to meet a specific need of a missionary family or a missionary organization. This is a wonderful way to make the congregation feel needed and useful and is an enormous blessing to the missionaries.

HAVENS. Missionaries who come home on furloughs often have many needs. Members can help provide clothing, housing, etc. A missionary haven -- a rent-free home on church property -- not only helps meet those needs, but also gives the congregation protracted exposure to some of God's choice servants.

PASTORAL TRIPS. If exposing the congregation to missionaries is so vital, so is exposing the pastor to the various mission fields which the church serves. Sending the pastor on these trips renews the pastor's vision for outreach and the enthusiasm he brings home is poured out upon the congregation, sharpening its vision as well.

FAITH PROMISES. A church must put its money where its mouth is. Lip-service is hypocritical. The faith promise is the best program today to encourage financial participation in missions. As the money comes in, the interest increases and people become excited about supporting the Lord's work. They learn firsthand that "where our treasure is, there will our heart be also."

Prescription # 10: REACH OUT INTO THE COMMUNITY & THE WORLD, has the power to prevent ingrownitis. Taken seriously, a church can maintain a healthy reproductive system capable of doing the work of an evangelist and living up to its Great Commission responsibilities to reach the world for Christ. Ingrownitis, on the other hand, makes a church so sick it can no longer dispense the only medicine on earth that has the power to save a soul from Hell -- the gospel of the Lord Jesus Christ. Of it Paul wrote:

> For I am not ashamed of the Gospel of Christ, for it is the power of God unto salvation to everyone that believeth; to the Jew first, and also to the Greek (Rom. 1:16).

Of that great power comes this exquisite and challenging comment from the pen of the 19th century's greatest preacher, Charles Hadden Spurgeon:

> Oh, the power, the melting and conquering, transforming power of that dear cross of Christ! My brethren, we have but constantly to tell abroad the matchless story, and we may expect to see the most remarkable spiritual results. We need to despair of no man now that Jesus has died for sinners. With such a hammer as the doctrine of the cross, the most flinty heart will be broken; and with such a fire as the sweet love of Christ, the most mighty iceberg will be melted. We need never despair for the heathenish or superstitious races of men; if we can but find occasion to bring the doctrine of Christ crucified into contact with their natures, it will yet change them, and Christ will be their King. [13]

And all God's people said, "Amen."

ENDNOTES

1. C. John Miller, *Outgoing the Ingrown Church* (Grand Rapids, MI: Zondervan Publishing House, 1986) book cover.

2. Donald McGavran, *Understanding Church Growth* (Grand Rapids, MI: Wm. B. Eerdmans Pub. Co., 1970) p. 15.

3. Donald McGavran, ibid, p. 87-88 (Amplification of types of church growth).

4. Donald McGavran, ibid, p.15.

5. Virgil Gerber, *A Manual for Evangelism Church Growth* (Pasadena, CA: William Carey Library, 1973) p. 14.

6. Bruce W. McDonald, *Bridge Evangelism* (cherry Hill, N.J.: Association of Baptists for World Evangelism, 1984) Chapter 6, pages 44-57.

7. Elwood McQuaid, "When No Offense Is the Best Offense" - article (Chicago, IL: *Moody Monthly*, Sept. 1983) p. 102.

8. Bruce W. McDonald, op. cit., p. 13-14.

9. Win Arn and Charles Arn, *The Master's Plan for Making Disciples* (Pasadena, CA: Church Growth Press, 1982) p. 6.

10. Elwood McQuaid, op. cit. , p. 104.

11. Rebecca Manley Pippert, *Out of the Saltshaker and Into the World* (Downers Grove, IL: Intervarsity Press) p. 13.

12. Elwood McQuaid, op. cit., p. 104.

13. Charles Haddon Spurgeon, see note on acknowledgment page.

11

Understanding the Times

Jesus Christ, as portrayed in some New Testament passages, is 'narrow-minded' and 'vindictive.' The Gospel writers 'twisted' the facts concerning Jesus' resurrection, which was never meant to be taken literally. The virgin birth of Christ is an unthinkable notion, and there is not much value in the doctrine of the Trinity, or in the belief that Jesus Christ was sent to save fallen humanity from sin. St. Paul, the missionary of Christianity to the Gentiles, was a repressed and 'self-loathing' homosexual. As for the Old Testament, it contains a 'vicious tribal code of ethics' attributed to a 'sadistic' god. The idea that Yahweh bestowed the Promised Land upon the Israelites is 'arrogance.' [1]

Thus saith the Episcopal Bishop John Spong in his book Rescuing the Bible from Fundamentalism, according to a February 8, 1991 review in Time Magazine. The review continues:

Excerpts from a tract by a staunch atheist? On the contrary, those are assertions offered by a bishop of America's Episcopal Church, John Spong of

Newark...Spong's unorthodoxy is of long standing, but it has now reached epic proportions. His
previous book, Living in Sin?, assailed Christian
dos and don'ts on sex and asserted that nonmarital
sex can be holy under some circumstances. After
the work appeared in 1988, Spong ordained a sexu-
ally active gay priest, inspiring the Episcopal House
of Bishops to 'disassociate' itself from Spong's action. [2]

The article said that Spong was reared in an atmosphere of
fundamental orthodoxy which gave him a "love of Scripture that
is no longer prevalent in the liberal tradition of the church." What
a confusing statement! How can anyone who truly loves the Scriptures reject them? How can anyone who has directly experienced
the personal love and forgiveness of Jesus Christ reject His re-
demptive work at Calvary?

How? Because these are perilous times. These are the last
days and Spong's statements typify the type of teaching about
which Paul warns the body of Christ. Prescription #11: UN-
DERSTAND THE TIMES, is essential preventative medicine for
any church that wants to avoid contracting an anemia that will
eventually grow into a self-defeating and tragically debilitating
lethargy.

Paul opens the third chapter of 2 Timothy with these words:
"This know, also, that in the last days perilous times shall come."
What is needed during these days is found in Chapter 12 of the
Old Testament book of 1 Chronicles. It contains a list of the men
of Israel who made David king. Verse 32 describes the children
of Issachar, calling them "men who had understanding of the times,
to know what Israel ought to do." These are the type of men the
church of Jesus Christ needs today. Men who understand the
times will know what the church ought to do to glorify God through
them.

This issue is obviously important because Paul returns to it on

R_x:

Understand the Times.

numerous occasions as he writes to young Timothy. Paul also uses alarming language as he warns Timothy concerning the "last days." As I noted earlier, I do not consider myself an expert on prophecy. As I was preparing to tackle this subject I found myself at Word of Life Inn listening to Dr. Donald Hubbard, at that time, senior pastor of the Boca Raton Community Church in Boca Raton, Florida. Dr. Hubbard's topic was, "Living in the Last Days."[3] He asked four excellent questions. Indeed, they were so good that I have borrowed them for the framework of this chapter.

1. What do we mean by the last days?
2. Are these the last days? If so, then:
3. Are these days the last of the last days?
4. What difference do the last days make anyway?

QUESTION #1: WHAT DO WE MEAN BY "THE LAST DAYS"?

The term "last days" in Scripture is translated in various ways in the English Bible. Sometimes it reads "the last hour," or "the latter times." Regardless, it is always prophetic terminology used to designate that period of time prior to the return of Jesus Christ to rapture His church. Though the word "days" is used, it actually refers to a prolonged period of time. In Scripture, the term "day" does not always refer to a 24-hour-period. The context determines the usage. When the term "last" precedes the word "days," it refers to that period of time that comes to a conclusion when the Lord returns for His church.

QUESTION #2: ARE THESE DAYS THE LAST DAYS?

Do the days in which we are living constitute the period of

time that will end when the Lord returns to rapture His church? The first key to answering the question is found in Hebrews Chapter 1, which states when "the last days" began.

> Hebrews 1:1-2 -- God, who at sundry times and in diverse manners spoke in time past unto the fathers by the prophets, Hath in these last days spoken unto us by His Son.

According to this verse, it is erroneous to believe that the last days constitute just the brief period of time immediately preceding the return of the Lord. They actually began with the earthly ministry of the Lord Jesus Christ. The Olivet Discourse of Matthew Chapter 24 also provides insight:

> Matthew 24:3-8 -- And as He sat upon the Mount of Olives, the disciples came unto him privately, saying, Tell us, when shall these things be? And what shall be the sign of thy coming, and of the end of the age? And Jesus answered and said unto them, Take heed that no man deceive you. For many shall come in my name, saying, I am Christ, and shall deceive many. And ye shall hear of wars and rumors of wars: see that ye be not troubled; for all these things must come to pass, but the end is not yet. For nation shall rise against nation, and kingdom against kingdom; and there shall be famines and pestilences, and earthquakes in divers (various) places. All these are the beginning of sorrows.

During that future period of sorrow, known as the tribulation period, catastrophic events will take place. Coming events often cast their shadow prior to their arrival, so when the beginning of what Jesus mentioned in Matthew 24 manifests itself, it is safe to conclude that the time is drawing closer.

Another passage that addresses the question, "Are we in the last days?" is found in the pastoral epistles of 1 Timothy 4, written some 30 - 35 years after the Lord's instruction in Matthew 24.

> 1 Timothy 4:1 -- Now the Spirit speaketh expressly that, in the latter times, some shall depart from the faith, giving heed to seducing spirits, and doctrines of demons.

In 2 Timothy 3:1 - 5 Paul lists 19 evils that will characterize the last days:

1. **Lovers of their own selves**---self loving.
2. **Covetous**--lovers of money.
3. **Boasters**--braggarts.
4. **Proud**--haughty, arrogant.
5. **Blasphemers**--evil speaking, slanderous, abusive people, disrespectful of God and their fellow man.
6. **Disobedient to parents**--breakers of civil and moral law. Under Roman law, to strike one's father was as bad as murder. In the Greek culture it could result in disinheritance. Honoring parents was also part of the Jewish Mosaic Law.
7. **Unthankful**--ungrateful, no appreciation.
8. **Unholy**--offenders of all that is holy.
9. **Without natural affection**--no family love.
10. **Trucebreakers**--unceasing enmity, so that men cannot be persuaded to enter into treaties with one another.
11. **False accusers**--slanderers.
12. **Incontinent**--without self control.
13. **Fierce**--brutal, savage, wild, untamed.
14. **Despisers of those that are good**--haters of good, whether in people or in things.
15. **Traitors**--treacherous, like those in Paul's day who turned Christians over to the Roman authorities because of their hatred for them.

16. **Heady**--rash, headstrong, reckless.

17. **High-minded**--conceited, from a word meaning "to raise smoke."

18. **Lovers of pleasure more than lovers of God.**

19. **Having a form of godliness, but denying the power of it**--people who maintain an external religiosity but who have no personal relationship with God and know nothing of true Christianity as a dynamic power to change lives.

After cataloging these evil characteristics Paul instructs Timothy: "From such turn away." At issue is a category of false teachers known as apostasizers. "Apostasy" simply means "departure." The major characteristic of biblical apostasy is a defection from the doctrine of the Scriptures. It is the deliberate rejection by professing Christians of (1) the deity of Jesus Christ and (2) redemption from sin through His atoning and redeeming sacrifice. Charles Ryrie, in his book, The Final Countdown, offers this identification:

> Apostates in the New Testament seem to be unsaved people who have made some sort of profession of faith, however shallow (2 Peter 2:1). Perhaps we could define apostasy as departure from truth which one professed to have accepted, or breaking a professed relationship with God. According to this definition, a true believer cannot apostasize, though he can be surrounded by apostasy in the organized church or denomination of which he is a part. [4]

When a defection in doctrine takes place there is always an accompanying decline in morality. We are in the last days. That is why Paul provided Timothy with such a lengthy list of reprehensible characteristics. That is why men like Bishop Spong can boldly write the things he writes and have many who even agree with him.

The Apostle Peter also warns of the evil of the last days:

2 Peter 3:3--Knowing this first, that there shall come in the last days, scoffers, walking after their own lusts.

John, writing so much later than Paul and Peter, echoes their epistles in unmistakable terms:

1 John 2:18--Little children, it is the last time; and as ye have heard that antichrist shall come, even now there are many antichrists, by which we know it is the last time.

The evidence is in. The last days began with the ministry of Christ and continue to the present. "Are these the last days"? Yes. These are the last days. And since the last days are now nearly 2,000 years in duration, a logical third question arises:

QUESTION #3: ARE THESE DAYS THE LAST OF THE LAST DAYS?

I believe they are, but it is unwise to become too dogmatic on the subject since it is impossible to know when the Lord will return. "Of that day and hour knoweth no man" (Acts 1:7). It seems reasonable, however, to answer this question in the affirmative based upon the evidence in four areas, as pointed out by Dr. Hubbard.

1. The Natural World--Matthew 24:4ff
2. The Theological World--1 Timothy 4:1ff
3. The Social World--2 Timothy 3:1ff
4. The International World--Revelation, etc.

The Natural World

The passage of import is Matthew 24, where Christ speaks primarily of conditions immediately following the rapture of the church. Since, as we have said, coming events often cast their

171

shadows prior to their arrival, it is reasonable to anticipate that the rapture may be closer than most people realize.

> Matthew 24:4-7--And Jesus answered and said unto them, Take heed that no man deceive you. For many shall come in my name, saying, I am Christ; and shall deceive many. And ye shall hear of wars and rumors of wars; see that ye be not troubled; for all these things must come to pass, but the end is not yet. For nation shall rise against nation, and Kingdom against Kingdom.

The Lord Jesus noted a series of natural disasters that will affect mankind: "And there shall be famines, and pestilences, and earthquakes in various places" (Matt. 24:7). Today, when any of these events occur anywhere in the world, sophisticated satellite communication networks beam the news around the globe even as the events are taking place. It is easier for Americans to turn on their televisions to watch flooding in Europe and earthquakes in Japan than it is to drive to the supermarket for a quart of milk.

Natural disasters, of course, are nothing new. Floods have been around since the days of Noah, and the earth quaked and opened to swallow Korah and all his cohorts during the days of Moses. Today, however, those events would have been beamed immediately into every house in America. Word of what takes place in one part of the world does not take long to reach the other parts. Man is more globally aware than ever before.

The Lord Jesus said that when we begin to see these natural, cataclysmic catastrophes we can know that we are in the last of the last days. We are seeing them today.

Not only are we seeing them, but we are seeing them at an ever-increasing rate. In 1982 Paul Lee Tan reported the following:

> During the 9th century, there was one major earthquake. In the 12th century, there were 2; in the

13th century, 3; in the 16th century, 2; in the 18th
century, 5; in the 19th century, 9 major quakes.
And so far in the 20th century, there have been
over 40 major quakes.[5]

The Theological World

> 1 Timothy 4:1-3--Now the Spirit speaketh ex-
> pressly that, in the latter times, some shall depart
> from the faith, giving heed to seducing spirits, and
> doctrines of demons, Speaking lies in hypocrisy,
> having their conscience seared with a hot iron,
> Forbidding to marry, and commanding to abstain
> from foods, which God hath created to be received
> with thanksgiving by them who believe and know
> the truth.

Paul instructs Timothy that as we come nearer to the last of
the last days we will begin to see religious leaders defect from
their professedly held convictions. Certainly that is common in
religious circles today. Paul repeatedly warns the church that in
the latter times it will experience from within a falling away from
the true faith (2 Thes. 2). In 1 Timothy 4 he points out that the
cause for such defection is not the "growing intelligence of men,"
but rather the same satanic deception that caused man's fall in the
Garden of Eden. Warren Wiersbe speaks to this issue:

> Down through the years, men have denied the
> Christian faith and attacked the basic doctrines of
> the Bible, on the basis that modern man is more
> intelligent and cannot "fall for" Bible teachings.
> The problem is not with the head but with the heart!
> They are under the subtle influence of Satan's de-
> monic forces, who, like their master, are liars and
> murderers.[6]

These individuals to whom Paul refers are "apostates," not believers who have simply erred or become confused. These people were never true Christians to begin with. John makes this clear in 1 John Chapter 2 where he deals with the identical subject of apostasy.

> 1 John 2:18--Little children, it is the last time; and as ye have heard that antichrist shall come, even now there are many antichrists, by which we know that it is the last time.

The antichrists noted here are plural and do not refer to the Anti-Christ who will surface during the tribulation. These antichrists to whom John is referring are individuals who oppose the historic Christ. This is a characteristic of an apostate. John refers, as does Paul, to a system of thought that represents a way of salvation that denies, downplays or even eliminates the necessity of Jesus' substitutiary, sacrificial death on the cross. Such thinking abounds in these days.

John continues in verse 19, "They went out from us." At one time these people were part of the professing Christian community. "They went out from us, but they were not of us," he continues. They may have sat with true believers in the same pews but they did not belong to the same God, namely the biblical and historical Lord Jesus Christ.

> For if they had been of us, they would no doubt have continued with us; but they went out, that they might be manifest that they were not all of us.

As the end of the age approaches, as mankind works its way through the "last of the last days," theological confusion will spread and intensify. That is, quite obviously, true today.

The Social World

> 2 Timothy 3:1--This know, also, that in the last
> days perilous times shall come.

What will the end of the last days be like socially? The answer is found in the word "perilous." That is the KJV translation of the Greek word chalepoi, which means that times will be "different, terrible, grievous and hard to live in." This word occurs only twice in the New Testament -- once here and once in Matthew 8:32 where Christ cast demons out of the man who lived in the tombs of Gadara (Matt. 8:28-34). There the word is translated as "violent." Hence, the times will be perilous, terrible and violent. What an apt description of the times we live in! The pages of any major city's newspaper attest to the violence permeating society. Another characteristic of the social structure of the last days is decadence (2 Tim. 3:2-5), a condition that certainly afflicts a good part of the world, particularly the United States.

It is virtually impossible to miss the connection between de-fective theology and decaying morality. The more a society re-jects the absolute teachings of God in the Bible, the more corrupt, base and violent the society becomes. "No wonder," said Dr. Hubbard, "that all hell breaks loose when the church is raptured because there will be no restraining force upon the world at that particular period of time" (2 Thes. 2:1-12).

The International World

This fourth area has so many technical and prophetic facets that the most effective way to overview it briefly is to thumb through the Book of Revelation. Here, according to Revelation 1:19, is a review of the past, the present and the future. In in-structing the elderly Apostle John, the Lord instructs him with these words:

Write the things which thou hast seen (chapter 1, the past), and the things which are (the church age, chapter 2-3, the present), and the things which shall be hereafter (Rev. 4-22, the future).

Eschatologically, I am premillenial and pretribulational. I believe that Christ will return prior to the millennium and that He will rapture His church prior to the tribulation. There is no prophetic event that must take place prior to the rapture. In The Future Explored, Timothy Weber writes concerning the signs of the times:

'Christ's second coming is imminent. The signs are everywhere. Read the daily newspaper and see for yourself. Biblical prophecies are being fulfilled every single day before our eyes. Jesus may arrive at any moment.'

We frequently hear that kind of statement these days. Each year scores of books are published and probably thousands of sermons are preached in an attempt to relate current events to some biblical prophetic scheme. How should we interpret the continuing Middle East crisis in light of Biblical prophecy? What does the inevitable energy crisis have to do with the coming tribulation? Is the European Common Market really the restored Roman Empire of the last days? In other words, to what extent can we find prophetic fulfillments in the events of our own day? Are the 'signs of the times' that obvious? [7]

Weber goes on to say:

Let's agree on one thing right at the beginning.

There is nothing perverse about these questions.
Anyone who firmly believes in the personal return
of Jesus Christ to earth is naturally concerned about
when it might occur. Christians would not be living up to Jesus' command to be watchful if they
did not ask themselves such questions.

But history has shown that when Christians become overly concerned about the times of the Second Coming, they get themselves into trouble.
Setting dates and miscalculating the arrival of
Christ have been the besetting sins of
premillennialism over the centuries. Not only do
such attempts bring considerable embarrassment
and shame on the people doing it, but they also
discredit the doctrine of the Second Coming in the
eyes of the rest of the world.[8]

Setting actual dates for the Lord's return is not only unbiblical;
it is irresponsible. But to be disinterested in His return would be
somewhat inconsistent with one's faith. Even the disciples were
interested (Acts 1:6). Following is an outline from Keith L. Brooks
as contained in Brief Outlines of Things to Come, compiled by
Theodore H. Epp. It gives ample evidence that, "Yes, we are
living in the last of the last days." The outline touches not only
pretribulational events, but events contained within the actual 7-
year tribulation period.

International Conditions Preceding
Christ's Second Coming

Constant rumors of war (Matt. 24:6).
Increasing world conflicts accompanied by pestilence and famine
(Matt. 24:7; Isa. 13:4,5).
Economic perils such as the nations have never known
(Matt. 24:21, 22; Mark 13:19; Dan. 12:1).

The people impotent to help themselves (Ezek. 7:17,18).

Gold and silver valueless as exchange (Ezek. 7:19).

Disastrous earthquakes (Matt. 24:7).

Increasing commotions within nations (Luke 21:9).

Fearful sights and great signs (Luke 21:11,25).

People's hearts failing for fear (Luke 21:26; Isa. 24:17, 18).

Perilous conditions in general (2 Tim. 3:1-5).

Collapse of great fortunes (James 5:1-8).

Nations utterly broken down (Isa. 24:19, 20; 51:6).

Days of darkness and gloominess (Joel 2:2).

Hellish war devices (Joel 2:3-5).

World empire attained; its final destruction (Dan. 2:40-45).

Many traitors, "fifth columnists" (Mark 13:12; Luke 21:16; 2 Tim. 3:3, 4)

National revival of Israel (Mark 13:28).

Russia and Germany, as one, eventually attempt to grab riches of Palestine (Ezek. 38, 39).

Increasing persecution of Christians and Jews (Dan. 7:21, 22; Jer. 30:7, 13-16; Matt. 24:9; Mark 13:13).

Final rise of an anti-God world dictator demanding allegiance of all (Dan. 7:24-26; Rev. 13:1-18); honors the god of forces (Dan. 11:36-39); overthrows many nations (Dan 11:41, 42).

Wastes of Palestine cultivated after many centuries of barrenness (Isa. 43:19,20; Ezek. 34:26, 27; 36:4-10, 30, 34, 35).

Hebrew language revived after being long dead (Zeph. 3:9).

The Jewish people return to the land of Israel in large numbers (Isa. 43:5, 6; 49:19; Jer. 23:3; 30:3; Ezek. 11:17, 18; Hos. 3:4, 5).

Seven years of consummation--the Great Tribulation--time of awful trouble for the Jewish people (Jer. 30:7; Dan. 9:27)[9]

The Scriptures certainly provide the evidence needed to conclude that these are, indeed, the last of the last days. All that being said, however, Dr. Hubbard's next question is the most critical.

QUESTION #4: WHAT DIFFERENCE DOES IT MAKE ANYWAY?

What difference does it make to Bible-believing Christians that these are the last of the last days? What difference does it make to those of us who are born again by the Spirit of God? The answer lies in 2 Peter 3 where on four occasions Peter uses the term "beloved."

2 Peter 3:1--"This second epistle, **beloved**..."
2 Peter 3:8--"But **beloved**..."
2 Peter 3:14---"Wherefore, **beloved**..."
2 Peter 3:17---"Ye therefore, **beloved**..."

Peter is coming to the close of an epistle that is very closely related to second-coming truth. He does so by linking the term "beloved" in each instance with an accompanying expression, and the text of the KJV describes his four points in a very beautiful fashion.

> *"Beloved"* (3:1); *"be mindful"* (3:2)

"Be mindful of the words which were spoken before by the holy prophets." Know what you believe. Base your convictions upon the Word of God. Of course, that necessitates studying it.

> *"Beloved"* (3:8); *"be not ignorant"* (3:8)

"Be not ignorant of this one thing, that a day is with the Lord as a thousand years, and a thousand years as one day...(10) the day of the Lord will come as a thief in the night."

179

"Beloved" (3:14); *"be diligent"* (3:14)

"Wherefore, beloved, seeing that ye look for such things, be diligent that ye may be found of him in peace, without spot, and blameless."

Believers must make sure that their lives before God their Father, the One whom they should aim to please, are pure and blameless.

"Beloved" (3:17); *"beware"* (3:17)

"Ye therefore, beloved, seeing that ye know these things before, beware lest ye also, being led away with the error of the wicked, fall from your own steadfastness."

Does it make any difference what Christians believe about the last days? Evidently Peter thinks it does. "Beloved":

Be Mindful
Be Not Ignorant
Be diligent
Beware

A church that takes **Prescription #11: UNDERSTAND THE TIMES,** will be filled with men and women who are like the men of Issachar. They will have an understanding of the days we live in and will know what to do. A local body that knows that the hour is late will translate that knowledge into action and will work diligently to reach out into its community to evangelize and make disciples. But a church that is unaware of the times will not get the job done.

In the Gospel of Luke, Chapter 2, Jesus and His earthly family went up to Jerusalem to celebrate the feast of the Passover. When the celebration was finished, the family began to return home. A day into the journey they realized that Jesus was not with them. They returned to Jerusalem and after three days they found their 12-year-old son, sitting in the temple debating with the teachers, astounding them with His understanding and answers. His mother rebuked Him with these words:

> Son, why hast thou thus dealt with us? Behold, thy father and I have sought thee, sorrowing (vs. 48).

He responded by saying:

> How is it that ye sought me? Knew ye not that I must be about my Father's business? And they understood not the saying which he spoke unto them (Lu. 2:49-50).

It is imperative that Christians understand what the Lord is trying to say and the lateness of the hour. Paul wrote in 2 Corinthians 6:2, "Behold, now is the accepted time; behold, now is the day of salvation." The church must be about its Father's business. It must never be lulled into unconsciousness by failing to understand the urgency of the days we are in.

Paul was an example for every Christian to follow. In his final letter to Timothy, this great saint encourages his young protege to remain faithful. As he does so, he rehearses his own life, looking back with no regrets on the life he has spilled out for God:

> For I am now ready to be offered, and the time of my departure is at hand. I have fought a good fight, I have finished my course, I have kept the faith (2 Tim. 4:6-7).

Then he looks ahead.

Henceforth there is laid up for me a crown of righteousness, which the Lord, the righteous judge, shall
give me at that day; and not to me only, but unto
all them also that love his appearing (2 Tim. 4:8).

Christ's appearing is not far off. With that awareness ever
before it, the church should march forward like it never has before, so Christians everywhere might say as did Paul, that they
"press toward the mark for the prize of the high calling of God in
Christ Jesus" (Phil. 3:14).

ENDNOTES

1. *Time* Magazine article, Feb. 9, 1991, p.62.

2. ibid, p. 62.

3. Donald Hubbard, *Living in the Last Days,* Message
   delivered at Word of Life Inn, Schroon Lake, N.Y.,
   July 17, 1991.

4. Charles C. Ryrie, *The Final Countdown* (Wheaton, IL:
   Victor Books, 1982, 1989) p. 69-70.

5. Paul Lee Tan, *Encyclopedia of 7700 Illustrations*
   (Rockville, MD: Assurance Publishers) p. 351-352.

6. Warren W. Wiersbe, *Whole Bible Study Course - Orig. by
   D. B. Eastep* (Covington, KY: Calvary Baptist Church
   Book Room, n.d.) notes from 1 Tim. 4.

7. Timothy P. Weber, *The Future Explored* (Wheaton, IL:
   Victor Books, 1978) p. 37.

8. Timothy P. Weber, ibid, p. 37-38.

9. Theodore H. Epp, *A Brief Outline of Things to Come* (Chicago, IL: Moody Press, 1952) p. 10-11.

12

Controlling the Flesh

Of all Paul's letters, 2 Timothy is the most personal. Written from Rome where Paul was imprisoned awaiting trial and certain death, it passionately encourages Timothy to be ready to step into Paul's ministerial shoes. Paul so desired his protegé to be true to his calling and to fulfill his ministry that he wove into this epistle not only exhortations to personal faithfulness, but the heartfelt pleas of a father to his son.

As the father of two sons, I can sympathize with Paul and the urgency of his plea. Many fathers are desperately concerned that their name be carried on for future generations. For Paul, it was not the survival of his name that concerned him; it was the survival of his ministry.

Paul now knows his death is near and he must pass the torch to Timothy, whom he has loved and nurtured from spiritual infancy. Patrick Fairbairn, in his commentary on the pastoral epistles, writes:

> We have no other instance of such a near, unbroken, and prolonged fellowship in the history of apostolic times, as that which appears to have subsisted between Paul and this youthful disciple; the more remarkable, considering the disparity of their

185

ages. From the period that Timothy entered upon his ministerial discipleship, he seems rarely to have been absent for any length of time from the apostle; and even when expressly mentioned among his companions, some turn in the affairs, or incidental expression, reveals the presence of the beloved disciple. [1]

Although many commentators have written about this father-son relationship, perhaps none states the case more clearly than the Apostle Paul himself when he wrote to the Philippian believers:

But I trust in the Lord Jesus to send Timothy shortly unto you, that I also may be of good comfort when I know your state. For I have no man like-minded, who will naturally care for your state; for all seek their own, not the things which are Jesus Christ's. But ye know the proof of him, that, <u>as a son with his father</u>, he hath served me in the gospel (Phil. 2:19-22).

Paul loved Timothy as a son. And it's out of that love that he writes this personal epistle, encouraging him through a number of different approaches to remain faithful to his charge and to follow Prescription #12: CONTROL THE FLESH AND ITS APPETITES.

Warren Wiersbe's outline [2] of 2 Timothy beautifully details the manner in which Paul proceeds to outline his charge to Timothy, first in a general fashion, then in a specific one.

<u>Chapter One--The Pastoral Appeal</u>

Paul reminds Timothy of his calling into the ministry and the responsibilities and privileges that go with it.

Chapter Two--The Practical Appeal

Paul deals in a very practical way with the local church and the pastor's special responsibilities. He presents several pictures of the local church, and shows the various ministries God has for His people and their pastor (to be amplified momentarily).

Chapter Three--The Prophetic Appeal

Paul explains the course of future events and the resultant necessity of holding fast to the Word of God.

R$_x$:
Control the Flesh and its Appetites

Chapter Four-- The Personal Appeal

Paul brings the letter to a close with a personal appeal directly from his heart, urging Timothy not to become another Demas.

The Wiersbe outline includes seven pictures of the Christian minister (in Chapter 2):

(1) The Steward	--	2 Timothy 2:1-2
(2) The Soldier	--	2 Timothy 2:3-4, 8-13
(3) The Athlete	--	2 Timothy 2:5
(4) The Farmer	--	2 Timothy 2:6-7
(5) The Workman	--	2 Timothy 2:14-18
(6) The Vessel	--	2 Timothy 2:19-22
(7) The Servant	--	2 Timothy 2:23-26

It is in point 6, the vessel, where Paul warns Timothy to "control the flesh and its appetites."

2 Timothy 2:19-22 -- Nevertheless, the foundation of God standeth sure, having this seal, The

Lord knoweth them that are his; and Let every one that nameth the name of Christ depart from iniquity. But in a great house there are not only vessels of gold and of silver, but also of wood and of earth; and some to honor, and some to dishonor. If a man, therefore, purge himself from these, he shall be a vessel unto honor, sanctified, and fit for the master's use, and prepared unto every good work. Flee also youthful lusts, but follow righteousness, faith, love, peace, with them that call on the Lord out of a pure heart.

Verse 20 employs the phrase "a great house." By application, this refers to the church, to "the household of God" (2 Tim. 3:15). Here Paul explains that within the house -- the church -- there are two general types of vessels: those of honor and much value (i.e., "gold and silver") and those of dishonor and little value (i.e., "wood and earth").

Various commentators have exegeted this passage in various ways. I agree with Homer Kent, who in his commentary The Pastoral Epistles,[3] lays the stress in this illustration not upon the usefulness of the vessels but rather upon their value or quality. As any housewife knows, the wood and earthen (pottery) vessels are probably used far more than fine gold and silver, which only make their appearance on special occasions. But the wood and pottery vessels eventually chip or break and must be replaced, whereas the gold and silver ones last forever. The same is true in the church. From time to time false teachers arise, but eventually their worthlessness is recognized and they are removed.

Kent notes the honored vessel must purge himself from other vessels.[4] When a dinner is complete and the guests have gone home, clean-up begins. The first dishes washed are usually the sterling silver and crystal. Then they are restored to safekeeping in the china closet or silver chest. They are not left with the pots and pans or piled indiscriminately with the common kitchen utensils in the drying rack. In fact, the silver utensils are never even to touch the stainless steel utensils in a dishwasher because the stainless tarnishes the sterling.

Likewise, the contamination that clings to the dishonored vessels must not be allowed to infect the honored ones. The true servant of God, says Paul, must "purge himself" from the company of the valueless, or dishonored. By so doing, he will separate himself from evil and be useful to the master of the household, who in this case is the Lord Jesus Christ.

Cleansing, however, is an ongoing process. It becomes the cleansed vessel's responsibility to maintain his value for His Master's sake by staying clean. This is a two-step process -- one negative and one positive. The negative aspect involves avoiding contamination; the positive requires following after righteousness. This dual approach is summed up in 2 Timothy 2:22: "<u>Flee</u> also youthful lusts, but <u>follow</u> righteousness, faith, love, peace, with them that call on the Lord out of a pure heart."

Unfortunately, many Christians do not realize the importance of following both steps of the procedure. Avoiding contamination, for instance, without seeking after righteousness will not produce the desired result in a person's life, and vice versa. That is why Paul cautioned Timothy to be faithful in both areas to be a servant fit for his Master's use. Otherwise his ministry would be valueless.

It is not difficult today to find ministries that have been wrecked because of a failure to heed Paul's instructions. Christians in visible positions have adopted lifestyles and practices that dishonor the Lord who called them "out of darkness into His marvelous light" (2 Pet. 2:9) and who commissioned them to His service.

PAUL'S ADVICE--NEGATIVE ASPECT
"Flee also youthful lusts (2 Tim. 2:22)

The phrase "youthful lusts" can easily be interpreted in a sexual context. While that is applicable, and certainly the primary emphasis in the text under consideration, the advice should not be construed to be limited to that area alone. There are many "lusts" which might easily entice a young man. Here are what some of the commentators have to say:

<u>Kenneth S. Wuest</u>: 'Lust...a craving, a passionate desire,' good or evil, depending upon the context...Here, the context refers to inordinate desires of uncontrolled youth.[5]

<u>Expositors</u>: Timothy had just been cautioned against errors of the intellect (2:15-18), he must also be warned against vices of the blood.[6]

<u>Patrick Fairbairn</u>: ...primarily, no doubt, sensual indulgence, yet not this alone, levity of spirit also, love of pleasure, vainglory, and things of a similar kind (Theodoret). Such an advice was still suitable to Timothy, who, though now in ripe manhood, was yet not beyond the period when the mind is liable to aberration or excess.[7]

<u>J. N. D. Kelly</u>: The advice to avoid youthful passions reminds us that Timothy is still a young man by ancient standards. The sequel with its reference to integrity, etc. suggests that the Apostle is not thinking so much of sensual temptations as of certain faults of character which headstrong young men are liable to display. He wants Timothy to wean himself of partiality, intolerance, quickness of temper, self-assertion, and the like, and thus to attain moral maturity.[8]

<u>Warren Wiersbe</u>: A useful human vessel must remain holy, and this means he must be separated from everything that would defile him. This includes sins of the flesh.[9]

<u>Homer Kent</u>: He must <u>flee</u> youthful desires. Those desires include not only bodily appetites, but all temptations

which particularly beset the young minister (older men can fall for them too). Pride, love of money, sex, contentiousness, display of knowledge -- all can ruin the usefulness of God's young servant. The only safe course is to continually flee from them. It is unfair to suspect Timothy of unusual weakness along this line. Paul may properly speak thus to every man.[10]

This is not the first time in his instructions to Timothy that Paul uses this negative/positive approach. In fact, it is not the first time he has used the "flee-follow" terminology. In 1 Timothy 6:11, after listing the evils money can generate, Paul tells Timothy,: "But thou, O man of God, <u>flee</u> these things, and <u>follow</u> after righteousness, godliness, faith, love, patience, meekness."

No doubt, there are times when running away would be considered cowardice. Nehemiah asked the question, "Should such a man as I flee?" (Neh. 6:11). But there are other times when fleeing demonstrates wisdom. Apt illustrations would be Joseph, who demonstrated godliness and wisdom when he fled the temptations of his master's wife (Gen. 39:12), and David, who fled when King Saul tried to kill him. (1 Sam. 19:10).

The word that Paul uses for "flee" in both 1 Timothy 6:11 and 2 Timothy 2:22 is <u>pheuge</u> and does not refer to a literal running away, but to the action of separating oneself from the issue in question. In 1 Timothy 6 it denotes separation from the evils of money and false teaching; in 2 Timothy 2 it denotes separation from those things to which youth is especially susceptible. In either case, the issue is separation.

True biblical separation is accompanied by balance. It is not simply negative; it is positive as well. It involves not only "fleeing" that which is evil, but "following" that which is good. When Paul writes to the Corinthians, he says:

> Wherefore, come out from among them, and be
> ye separate, saith the Lord, and touch not the un-

clean thing; and I will receive you, And will be a
Father unto you, and ye shall be my sons and daugh-
ters, saith the Lord Almighty (2 Cor. 6:17-18).

The Scofield Reference Bible note, in part, gives this summary of
separation:

> Separation in Scripture is two-fold: (a) from
> whatever is contrary to the mind of God; and (b)
> unto God Himself. The underlying principle is that
> in a moral universe it is impossible for God to fully
> bless and use His children who are in compromise
> or complicity with evil. [11]

It continues:

> Separation from evil implies (1) separation in de-
> sire, motive, and act, from the world, in the ethi-
> cally bad sense of their present world system; and
> (b) separation from false teachers, who are de-
> scribed as being "vessels...to dishonor" (2 Tim.
> 2:20-21; 2 John 9-11). [12]

Not only that, but:

> The reward of separation is the full manifestation
> of the divine fatherhood (vs. 17-18; unhindered
> communion and worship (Heb. 13:13-15), and
> fruitful service (2 Tim. 2:21), as world conformity
> involves the loss of these, though not of salvation.[13]

For "lust" Paul uses the Greek word epithumia, which means
"desire, longing , craving." By definition it does not always have
a negative connotation. To desire, long for or crave something is
not evil. In fact, more often than not the use of the word epithumia

in the New Testament is positive. Paul, however, in this instance does not use it that way. His usage is negative.

To Paul, <u>epithumia</u> is the motivator behind the actions of fallen man. The "old man" is corrupt "according to the deceitful lust" and contrasts with the "new man" of the believer, "which after God is created in righteousness and true holiness" (Eph. 4:22-24). That new creation, the result of one's salvation, is not home free, however. Though salvation is secure, the old nature remains annoyingly intact and will constantly attack and challenge a believer's new nature. Paul tells Timothy, "Do not let these sinful inclinations rule your life. If you do, your life will be valueless, and your ministry will be ruined."

James considered lust an enticer that lures man to sin (Ja. 1:14). Peter wrote of the "former lusts" (1 Pet. 1:14), those desires which belonged to the old life. A believer is to avoid these since they wage war against the soul (1 Pet. 2:11). Unfortunately, these lusts encompass more areas than one would notice at first glance.

Sexual Lust

This is probably the first association people make when they hear the word "lust." To desire a sexual union is not wrong. Sex is one of the God-given and God-sanctioned desires of mankind. But those desires are only God-approved within marriage. Sex outside of marriage is not only unacceptable, it is sin.

Power Lust

This is a passion to be Number One and to be in control of everything. It is characterized by the selfish attitude, "I will have my way." This is carnality and carnality is sin. Satan is the father of such corruption as illustrated in Isaiah Chapter 14, where, in just two verses, Satan uses the phrase "I will" five times. He craves to be above God, in the position of utmost preeminence.

Ego Lust

This really is pride, a sin that God says He actually hates (Prov. 6:16). An ego-centric person is one who is overly concerned with himself, one who is self-centered. It is closely related to power lust.

Pleasure Lust

This is the "eat, drink and be merry" mentality of the individual whom God calls a "fool" (Lu. 12:19-20). Everything is fun and games to this person, and unless life is one continual blast it is not worth living. This mentality is demonstrated by the bumper sticker that says: "He who dies with the most toys, wins!" A sequel bumper sticker is more accurate: "He who dies with the most toys, wins -- nothing!"

Approbation Lust

This is the desire for applause or praise. People who suffer from approbation lust may often do good things, but they do them not to please God but to satisfy their craving for praise and approval from men. The Lord deals with this in Matthew 6:1, where He says: "Take heed that ye do not your alms before men, to be seen by them; otherwise, ye have no reward of your Father, who is in heaven."

Materialism Lust

This is a desire to "keep up with the Joneses" or to inordinately strive for security in the financial realm. Christians should not be preoccupied with either the vastness or the meagerness of their material possessions. Christ addressed this in Matthew 6:31-33:

> Be not anxious, saying, What shall we eat? or, What shall we drink? or, With what shall we be clothed?...for your heavenly Father knoweth that ye have need of these things. But seek ye first the kingdom of God, and his righteousness, and all these things shall be added unto you."

Our preoccupation should be to seek after righteousness, not financial security. Paul also addresses this subject in 1 Timothy 6:8-11, where he writes:

> But they that will be rich fall into temptation and a snare, and into many foolish lusts, which drown men in destruction and perdition. For the love of money is the root of all kinds of evil, which, while some coveted after, they have erred from the faith, and pierced themselves through with many arrows...But thou, O man of God, <u>flee these things</u>.

Earnestly wanting Timothy to succeed in his walk with the Lord and in his ministry, Paul warns him to "flee" the lusts of the flesh. Many a prominent Christian leader has destroyed his ministry by failing to heed this warning.

PAUL'S ADVICE--POSITIVE ASPECT

To be a "vessel unto honor," fit for the Master's use, one must flee, then remain separated from evil. On both the occasions where Paul tells Timothy to flee, he also tells him to follow. The word "follow" means "to run swiftly in order to catch some person or thing, to run after, to pursue." Metaphorically it means "to seek eagerly, to earnestly endeavor to acquire." Practically, it means that nothing should be more important. It is a process to be tackled with vigor. The stress is the same here as in Romans 12:21: "Be not overcome by evil, but overcome evil with good."

1 Timothy 6:11--But thou, O man of God, <u>flee</u> these things, and <u>follow</u> after righteousness, godliness, faith, love, patience, meekness.

2 Timothy 2:22--<u>Flee</u> also youthful lusts, but <u>follow</u> righteousness, faith, love, peace, with them that call on the Lord out of a pure heart.

There are seven specific ingredients inherent in the lifestyle that believers should follow. Six are found in 1 Timothy, three are repeated in 2 Timothy and one is added. They are:

> Righteousness

Paul is not using this term in the normal dogmatic, theological sense. Here it means "giving God and men their due," or doing what is right. It is used the theological way in Ephesians 5:9: "For the fruit of the Spirit is in all goodness and righteousness and truth."

> Godliness

This is one of Paul's favorite words. He uses it in the pastoral epistles at least 11 times. It is a shortened form of "god-likeness." Since God is our Father, our behavior should exhibit a family resemblance. It should manifest the character of God.

> Faith

The connotation is fidelity and faithfulness. Along with love, this is one of the primal virtues of Christianity. It is a positive characteristic of trusting God as keeper of all that He has promised and believing that God is of such character that all He does is always right. It should be noted that without this characteristic "it is impossible to please God" (Heb. 11:6).

Love

The Greek word here is <u>agape</u> -- God's love as produced by the Holy Spirit in the heart of the yielded believer. It is part of the fruit of the Spirit (Gal. 5:22) and the essence of Christ's new commandment (Jn. 13:34).

Patience

This refers to an endurance and steadfastness that perseveres even in the worst of circumstances. It comes from two Greek words, <u>hupo</u> meaning "under" and <u>meno</u> meaning "remain," indicating the characteristic of being able to bear up under pressure.

Meekness

This is a description of the attitude of the servant of God toward opponents and adversity in general. It is a gentleness of spirit that is the opposite of the argumentative, divisive, envious spirit that often characterizes people who are preoccupied with the things of the world.

Fairbairn quotes Huther in a way that ties these six characteristics together beautifully.

> As Christian virtues to which Timothy must apply himself, Paul names six, of which each pair stand in a close relation to one another: the two most general ideas go first -- <u>righteousness</u> and <u>godliness</u>; then follow <u>faith</u> and <u>love</u> as the fundamental principles of the Christian life; and finally, <u>patience</u> and <u>meekness</u> of spirit, which denote the conduct proper to a Christian amid the enmity and opposition of the world to Christ's gospel.[14]

These six ingredients/virtues are all found in 1 Timothy 6. In the 2 Timothy 2:22 passage, Paul repeats righteousness, faith, love and adds

> ### Peace

Paul also uses this term in many of his salutations, including all three pastoral epistles.   In the Hebrew it is the word <u>shalom</u>, which was a common greeting among Jewish people. In the Christian context it was more than just a common greeting like "hello." When Jesus used the term in John 14:27 He referred to the total well-being and inner rest of spirit that comes from fellowship with God. It is also part of the fruit the Spirit produces in the life of the believer (Gal. 5:22).

Separation, therefore, involves more than the negative command to flee. Effective separation unto God also depends upon obedience to the positive command to follow.

In 1 Timothy 6:11 Paul adds a third command: Fight. The Greek word is <u>agonizomai</u> which means "contend for a prize." Thus, the sequence is: **FLEE, FOLLOW, FIGHT:**

<u>FLEE</u>	**<u>FOLLOW</u>**	**<u>FIGHT</u>**
anything that would keep you from being an honored vessel in the household of God.	after the virtues that the Spirit of God produces in the life of a believer.	to pursue the path of fleeing and following.

As Paul notes many times throughout his epistles, the believer is at war. When Timothy was called into the Lord's service in Acts 16:3, that call was couched in military language. "Him would Paul have to go forth with." The phrase "go forth" literally means "to take to the field as a soldier." Timothy was enlisted as are all believers, into the army of the King. 2 Timothy 2:3-4 is more specific concerning the call and subsequent service:

> Thou, therefore, endure hardness, as a good soldier of Jesus Christ. No man that warreth entangleth himself with the affairs of this life, that he may please him who hath chosen him to be a soldier.

Christians are indeed soldiers marching under orders that come directly from the Lord Jesus Christ. Like soldiers in any battle, we must learn how to endure hardness, how to "tough it out" no matter how difficult the circumstances. It is clear from Paul's letters that Timothy was not the "John Wayne" type. Persecution discouraged him. But every believer should expect opposition; Satan is a formidable enemy. "The Christian life," says Warren Wiersbe, "is not a playground. It is a battlefield. We do not have the strength ourselves, but by His grace we can endure and stand against the wiles of the devil."[15]

Endurance is not the only quality required of a soldier; non-entanglement with the affairs of life is another. Nothing is to draw the soldier away from his "military" duties. His job is to "please him who hath chosen him to be a soldier." Anything less than total commitment is unsatisfactory and likely to produce defeat.

When Paul exhorts Timothy and, in effect, all believers, to "fight the good fight of faith," he is not asking others to do anything he has not done himself. The Christian's battle is not only against Satan, who is bent on destroying one's effective service for the Lord, but it is also against the old nature from which emanate the appetites of the flesh. This internal battle, between the old sin nature and the new, spiritual nature that arrives with the indwelling of the Holy Spirit, is one that will last all life long. Paul speaks of his own battle in this area in Romans 7:

> Romans 7:15--For that which I do I allow not: for what I would, that do I not; but what I hate, that do I (KJV).

199

The word "do" appears here three times. However, only once is that really the proper translation. The three Greek words used are:

(1) <u>Katergazomai</u> - something on the inside working its way out.

(2) <u>Prasso</u> - to practice.

(3) <u>Poieo</u>- to do.

With these definitions in mind, here is how Paul describes the battle raging inside him:

> For that which keeps on working out of me I do not understand; for what I desire, that I do not practice; but what I hate, that is what I am doing.

In other words, what Paul desired to do -- to honor the Lord -- was not what he was practicing. The subsequent verses of chapter seven explain the problem. The old indwelling sin nature was generating the appetites of the flesh. Unless that nature is repressed (the intent of Paul's "flee" admonition) and the new nature nurtured (the intent of Paul's "follow" admonition), the "fight" will be lost. Paul explains how to accomplish this difficult task in Romans Chapter 6.

> <u>Romans 6:11-13</u> -- Likewise, reckon (count on, rely upon) ye also yourselves to be dead indeed unto sin (the sin nature), but alive unto God through Jesus Christ, our Lord. Let not sin (the sin nature), reign in your mortal body, that ye should obey its lusts. Neither yield ye your members as instruments of unrighteousness unto sin (the sin

nature), but yield yourselves unto God, as those
that are alive from the dead, and your members as
instruments of righteousness unto God.(Note:
"sin" in the N.T., when in the singular, usually refers to the old sin nature man is born with.)

FLEE...FOLLOW...FIGHT. Therein is the three-point procedure that will enable Christians to appropriate Prescription #12:
CONTROL THE FLESH AND ITS APPETITES. Failure in this
area leads to a wide range of consequences, particularly for people
in church leadership such as pastors and deacons who are singled
out to provide a visible pattern of a God-like lifestyle. Unfortunately, however, failures do occur. The question arises: When a
leader suffers a moral failure, can there be restoration?

The answer is two-fold. First, there is no sin in life that cannot
be forgiven. Therefore, restoration to fellowship is always possible, providing the sinning individual takes the biblical steps to
correct the matter. However, restoration to fellowship is not the
same as restoration to a position of leadership within the church.
The answer here is "No." Once it has been determined that a
leader is guilty of sin that would disqualify him from office, that
disqualification is permanent. He will never again be able to function as pastor or deacon with the approval of God.

This in no way means that he can never serve the Lord. But
his place of service has been narrowed. Although this stand may
seem hard to some, it is in keeping with the attempt to give God a
church that is "holy and without blemish" (Eph. 5:27). The objective is not to penalize the sinner, although that inevitably becomes part of the natural consequence, but to provide a clear
picture of righteousness in a world that is becoming increasingly
dark, with less and less illumination coming from the church.

Of course, it is imperative before such action is taken, that the
biblical procedures of getting and appraising the facts, without
partiality, be carefully and prayerfully followed (see 1 Tim. 5:19-
21).

Paul spoke to this subject in other places. Perhaps the clearest and most direct example is in 1 Corinthians 9:27 where he was so concerned that he himself might be "put on the shelf," that he wrote that he would "keep under my body, and bring it unto subjection, lest that by any means, when I have preached to others, I myself should be a castaway." The term "castaway" comes from the Greek word <u>adokimos</u>, meaning one who is disapproved, or "put on the shelf." To permit one to function in a biblically ordained role following such a failure would bring discredit and shame to the cause and work of Christ. In the final analysis, the issue is not the fate of one individual, but rather the integrity of church leadership, and the resultant fate of the Church of Jesus Christ.

Jack Wyrtzen, in an article for the 1989 <u>Word of Life Annual</u> entitled "Restoration: Fellowship or Leadership?" notes:

> There is no New Testament record of a leader being restored to leadership after a moral failure. Indeed, all the passages that address restoration speak of restoration to fellowship, not leadership (see Gal. 6:1; 1 Cor. 2:7; 2 Thess. 3:15; Heb. 12:13 and Ja. 5:19-20).[16]

People in Christian leadership should be acutely aware of their higher responsibility. They must walk in a manner that would never discredit the Savior. "To whom much is given, much shall be required" (Lu. 12:48).

ENDNOTES

1. Patrick Fairbairn, *Commentary on the Pastoral Epistles* (Grand Rapids, MI: Zondervan, 1956 reprint of T. T. Clarks 1874 edition) p. 32.

2. Warren W. Wiersbe, *Be Faithful* (Wheaton, IL: Victor Books, 1981) p. 123.

3. Homer A. Kent, *The Pastoral Epistles* (Chicago, IL: Moody Press 1982 Rev.) p. 268-269.

4. Homer A. Kent, ibid, 269.

5. Kenneth S. Wuest, *The Pastoral Epistles in the Greek New Testament* (Grand Rapids, MI: Wm. B. Eerdmans Pub. Co., 1952) p. 140.

6. Robertson Nicoll, *Expositors Greek Testament* (Grand Rapids, MI: Wm. B. Eerdmans Pub. Co., Reprinted, 1970-Orig. 1909) Vol. 4, p. 168.

7. Patrick Fairbairn, op. cit., p. 355-356.

8. J.N.D. Kelly, *The Pastoral Epistles* (Peabody, MA: Hendrickson, 1987).

9. Warren W. Wiersbe, op. cit., p. 147.

10. Homer A. Kent, op. cit., p. 269-270.

11. C.I. Scofield (E. S. English, rev.) *The New Scofield Reference Bible* (New York: Oxford University Press, 1967) p. 1257.

12. C.I. Scofield, ibid, p. 1257.

13. C.I. Scofield, ibid, p. 1257.

14. Patrick Fairbairn, op. cit., p. 240.

15. Warren W. Wiersbe, *Whole Bible Study Course - Orig. by D. B. Eastep* (Covington, KY: Calvary Baptist Church Book Room, n.d.) notes from 2 Tim. 2.

16. Jack Wyrtzen, "Restoration: Fellowship or Leadership?" - article in <u>*1989 Word of Life Annual*</u>, Schroon Lake, NY: Word of Life Fellowship).

13

Storing Up Treasure

Did you know that Jesus Christ had more to say about money than He did about His Second Coming? Did you know that of Christ's 38 parables, 19 of them dealt with some aspect of stewardship, and that approximately one verse out of every four in the New Testament also addresses the same subject? How Christians handle the material things of the world which God has entrusted to them, including money, is obviously a matter of deep importance to the Lord.

Dr. Charles Ryrie, in his book <u>Balancing the Christian Life</u>, says:

> Our love for God may be proved by something that is a major part of everyone's life, and that is our use of money. How we use our money demonstrates the reality of our love for God. In some ways it proves our love more conclusively than depth of knowledge, length of prayer or prominence of service. These things can be feigned, but the use of our possessions shows us up for what we actually are. [1]

How many local churches today struggle to make budget because believers are not committed to giving to the Lord's work? And how many churches say they want to see souls saved, but spend money on non-essentials while refusing to allocate sufficient funds to missions or youth programs? Most people, and, indeed, most local churches, put their money where their priorities are. To avoid bankruptcy a church must take prescription #13 and dispense it regularly to the congregation: HANDLE MONEY WISELY.

Paul addresses this matter of financial stewardship several times in his instructions to Timothy and Titus. He deals with three areas:

1. Qualifications for Leadership
2. Advice to the Wealthy
3. Support of Others

QUALIFICATIONS FOR LEADERSHIP

In Paul's lists of qualifications for pastor and deacon, he says the following:

Pastors	**Deacons**	**Pastors**
not greedy of	not greedy of	Not greedy of
filthy lucre	filthy lucre	filthy lucre
(1 Tim. 3:3)	(1 Tim. 3:8)	(Titus 1:7)

Although several different Greek words are used, all three say basically the same thing. In 1 Timothy 3:3, the Greek word is aphilorguron, which comes from phileo meaning "to love" and arguros, meaning "silver." The alpha privative prefix a means "not," rendering the word: "not a lover of silver, or money." No man in the ministry should have financial reward as his goal. The church's reputation has often been damaged and its spiritual growth hindered because of the covetousness of her leaders. Homer Kent states:

The poverty of many Christian ministers does not remove this temptation from them. In a materialistic world, the elder must wage an unceasing battle to keep material things in their proper perspective. The love of money often leads to other sins. Calvin quotes the old Latin proverb: 'He who wishes to become rich also wishes to become rich soon.'[2]

The word Paul uses in 1 Timothy 3:8, as well as in Titus 1:7, is aischrokerdeis(and aischrokerde).

R$_x$:
Handle
Money
Wisely

It means "greedy of, or fond of, disgraceful, shameful, or dishonest gain." It is the picture of a man who does not care how he gets money as long as he gets it. Obviously this is not a quality to be desired in the life of a leader. It would be a severe defect not only in the character of a pastor, but also in a deacon whose duties involve distribution of funds to the needy (see Acts 6), a responsibility that would lend itself exceptionally well to the opportunity for embezzlement. Anyone with access to church finances has ample opportunity to misuse them. As Erdman has stated: "Judas was not the last treasurer who betrayed his Lord for a few pieces of silver."[3]

ADVICE TO THE WEALTHY (or to anyone desirous of wealth)

1 Timothy 6:6-19 -- But godliness with contentment is great gain; For we brought nothing into this world, and it is certain we can carry nothing out. And having food and raiment let us be therewith content. But they that will be (lit., desire to be)

rich fall into temptation and a snare, and into many foolish and hurtful lusts, which drown men in destruction and perdition. For the love of money is the root of all (i.e. all kinds of) evil, which while some coveted after, they erred from the faith, and pierced themselves through with many sorrows... Charge them that are rich in this age, that they be not highminded, nor trust in uncertain riches but in the living God, who giveth us richly all things to enjoy; That they do good, that they be rich in good works, ready to distribute, willing to share, Laying up in store for themselves a good foundation against the time to come, that they may lay hold on eternal life.

Once again, Paul uses the negative-positive approach in his teaching. First, he states the negative (vs. 6-10), followed by the positive (vs. 17-19).

The Negative (vs. 6-10)

```
Wealth Does Not Bring Contentment (6:6)
```

This truth seems fairly obvious. We all know rich people who have been miserably discontent, and poor people who have enjoyed peace and great contentment. In 1 Timothy 6:5, just preceding this section, Paul writes that those who are "destitute of the truth" suppose that "gain is godliness; from such withdraw thyself." Then he says that "godliness with contentment is great gain" (1 Tim. 6:6). So beware of covetousness, an evil that God speaks against directly in the Law.

```
Wealth Does Not Last (6:7)
```

Job, that great Old Testament saint who was asked to bear

208

what would seem to be unbearable burdens and to suffer unpassable tests, supported this point when he said, "Naked came I out of my mother's womb, and naked shall I return there" (Job 1:21). As Job so wisely understood, material wealth does not follow us beyond the grave. Riches cannot be carried off into eternity. Someone once asked concerning a recently departed millionaire, "How much did he leave behind?" The answer: "Everything."

Our Basic Needs Are Easily Met (6:8)

The issue here is food, clothing, shelter, etc. The Lord has promised to meet these needs for all His children, though sometimes that is conditional. In the Lord's Sermon on the Mount, He says:

> Matthew 6:31-33 -- Be not anxious, saying, what shall we eat? or, What shall we drink? or, With what shall we be clothed... your heavenly Father knoweth that ye have need of all these things. But seek ye first the Kingdom of God, and His righteousness, (that's the condition) and all these things shall be added unto you.

A Desire for Wealth May Lead to Sin (6:9-10)

These two verses can be easily misunderstood. Paul is warning those who have set their sights on becoming rich. The road to achieving such a goal can be deeply pitted with temptations and snares that lead to eventual destruction. Lot, Abraham's nephew, lost everything because he set his eyes upon the rich plain of Sodom and coveted what he saw. Haman, in the book of Esther, set his eyes upon riches and honor and wound up hanging on his own gallows. The verse, "The love of money is the root of all evil" (vs. 10), would be better translated: "The love of money is the root of all kinds of evil."

209

Certainly evil can exist where no money is involved. Money itself is a rather neutral commodity. The way it is used and the heart motive behind that use determine its character. While it is true that "you can't take it with you," what many people do not seem to realize is that you can "send it on ahead." The Lord says to "lay up for yourselves treasures in heaven, where neither moth nor rust doth corrupt, and where thieves do not break through or steal" (Matt. 6:20). Money can be invested, so to speak, in the bank of eternity when it is used to bring Christ to a lost world. By the same token, it can become the instrument that sends a man to Hell by becoming his god.

The Positive

In verses 17 through 19, Paul instructs God's people who are rich in this world's goods to use them for the glory of God.

> Be Humble (vs. 17)

"Be not highminded." Recognize that wealth is a gift from the hand of God, so focus upon the Giver and not the gift.

> Be Appreciative (vs. 17)

What God has given, He has given us to enjoy, and to enjoy richly.

> Be Useful (vs. 18)

What God has given is intended not only for our enjoyment, but also for our employment. Our possessions are meant for "good works" and should be shared. Hoarding stems from selfishness and contrasts sharply with the characteristics manifested by our Giver, the Lord Jesus, who, "though He was rich, yet for your sakes He became poor, that ye through his poverty might be rich" (2 Cor. 8:9).

Be Visionary (vs. 19)

Christians should be looking ahead, past the every day to the everlasting. What God has given should be invested in something that will pay dividends for all eternity, "laying a good foundation against the time to come." This is what Christ means by storing up "treasures in heaven" (Matt. 6:20).

SUPPORT OF OTHERS
Paul commands that two categories of individuals be financially supported by the church body:

> Widows -- Honor widows that are widows indeed (1 Tim. 5:3).
> Pastors -- Let the elders that rule well be counted worthy of double honor, especially they who labor in the word and doctrine. For the Scripture saith, Thou shalt not muzzle the ox that treadeth out the grain; and, The laborer is worthy of his reward (1 Tim. 5:17-18).

The word "honor" is used with regard to both widows and pastors. It comes from the Greek word _timae_ meaning "to fix the value." It is the thought behind the "honorarium," the fee given to one who ministers spiritually to God's children. Thus financial support of widows is clearly in view in 1 Timothy 5:3 and 5:17.

The Support of Widows (1 Tim. 5:3)
Under the Mosaic law of the Old Testament, Exodus 22:22-24, the widow, the orphan and the poor fell under the protection of God Himself:

> Ye shall not afflict any widow, or fatherless child. If thou afflict them in any way, and they cry at all

> unto me, I will surely hear their cry; And my wrath
> shall burn, and I will kill you with the sword; and
> your wives shall be widows, and your children fa-
> therless.

Strong words, indeed. God designed a system to insure that widows were cared for (see Deut. 24:19-20; Deut. 25:5-10; 14:28-29; Lev. 19:9-10), then went one step better and appointed Himself the One to enforce it.

> For the Lord your God is God of gods, and Lord
> of lords, a great God, a mighty, and an awesome,
> who regardeth not persons, nor taketh reward. He
> doth execute the justice for the fatherless and
> widow, and loveth the sojourner, in giving him food
> and raiment (Deut. 10:17-18).

Joining His sovereignty with human responsibility, this great God of Israel commands His children to follow His example (Deut 10:19-22). This dictum is placed upon Israel throughout the Old Testament, a reasonable pattern of behavior to expect from a re-deemed people who have been entrusted with the standards of their Redeemer.

When Paul instructs Timothy regarding widows, he first says to determine which widows are genuinely needy, ("Honor wid-ows that are widows indeed"). Then he lists all the qualifications a woman must meet if she is to be included on the widows' roll (See Chapter 9). She must:

1. Be unable to support herself and have no one else to do so (1 Tim. 5:3-4).

2. Have lived a life that did not smack of self-indulgence (1 Tim. 5:5-16).

The primary group responsible for a widow's care is her family (vs. 4, 8, 16). The secondary group is the church. Failing to provide in such cases demonstrates a shallow commitment to biblically mandated principles and displeases the Lord. James wrote:

> Pure religion and undefiled before God and the
> Father is this: to visit the fatherless and widows in
> their affliction, and to keep oneself unspotted from
> the world (Ja. 1:27).

By "visit," James meant far more than to stop by for a cup of tea. It entails becoming involved in the lives of these women in order to help meet their needs, be it mowing the lawn, making home repairs or actually providing money. The church today must realize that this is part of its stewardship obligation and God's household must be found faithful (see 1 Cor. 4:2).

Every church body should take the time to compile a list of its widows, determine if they have needs that the church should meet based on 1 Timothy Chapter 5, and then meet those needs. By doing so the church appropriately becomes the arms and legs of the Lord Himself, reaching out through the Body of Christ to fulfill His promise in Deuteronomy 10:18.

THE SUPPORT OF PASTORS (1 Timothy 5:17)

The issue of the support of pastors is one I approach with hesitancy, being a pastor myself. In Charles Wagner's book, <u>Laborers Together</u>, Dr. Wagner, former president of Grand Rapids (MI) Baptist College and Seminary, wrote:

> Many times a pastor may want to sit down with
> his people and unburden his heart regarding mat-
> ters of money -- but he usually doesn't. Actually,
> if it were not for the fact that I am no longer in the
> pastorate, I would probably eliminate this chapter

(entitled: "Let's Talk About Money Matters"). But we need to face these issues head-on.[4]

Unfortunately, too many men in the ministry have had to "bail out" and seek more gainful employment in order to support their families. Others have had to change churches to do so. Many pastors who go home to be with the Lord leave behind widows and families with no visible means of adequate support.

Because I am still in the pastorate, I thought it best to ask someone else to write the majority of this section. Following is an article by Dr. John R. Master, professor of Bible at Philadelphia College of Bible in Langhorne Manor, Pa. He deals with the issue of pastoral support.

Paying the Pastor
By John R. Master, Th.D.

Like cod liver oil, talk of paying the pastor well may seem hard for a church to swallow. But how a church digests biblical teaching on the subject is crucial to its spiritual health.

In Matthew 22:34-40 Jesus summarized the message of the entire Old Testament "law and prophets" as, "thou shalt love the Lord thy God with all thy heart, and with all thy soul, and with all thy mind. This is the first and greatest commandment. And the second is like unto it. Thou shalt love thy neighbor as thyself." Jesus presented these commands as a unit. The command to love God does not stand by itself nor does the command to love our neighbor.

John echoes this perspective by explaining that if someone says he loves God, whom he cannot see, but does not love his brother, whom he can see, he is lying (1 Jn. 2:4,9). The relationship between loving God and loving our neighbor is integral.

The Apostle Paul develops the same idea throughout his epistles. In Galatians 5:14 he repeats "thou shalt love thy neighbor as thyself" as the background to his continued discussion in the book, including Galatians 6:6: "Let him that is taught in the word share with him that teacheth in all good things." According to Galatians, loving your neighbor as yourself involves sharing with the one who teaches you the Word.

How many Christians routinely turn down an offered raise? Not many. Most are interested in having more for ourselves and our families. Most would like to be able to give more money, to send their children to college, to afford some time away. If such desires are legitimate for you, you should want them for your neighbor as well, especially for that neighbor who teaches you the Word.

Paul presents the same idea in a bolder way in 1 Corinthians 9:14: "Even so hath the Lord ordained that they who preach the gospel should live of the gospel." He puts this injunction in the context of nature and of the Old Testament (1 Cor. 9:7-13). In the Old Testament God had organized the nation of Israel around His very presence. He designed the priests to minister in holy things, the Levites to assist the priests, and the congregation to support the priests and Levites. According to Paul, this design shows that the one who labors in the work of God is to be supported by the people of God.

"But," a congregation may argue, "didn't Paul himself refuse to take support from the Corinthian church?" (1 Cor. 9:12b). Yes. His reasons for accepting support from the Philippians, however, provide a key insight. In his thank you letter to that church, Paul noted that "even in Thessalonica ye sent once and again unto my necessity. Not because I desire a gift: but I desire fruit that may abound to your account" (Phil. 4:16-17). Notice Paul's

215

motivation. He did not speak as head of the "pastor's union." He did not even point to his need. When Paul put out his hand for the pastors, he wanted something for the people.

Christian fruitfulness often reminds us of John 15:4: "He that abides in me and I in him, the same bringeth forth much fruit, for without me, ye can do nothing." Philippians teaches that one of the ways to produce fruit, one of the evidences of abiding in Christ, is the desire to give to the one who ministers the Word.

Exactly how much should the pastor be given? Some Christians believe that poverty encourages his spirituality. Paul did not agree. In one of his last letters (1 Tim. 5:17) Paul taught the radical truth that "the elders who rule well be counted worthy of double honor," the portion belonging to the first born. According to this principle, those in charge over the church may deserve even more than anyone else in the church!

What does all this mean in practical terms? When you go to the store, you look at the price tag and evaluate, "That's too expensive" or "I'll take that; it's a good buy today." When you pay the pastor a poor salary, you've made a similar value judgment. But this judgment reflects your spiritual life. You cannot live in fellowship while continuing to promote a practice contrary to God's Word.

A church should pay its pastor well because the believers love their neighbors as themselves, a command related to their love for God.

A church should pay its pastor well because God has ordained that the one who preaches the gospel should live by the gospel -- to the extent of a double portion.

A church should pay its pastor well because "he that is faithful in that which is least is faithful also in much... If therefore ye have not been faithful in the unrighteous money, who will commit to your trust the true riches?"

(Lu. 16:10).

A church should pay its pastor well because, though the subject may be as uncomfortable as cod liver oil, each member desires to be a well-nourished Christian, eligible for more blessings from God.

PRINCIPLES AND PRIORITIES

The use of our possessions, does indeed, "show us up for what we are." Dr. Earl Radmacher, in a booklet entitled <u>Biblical Priorities in Financial Stewardship</u>, says that "how a man thinks about money is our most tangible way of evaluating his spirituality." He continues:

> A wise man must give careful consideration to how his money is being spent. It is the key to his future. Humanly speaking, he must meet all of his current personal and family obligations. Next, he must build a hedge against emergencies that may arise in the future. Finally, he must prepare for retirement years.
>
> But what about the Christian? What are his financial obligations? Are they any different from that of an unbeliever? Does he have any additional financial responsibility?[5]

Dr. Radmacher answers his own questions by providing two scriptural principles that Christians can use to evaluate their use of material things, and then he outlines three priorities for the believer in his stewardship practices.

Scriptural Principles:

<u>Matthew 6:19-21</u> -- Lay up not for yourselves treasures upon earth... but lay up for yourselves treasures in heaven... For where your treasure is, there will your heart be also.

217

> Principle #1: It is more important
> to lay up treasure in heaven than to
> accumulate treasure on earth.

Matthew 6:33 -- Seek ye first the Kingdom of God, and his righteousness, and all these things (every need we have) shall be added unto you.

> Principle #2: Placing God first in
> all areas, including financial
> stewardship, is fundamental to
> the Christian life.

Priority #1 -- Local Church Ministry

> 1 Corinthians 9:13-14 -- Do ye not know that they who minister about holy things live of the things of the temple... Even so hath the Lord ordained that they who preach the gospel should live of the gospel (NEB - should earn their living by the gospel).

When Paul wrote to Timothy, he instructed:

> Elders who do well as leaders should be reckoned worthy of a double stipend, in particular those who labor at preaching and teaching (1 Tim. 5:17, NEB).

The Scripture clearly and definitely requires Christians to provide well for the pastor and to underwrite the cost of administering the work of the local church.

Priority #2 -- Formal Training of Evangelists, Pastors and Teachers

"How shall they hear without a preacher?" Paul asks in Romans 10:14. It is imperative to evangelism that preachers and teachers be trained so they can build up the church and propagate the gospel around the world. The responsibility for such training rests upon the churches -- the body of Christ -- of which we are members. How many of us would intentionally go to court with an untrained person acting as our attorney, or entrust ourselves to a "surgeon" who had never been to medical school? Why then should we think it okay to send preachers and missionaries into a lost and dying world without adequately teaching them how to dispense the only medicine that can promote healing -- the Word of God. The church cannot afford to settle for anything less than the most complete preparation possible for those who are charged with preaching the sacred Word.

Priority #3: -- Sending Missionaries into the World

> Acts 13:2 -- As they ministered to the Lord, and fasted, the Holy Spirit said, Separate me Barnabas and Saul for the work unto which I have called them.

To obey the call "go ye," and to fulfill the injunction "occupy until I come," the church must send gospel messengers into all the world.

Priority #1	**Priority #2**	**Priority #3**
Supporting the Local Church Ministry	Formally Training Evangelists, Pastors, Teachers	Sending Missionaries into All the World

These three comprise the main priorities for giving on the part of believers. There are, no doubt, many other good causes. But if a church is to follow the scriptural pattern for stewardship then these three must be first and foremost. The others, of necessity, must be secondary.

PERSONAL PRACTICES

It would be well to note here how the Bible says an individual should give. The key passage is 1 Corinthians 16:2, which reads:

> Upon the first day of the week let every one of
> you lay by him in store, as God hath prospered
> him, that there be no gatherings when I come.

Dr. Ryrie, in his book <u>Patterns for Christian Youth</u>,[6] uses a rather concise outline based upon this passage that clearly illuminates four basic principles.

> Giving Is Incumbent On Each Person

"...let every one of you..." Grace does not make giving optional; it is the privilege and responsibility of every believer.

> Giving Is To Be Proportionate

"... as God hath prospered him..." In the Old Testament (under law) giving was very specific (10%, 20%, 23 1/3%). But in the New Testament and into the Church Age giving is to be directly related to God's financial blessing. For some, 10% may be too high; for others, 50% may be too low. "To whom much is given much shall be required," is an applicable principle.

> Giving Is To Be In Private Deposit

"... lay by him in store..." The Greek word "in store" means to gather and lay up, to heap up, to treasure. The reflexive pronoun "to himself" indicates that the gift is to be kept in private, not public, deposit. The picture here is of a private gift fund into which the believer places his proportionately determined gifts, so that when giving time comes he is prepared to give as the Spirit directs.

Giving Should Be Planned

"Upon the first day of the week..." Giving is to be consistent, not erratic. It is to be done on Sunday, the first day of the week. The Scripture does not say much about what the Christian should do on Sunday except that he should assemble with other believers in worship (Heb. 10:25) and do his giving then (1 Cor. 16:2).

Thus, every believer should practice regular, weekly, proportionate giving. By doing so a Christian acknowledges that everything he has is a gift from the good hand of God, and that his giving is an act of grateful reciprocity for God's goodness to him. We give not because we have to, but because we want to, and, to paraphrase Ryrie and Radmacher, because our giving demonstrates to God our genuine love for Him.

Prescription #13: HANDLE MONEY WISELY, is potent medicine, particularly in a day and age when materialism is the god of millions and restraint is looked upon as old-fashioned and prudish. Many a church has failed to meet its budget because its members have failed to mature sufficiently in this area. And when church after church fails to meet its budget, and missionary after missionary struggles to raise the needed support to get to the field, it becomes very clear that the body of Christ has its priorities out of order.

Satan is so subtle. He is a liar and a thief and is stealing from unsuspecting Christians what God has given them to use for God's own glory. If we give back to God what He has given to us, we will be rich, indeed, when we go to live with Him.

As Jim Elliott, who gave his life on the mission field, once said in a statement that has been oft-repeated:

He is no fool who gives what he cannot keep, to
keep that which he cannot lose.

ENDNOTES

1. Charles C. Ryrie, *Balancing the Christian Life* (Chicago, IL:
   Moody Press) p. 84.

2. Homer A. Kent, *The Pastoral Epistles* (Chicago, IL: Moody
   Press, 1982, rev.) p. 129.

3. Charles R. Erdman, *The Pastoral Epistles of Paul*
   (Philadelphia, PA: The Westminister Press, 1925) p. 43.

4. Charles U. Wagner, *Laborers Together* (Schaumburg, IL:
   Regular Baptist Press, 1988) p. 79.

5. Earl D. Radmacher, *Biblical Priorities in Financial
   Stewardship* (Portland, OR: Western Conservative
   Baptist Seminary, n.d.) In-house publication.

6. Charles C. Ryrie, *Patterns for Christian Youth* (Chicago, IL:
   Moody Press, 1966), p. 63-64.

14

Praying The Father

The great 18th Century English clergyman John Wesley once said, "God does everything with prayer and nothing without it." Geoffrey R. King concurs: "I believe Wesley was absolutely right. I know the importance of prayer, not so much by my success in praying, which is very meagre, nor by wonderful answers to prayer, as by this, that there is nothing in my life Satan tries to contest more than my prayer time."[1] The comments of both Wesley and King should be taken very seriously, for there is no doubt that God commands us to pray. It is a command that we must be careful not to ignore. This is especially true for a pastor because praying the Father and teaching the Word of God are the two most significant aspects of his entire ministry. I know, because reflecting on over 30 years of ministry I can see where I failed to understand the importance of prayer, and consequently failed to communicate its importance to my people.

Prescription #14: UNDERSTAND THE IMPORTANCE OF PRAYER. It is life-giving medication for any local church that truly wants the power of God to flow through its veins. Christians who value prayer will pray; Christians who don't, won't.

The Apostle Paul had much to say about prayer. He understood it profoundly; he practiced it diligently and he encouraged its use regularly. When he wrote to the church at Rome he told believers that "without ceasing" he made mention of them in his prayers (Rom. 1:9). When he wrote to the believers at Thessalonica he admonished them to "pray without ceasing" (1 Thes. 5:17). And clearly, when he writes to Timothy, his young son in the faith, he makes it plain that prayer deserves a place of high priority in the life of a believer and in the life of the church. Lack of prayer is an invitation to failure, both in life and in ministry. Paul wants Timothy to succeed so he instructs him, stating his goal in 1 Timothy 3:15, which is the overriding theme of the pastoral epistles.

> But if I tarry long, <u>that thou mayest know how thou oughtest to behave thyself in the house of God</u>, which is the church of the living God, the pillar and ground of the truth.

In the first two chapters Paul zeroes in on the two key ministries of both the church and its leadership:

The Ministry of Prayer	The Ministry of The Word

In chapter one Paul emphasizes the Word, rebuking false teachers, branding their teaching as "contrary to sound doctrine" (1 Tim. 1:10b), and exposing their ignorance of the truth of the gospel message and the place of the law (1 Tim. 1:7-10a). The issue was "the glorious gospel of the blessed God which was committed to my trust" (1:11), and which Paul was now committing to Timothy, his son in the faith (1:18).

Then, having emphasized the importance of an effective ministry of the Word, he turns his attention to the importance of an effective ministry of prayer.

> I exhort, therefore, that first of all, supplications, prayers, intercessions, and giving of thanks, be made for all men (1 Tim. 2:1).

Prayer and the ministry of the Word are, as any pastor should know, his two major responsibilities. Of course there are other responsibilities, but these two are inescapably, biblically and pre-eminently important. Luke makes this clear when he records the selection of the first deacons in Acts Chapter 6. The apostles, unable to do all they found themselves saddled with, had to devise a way to care for the widows. So:

The twelve called the multitude of the disciples unto them and said... look ye out among you... men... whom ye may appoint over this business (meeting the needs of the widows)... we will give ourselves continually to prayer and to the ministry of the word (Acts 6:2-4).

R$_x$:

Understand the Importance of Prayer

Many of us in the ministry, however, do not treat these two great responsibilities with equal importance. The ministry of the Word seems to receive a greater prominence and a greater commitment of time. After all, it is a highly visible ministry. Whereas few preachers would ever consider entering a pulpit without a sermon, far too often we enter that same pulpit without adequate prayer. Fervent prayers encourage dynamic answers. Yet, maintaining a consistent, disciplined prayer life is not easy.

In a little Radio Bible Class publication entitled *Jesus' Blueprint for Prayer*, Dr. Haddon Robinson discusses what he calls his "life-long struggle with prayer."

I admire men who give prayer high priority in their lives. Frankly, prayer has proved to be the most demanding discipline in my life. At different times

I have found it strenuous, boring, frustrating, and confusing. Over the years, a solid prayer life has been more intermittent than persistent. Occasionally I have grabbed hold of the hem of a garment, only to discover I could not sustain the grip. Out of my experience I have learned that you cannot simply "say your prayers." Prayer, real prayer, is tough, hard business. [2]

Indeed it is. Geoffrey R. King writes: "I believe that prayer is Priority Number One for every Christian and for every church." [3] The disciples held prayer in such high regard that they asked the Lord to teach them how to pray. It is interesting to note that they never asked Him to teach them how to preach, or how to counsel -- just how to pray. The Savior Himself spent an incalculable amount of time in prayer. A brief review of 20 of His prayers reveals:

1. Prayer re:
   the Holy Spirit
   on His Ministry
   Luke 3:21-23

2. Prayer
   indicating His own
   discipline
   Mark 1:35-38

3. Prayer while
   withdrawing from
   human acclaim
   Luke 5:16

4. Prayer for
   wisdom
   Luke 6:12

5. Prayer for
   sanctification
   John 6:15;
   Matthew 14:23

6. Prayer for
   discernment
   in disciples
   Luke 9:18

7. Prayer for
   the revealing
   of His glory
   Luke 9:28-29

8. Prayer for
   rejoicing
   Luke 10:17-24

9. Prayer for
   inciting
   disciples to pray
   Luke 11:1

10. Prayer for
    sympathy
    at grave
    John 11:32-43

11. Prayer for
    concern at
    the cradle
    Matthew 19:13-15

12. Prayer that
    His Father
    be glorified
    John 12:20-28

13. Prayer for
    Peter and
    his faith
    Luke 22:31-34

14. Prayer
    giving thanks
    at communion
    Luke 22:19-20

15. Prayer for
    the Comforter
    John 14:16-18

16. Prayer for
    intercession
    John 17

17. Prayer for
    submission to
    the will of God
    Matthew 26:36-46

18. Prayer for
    sinners
    Luke 23:33-34

19. Prayer of
    His own agony
    Matthew 27:46

20. Prayer of
    commitment
    Luke 22:46

Simply put, prayer is talking directly with God. It is a privilege reserved in its most complete sense for believers only. While others may ritually offer what they call prayer, their communication is one way. Before a two-way line can be opened a person must have a personal relationship with God through faith in the finished work of Christ on the Cross. Once that relationship is established, true prayer becomes possible. This is the concept Paul teaches in Romans 5:1-2:

> Therefore, being justified by faith, we have peace
> with God through our Lord Jesus Christ, by whom
> we have access by faith into the grace wherein we
> stand (Rom. 5:1-2).

First comes faith, then comes access. John Bunyan put it this way: "Prayer is a sincere, sensible journey out of the soul into God, through Christ, and in the strength and assistance of the Holy Spirit for such things as God has promised."

Failing to pray is both sin and foolishness. The God of the universe has made it possible for us to enter directly into His presence. Not to take advantage of that unparalleled privilege is an act of spiritual retardation of unlimited dimension. Yet many of us are guilty of exactly that.

Having defined prayer as "the act of talking with God," two verses immediately come to mind:

> 1 Thessalonians 5:17 -- Pray without ceasing.

> Matthew 6:6 -- But thou, when thou prayest, enter into thy closet, and when thou hast shut thy door pray to the Father who is in secret, and thy Father who seeth in secret shall reward thee openly.

Both concern the practice of prayer, yet on the surface they seem contradictory. Whereas one says to pray to the Father at all times, the other says to do it only at restricted times, i.e., when privacy can be observed. How can these two both be right?

The answer is seen in the fact that each set of directions depicts a different facet of prayer. To "pray without ceasing" involves an attitude. Entering into one's closet involves an action. While it is not always possible to carry out the action, the attitude should always exist.

Paul's instruction to the Thessalonians to "pray without ceasing" literally means to pray "unremittingly." It is a word that can be understood in the illustration of an incessant cough, a cough that just won't go away. It is always there. This does not mean that the afflicted individual is always coughing, or "coughing without ceasing," but that the cough is unremitting -- it is constantly recurring; it is always there. That is the intent behind Paul's instruction to "pray without ceasing." The action may not always be there, but the attitude is. There is always an "open line," so to speak, so that the two-way communication secured for the believer at the cross with his Father in Heaven never ceases.

Paul goes a step further, however, when he writes to Timothy. He gives him specific instructions concerning the act of prayer, not the attitude. First he emphasizes its priority, then he describes its nature, or the forms it is to take.

> 1 Timothy 2:1 -- I exhort, therefore, that first of all, supplications, prayers, intercessions, and giving of thanks, be made.

THE NATURE OF PRAYER

> Supplications

This is primarily self-centered, and properly so. Here the believer presents his personal requests to God. Paul calls these "supplications." It is a term he used with the Philippians:

> Be anxious for nothing, but in everything, by prayer
> and <u>supplication</u> with thanksgiving, let your re-
> quests be made known unto God (Phil. 4:6).

The word itself means "an earnest request." God invites us to place our earnest requests before Him.

Paul is not recommending something he did not practice him-self. In Romans Chapter 15, Paul was in Corinth preparing to go to Jerusalem and then to Rome. He prayed for three things: (1) safe deliverance, (2) acceptance by the saints in Jerusalem and (3) a refreshing journey to Rome. Though his requests were not an-swered exactly as he had hoped, they were answered in keeping with his challenge to the Philippians (4:6). God gave him peace in the midst of difficult circumstances.

The Bible teaches much about supplication. "Ye have not be-cause ye ask not" (Ja. 4:2). "Ask in faith, nothing doubting." In asking, however, certain conditions must be taken into consider-ation:

Relationship
"Whatsoever ye
ask <u>in my name</u>"
(John 14:13).

Unity
"If two of you <u>agree</u>
as touching anything"
(Matthew 18:19-20).

Abiding
"If ye <u>abide in me</u> ye
shall ask what ye will"
(John 15:7).

Obedience
"<u>Ye ask</u> and receive not,
because ye ask amiss"
(James 4:3).

Faith
"Whatsoever you <u>ask</u> in
prayer, <u>believing</u>, ye shall receive"
(Matthew 21:22)

Of course, it is important not to make supplication the <u>only</u> aspect of regularly practiced prayer. But it is important to practice it regularly, bearing in mind that the answer is up to God. He will hear and is willing and able to answer (Ja. 1:17; Matt. 7:9-11). He may answer "yes," as He did to Hezekiah (Is. 38:5); He may answer "no" as He did in denying Moses access to the promised land. He may delay His answer, as He did in giving Hannah a son. The asking is up to us, but the answer is up to Him.

Prayers

This probably suggests worship and adoration. The psalmist writes: "Bless the Lord, O my soul, and all that is within me, bless His Holy Name" (Ps. 103:1). Later he writes: "How precious are thy thoughts unto me, O God! How great is the sum of them!" (Ps. 139:17). When the Lord taught His disciples to pray, in the model prayer of Matthew 6:9-13, He began by saying:

> After this manner therefore pray ye: Our Father,
> who art in heaven, hallowed be thy name (vs. 6).

He says: "Begin with a petition for the glory of God. Lift up His name in praise!" The very mention of God's name should generate praise. In His name He has revealed Himself to us as the self-existent One (Jehovah, "I Am"); as the strong faithful One (Elohim); and as Lord and Master (Adonai). And those are just a few. The names of God go on and on, revealing His attributes to mankind. How in the world can anyone pray without including some degree of worship and adoration? The answer: he can't.

Intercessions

These are prayers sent up on behalf of others. Paul, in his second letter to Timothy, says "that without ceasing I have remembrance of thee in my prayers night and day" (2 Tim. 1:3b).

He includes similar comments in his letters to the believers at both Philippi and Thessalonica:

> <u>Philippians 1:3-4</u> -- I thank my God upon every remembrance of you, always in every prayer of mine for you making request with joy.

> <u>1 Thessalonians 1:2-3</u> -- We give thanks to God always for you all, making mention of you in our prayers; Remembering without ceasing your work of faith.

If it is true that "we have not because we ask not" (a failure in supplication), then no doubt it is just as true that "they have not because we ask not" (a failure in intercession). Dr. Harry Ironside once gave this personal illustration about intercessory prayer. He had been preaching in a Midwestern American church that had some unusual practices. Although it held Sunday services as well as mid-week meetings, the members did not get together for prayer. When he asked why, they replied, "Oh, we don't need to meet for prayer. We have no spiritual needs, for the Bible says that we have all spiritual blessings in Christ Jesus. And we have no need of material things, for we are well provided for. So we don't pray."

Ironside replied, "Well, that's unfortunate. At the very least, you should pray for me that God will give me freedom of speech as I go about preaching the gospel."

They didn't seem to get the point and Ironside left. Sometime later he collapsed in the pulpit, the result of typhoid fever and a 106 degree temperature. In time he recovered and returned the following year to the same church. "You know," they told him, "when we heard that you were sick with typhoid fever we began to pray for you. We prayed for you twice a week, but after we heard that you had recovered we stopped."

"Well," said Ironside, "that is unfortunate also. As long as I was in the hospital room I was all right. All I had was typhoid fever. But now that I am out preaching the gospel, I am faced with all of the spiritual temptations that come to a Christian minister. Now I need your prayers more than ever." [4]

Intercession is prayer that is "other-centered." It reduces occupation with self and increases occupation with others. Real intercessors pray fervently for both the temporal and spiritual needs of others. They "travail," as Paul did for the Galatians: "My little children, of whom I travail in birth again until Christ be formed in you," (Gal. 4:11). This form of prayer obviously does not come easily.

Giving of Thanks

Although this form of prayer seems easily understood by definition, by observation it is sometimes non-existent. There ought to be in the heart and on the tongue of every believer an unending string of gratitudes for the incalculable blessing that God has directed our way, beginning with the privilege of being joined to the body of Christ as a result of our salvation to the "much mores" that we have received since then. Paul emphasizes exactly that when he says in Romans Chapter 5 that the greatest thing God could ever do for any member of the human race would be to provide for him the free gift of salvation through the death of His Son.

But it doesn't stop there. After God saves a sinner, He then does "much more" for him. The phrase "much more" appears five times in Romans 5:9, 10, 15, 17, and 20. If every Christian just kept in mind his salvation and the "much mores" when he prayed, he would never cease to give thanks for what God has done for him.

It is interesting to note that when Paul lists the characteristics of the apostates of the last days, he includes an <u>unthankful</u> attitude (2 Tim. 3:2). He also notes in Romans 1:21 that those who reject the gospel of Christ are marked by unthankfulness. All prayer should come from a grateful heart with an attitude of thanksgiving, as Paul wrote in Philippians 4:6: "In everything, by prayer and supplication with thanksgiving, let your request be made known unto God." He said the same thing when he wrote to the Colossians: "Continue in prayer, and watch in the same with thanksgiving" (Col. 4:2).

Unfortunately, many Christians probably spend far more time asking God for things than thanking Him for the things He has already done. Geoffrey King makes an interesting and valid observation:

> We need to get into David's proportion. In one of the Psalms David said: "Seven times a day do I praise Thee." In another, David said: "Morning, noon and night will I pray." Well now, get that proportion. Seven times praising, saying "Thank you," for every three times saying "Please," asking for anything. Is not our proportion usually the reverse? Seven times pleading for three times praising? Or even much more asking? I do feel strongly that we ought to give ourselves much more than we do to this vital matter of thanksgiving. [5]

So Paul writes Timothy, telling him "PRAY."

THE OBJECTS OF PRAYER (in context of 1 Timothy)

For All Men 1 Timothy 2:1	**For Kings** **And All in Authority** 1 Timothy 2:2a

THE PURPOSES OF PRAYER (in context of 1 Timothy)

To Have Peace in Society	To Please God	To Win Souls
"That we may lead a quiet and peaceable life in all godliness and honesty." (1 Tim. 2:2b).	"For this is · good and acceptable in the sight of God, our Savior (1 Tim. 2:3).	"Who will have all men to be saved and to come unto the knowledge of the truth." (1 Tim. 2:4).

To Have Peace In Society

It is through prayer that God overrules and protects His church. While the pendulum has begun to swing in an anti-God direction here in America, to date American society has experienced and enjoyed a peace that few peoples have ever known. For Christians, this has translated into an ability to worship and serve the Lord with minimal interruptions or objections from the legal powers that be. Paul and Timothy did not enjoy such freedoms. Christianity was illegal and the authorities provided severe interference followed later by overt persecution.

To Please God

If Christians were to pray solely to have their needs met, then Christianity would be demonstrating a rather low view of God. It would reduce God to the status of a servant. Indeed, we are the servants. God is the Master. It is our job to do His will, not His job to do ours. We should pray because we delight in the opportunity to communicate with the One who loves us so and who continues to demonstrate that love to us each day. That is the kind of prayer that deeply pleases Him.

To Win Souls

This is, of course, the reason Christ Jesus came into the world. As Paul said:

> This is a faithful saying, and worthy of all acceptance, that Christ Jesus came into the world to save sinners, of whom I am chief (1 Tim. 1:15).

This purpose of prayer clearly supports the great doctrine of unlimited atonement, a doctrine spoken of by at least two other apostles besides Paul. Concerning Jesus Christ, the Apostle John wrote:

> He is the propitiation for our sins, and not for ours only, but also for the sins of the whole world (1 Jn. 2:2).

That is a verse that needs no explanation. Its meaning is unmistakable. The Apostle Peter also addresses the subject.

> The Lord... is longsuffering... not willing that any should perish, but that all should come to repentance (2 Pet. 3:9).

The same truth surfaces in 1 Timothy 2:4 regarding the will of God and the salvation of the lost. The NIV translates the verse this way:

> This is good and pleases God our Savior who wants all men to be saved and come to the knowledge of the truth.

"All," quite simply, means everyone. Everyone is encompassed in the love of God, and while salvation will be experienced only by those who accept His gracious gift of eternal life, His gift nonetheless is available to all. Salvation is not limited by God's willingness, but rather by the reluctance and unbelief of those who reject the message. And since salvation is inseparable from faith, and therefore from knowledge, Paul urges Timothy and his churches to pray that the lost will come to the "knowledge of the truth."

THE REQUIREMENTS OF PRAYER (from 1 Timothy)

Paul implies three preliminary ground rules for praying in his instructions to Timothy. They are all found in 1 Timothy 2:8: "I will, therefore, that men pray everywhere, lifting up holy hands, without wrath and doubting."

> ### Lifting Up Holy Hands

The issue here is not the position of one's appendages. Prayer can be offered with uplifted hands (Ex. 9:33); sitting (2 Sam. 7:18); standing (1 Sam. 1:26); kneeling (Dan. 6:10); or even with one's eyes open (Mark 6:41; 7:34). The issue is not external position but rather internal condition. Is the heart clean?

Pontius Pilate tried unsuccessfully to demonstrate this when he washed his hands and said, "I am innocent of the blood of this righteous person" prior to sending Christ to be sacrificed (Matt. 27:24). By washing his hands he was attempting to say "my heart is clean."

Applied to prayer, this means that Christians should approach the throne of grace "confessed up," with the sin in one's life dealt with and fellowship with the Father fully intact (see 1 Jn. 1:9).

> ### Without Wrath

Wrath is unconfessed sin in one's heart. It is useless to come to God in such a condition. The prophet Isaiah made this clear when he wrote:

> Behold, the Lord's hand is not shortened, that it
> cannot save; neither His ear heavy, that it cannot
> hear. But your iniquities have separated between
> you and your God, and your sins have hidden His
> face from you, that He will not hear (Is. 59: 1-2).

The Scripture does not say that God cannot hear. It says He will not hear. Not only does He refuse to listen when you come in wrath, but you will probably not even come in that condition. It is exceedingly difficult to go to the throne of grace when you are out of fellowship with the King who sits on it. That is one of the consequences of sin.

Without Doubting

Doubt is the opposite of faith. To pray without faith is to run the risk of receiving no answer. In Mark 11:20-26 Christ speaks of the prayer of faith. After He and His disciples have taken note of the cursed fig tree, withered up because of its failure to produce, the Lord says:

> Have <u>faith</u> in God. For verily I say unto you, who-
> soever shall say unto this mountain, Be thou re-
> moved, and be thou cast into the sea; and shall <u>not</u>
> <u>doubt</u> in his heart, but shall <u>believe</u> that those things
> which he saith shall come to pass, he shall have
> whatever he saith. Therefore, I say unto you,
> whatever things ye desire, when ye pray, <u>believe</u>
> that ye receive them, and ye shall have them (Mk.
> 11:22b-24).

John, in his first epistle, echoes those words:

> And this is the confidence that we have in Him,
> that, if we ask anything according to His will, He

heareth us; and if we know that he hear us, whatever we ask, we know that we have the petitions that we desired of him (1 Jn. 5:14-15).

"I will, therefore," writes Paul, "that <u>men</u> pray" (1 Tim. 2:8). Keeping in mind Paul's goal that Timothy and his people may "know how to behave" themselves "in the house of God" (1 Tim. 3:15), it is appropriate to suggest that public prayer in the assembly be led by the men. It is the men who have been assigned the role of spiritual leadership and certainly there is no more important spiritual leadership role than representing the congregation before the throne of God's grace.

One of the wonderful things about prayer is that it can take place anytime and any place. Geoffrey King, in his book, <u>Let Us Pray</u> has an especially appropriate example.

> I think perhaps the loveliest illustration of this came from the Indian mission field, where one of our missionaries was refereeing a football (soccer) match for Indian lads. One of the boys, just recently converted, got the ball to his feet and maneuvered it and shot a splendid goal. The missionary was standing by just when he made that fine kick. As the boy saw the ball swinging through the goal posts -- the missionary heard him say: "Lord Jesus, look!" Well now, that boy had the secret of the whole thing. Quite simply and naturally he would share a good kick on the football field with the Lord. That cultivated companionship (what we call fellowship) with God is prayer at its best. [6]

For a church to effectively move out for God, it must be in constant communication with Him. Prescription #14: UNDERSTANDING THE IMPORTANCE OF PRAYER is the medicine that opens the veins so the power of God can flow through the

Body of Christ. Without prayer, a church limits the work of God, not because He cannot work, but because He will not. And without the Lord, what can any man do that will endure for all eternity?

ENDNOTES

1. Geoffrey R. King, *Let Us Pray* (Fort Washington, PA: Christian Literature Crusade, n.d.) p. 16.

2. Haddon W. Robinson, *Jesus' Blueprint for Prayer* (Grand Rapids, MI: Radio Bible Class, 1989) p. 2.

3. Geoffrey R. King, op. cit., p. 16.

4. H. A. Ironside, *In the Heavenlies* (New York: Loizeaux Brothers, 1946) p. 333-335 (this illustration used elsewhere in Ironside's writing with details insignificantly different).

5. Geoffrey R. King, op. cit., p. 49.

6. Geoffrey R. King, ibid, p. 17.

15

Too Soon To Quit

A number of years ago a pastor in Oregon wrote in his journal: "Today I feel as though I'd like to quit, take a leave of absence, resign from the world or something."[1] Problems were mounting in his congregation. A potential staff member refused his call; a young missionary from his church had been killed in a car accident in Africa; his leadership team was stuck on dead center; his minister of visitation went home to be with the Lord after a brief illness; four letters marked "personal" arrived the same day, all with bad news; and a staff member turned in his resignation, the third such resignation within a year.

This particular pastor did not quit, praise God. But how many others would have given the same circumstances? Pastoring a church can be discouraging and far too many men leave before they have put in the time to build a lasting ministry. Paul evidently was trying to share this concept with Timothy and Titus, who may well have had thoughts of quitting the difficult situations they found themselves in. Paul writes:

> To Timothy--I besought thee to abide still at Ephesus...that thou mightest charge some that they teach no other doctrine (1 Tim. 1:3).

241

> To Titus--For this cause left I thee in Crete, that
> thou shouldest set in order the things that
> are wanting (Titus 1:5).

Paul is a great example of the mentality summed up by V. Raymond Edman: "It's always too soon to quit." Paul persevered under unbelievably difficult circumstances. His physical condition was deplorable, as evidenced by passage after passage in Scripture (2 Cor. 4:10; 10:10; 12:7; Gal. 6:17; Acts 14:9). He is described as "weak" in bodily presence; "contemptible" in his speech; bearing in his body "the marks of the Lord Jesus," apparently from his numerous lashings; and constantly plagued by a "thorn in the flesh." This may have been an eye affliction, necessitating that he write in the large letters mentioned in his epistle to the Galatians (Gal. 6:11).

Paul does not fare any better in comments made by extra-biblical writers either. In the apocryphal <u>Acts of Paul and Thecla</u> he is described as being "of low stature, bald, crooked thighs...hollow eyed; had a crooked nose." In the fourth century Paul is ridiculed in the Philopatris of the Pseudo-Lucian as "a bald-headed, hook-nosed Galilean." John of Antioch, writing in the sixth century, preserves the tradition that Paul was "round-shouldered, with a sprinkling of gray on his head and beard, with an aquiline nose, with a mixture of pale and red in his complexion." Holzman speaks of the "small, emaciated figure for the man of Tarsus." Giordani describes Paul as "small of stature and all nerves," a man "infirm in health" with "a miserable physique." He depicts "Paul with his sore eyes" as repulsive. Shaw speaks of Paul's "insignificant stature," his marred visage, his weak and often distorted frame." Stalker observes that Paul appears to have been small of stature, and that his bodily presence was weak. He says "This weakness seems to have been aggravated by disfiguring disease."[2]

What is the point of all this? Paul is writing to two much younger men, who are hinting that they would like to pack it in -

- the assignment is too difficult. His response, in effect, is: "You? You want to pack it in? You, with all of your youth and vigor? Look at me! Look at what I've been through. Look at my condition."

R$_x$:

**Keep On
Keeping On**

Paul was whipped, beaten stoned, shipwrecked, imprisoned, hungry, thirsty, cold and naked -- all because he served the Lord Jesus Christ (2 Cor. 10:23-27). And if that were not enough, his mind was occupied daily with "the care of all the churches (2 Cor. 10:28). How many church leaders today can say the same? Prescription #15 is for the saints who feel discouraged, who feel weary and faint, who feel unequal to the task before them. KEEP ON KEEPING ON. It is always too soon to quit.

WITH REGARD TO THE PASTOR

Many years ago, while working on my doctorate, I wrote that a church must set goals if it is to achieve any measure of success. Few churches ever set goals, however, and there are three major reasons why.

A Fear of Failure

If there is no goal, there is no visible mark of failure.

An Unwieldy Church
Government

A local church whose governmental structure fails to follow the simplistic format outlined in Scripture is often too encumbered to set goals.

A Short-term Mentality

Too many pastors lack the determination to stay at their churches long enough to make them great. As I wrote those many years ago:

> The result is short-sighted leadership. Three and five-year pastorates are common if not average. As a result the average church has no long-range plan. In fact, it may not even be sure of what it will be doing next week. Pastors come, pastors go and next to nothing gets done. I used to think that it would take about three to four years to be able to develop a plan that would in some way begin to help a church accomplish its Great Commission goals. Seven to eight years is more realistic. You cannot build a lasting ministry overnight.[3]

Nothing has happened in all the years since I have written that to change my mind. On the contrary, I believe it now more than ever. Christians are in a warfare. "Chucking it all" is not an option. Paul reminds Timothy of that fact on a number of occasions.

> 1 Timothy 1:18--This charge I commit unto thee, son Timothy, according to the prophecies which pointed to thee, that thou by them mightest war a good warfare.

> 1 Timothy 6:11-12--But thou, O man of God, flee these things, and follow after righteousness, godliness, faith, love, patience, meekness. Fight the good fight of faith, lay hold on eternal life, unto

which thou art also called and hast professed a good profession before many witnesses.

2 Timothy 2:3-4--Thou, therefore, endure hardship, as a good soldier of Jesus Christ.

No man that warreth entangleth himself with the affairs of this life, that he may please him who hath chosen him to be a soldier.

2 Timothy 4:7--I have fought a good fight, I have finished my course, I have kept the faith.

It is absolutely incumbent upon a pastor in particular, that he develop the mentality that Paul had. It enables the Lord to carry him victoriously through the many storms that he will doubtless face in the ministry.

Storms, by the way, are not always bad. Often they either build character or reveal the lack of it. In the ministry the storms are almost always people related, and no pastor can flee from people. My father-in-law once wisely told me: "The problems are always the same--they just wear different skins."

If a man expects to successfully serve the Lord as a pastor, he should reject the concept of a short-term pastorate and treat his call as if it were for life. Dr. Raymond Linquist, who for years pastored the First Presbyterian Church of Hollywood, California, used to challenge prospective pastors never to take a church "unless you can envision spending your life there." Frederick Agar, in a book entitled The Minister and His Opportunity, wrote: "Short pastorates generally creates weak ministers as well as ill-conditioned churches." The flip side of the equation is this: "It is no accident that, practically without exception, the most successful churches are those that have had long pastorates" (Gaines Dobbins in Building Better Churches.)

Obviously, God may want to move a pastor from one church

to another. Sometimes circumstances will indicate when that move is of the Lord. But every man in the pastorate should be extremely careful not to move preemptively. Says Gerald W. Gillaspie in The Restless Pastor:

> If one has been led of God to accept the undershepherd of a congregation, if he is being blessed in his work, if he enjoys the confidence and affection of the people, if there is wise building for the future of the church, then...he should move only when it is clear to him that he is obeying the voice of God. If he is able, efficient, faithful and loved, the longer he remains in a field, the greater will be his ministry and influence.[4]

WITH REGARD TO THE DEACONS

The mentality of the men in this office should be similar to that of the pastor. It is always too soon to quit. A good deacon willingly shoulders the responsibility of caring for people within the congregation, thereby liberating the pastor to pray and teach the Word (see Acts 6:1-4). When this system works the way it should, it produces a congregational harmony that goes a long way toward generating long-term pastorates and enhancing the church's ability to successfully accomplish its goals. A deacon leaving in mid-term can disrupt that harmony and even provoke gossip that opens the door for an organizational crisis.

A pastor and his deacons are a team. As such, they are obligated before God to get along with one another. That obligation can only be met if both approach their responsibilities with great, Spirit-directed seriousness. As a pastor I have interacted with many fine deacons. When the relationships were good the ministry moved forward beautifully; when they were strained the ministry suffered. But quitting is not the way to solve problems. It is much better for the church body and the ministry if the leaders resolve their differences in a biblical manner.

WITH REGARD TO THE SAINTS

In Ephesians 2:8-10, Paul makes it clear that one is not saved by works, but when one is saved he works.

The Process of Salvation	The Result of Salvation
"For by grace are ye saved through faith; and that not of yourselves, it is the gift of God - Not of works lest any man should boast." (Ephesians 2:8-9)	"For we are his workmanship, created in Christ Jesus unto good works, which God hath before ordained that we should walk in them." (Ephesians 2:10)

Christianity is not a dead faith; it is a living faith; it is a follow-through faith. It is Jesus Christ living out His life through His purchased possessions, men and women who are empowered by the indwelling presence of the Spirit of God. Born again of incorruptible seed (1 Pet. 1:23), which is the Word of God, the baby Christian grows by drinking the milk of the Word (1 Pet. 2:2). As he matures he graduates to the meat of the Word (1 Cor. 3:2) and produces the fruit of the Spirit (Gal. 5:22-23). That fruit is to be visible. We are to "show forth the praises of him who hath called us out of darkness into his marvelous light" (1 Pet. 2:9).

This sequence of birth, maturity and productivity -- the signature of the reality of one's faith -- is what Paul endeavors to impress upon Titus and Timothy as he sends them written instructions for church life. As we said earlier, the natural sequence of the three pastoral epistles is:

1 Timothy Church Organization	2 Timothy Sound Doctrine	Titus Consistent Christian Living

The church is organized (1 Timothy) so that the Word of God may be taught (2 Timothy) so that believers will lead a consistent Christian life, walking under the control of the Holy Spirit (Titus) and bearing much fruit for the Kingdom of God. The book of Titus, in fact, often refers to "good works," which Paul says in Ephesians 2:10 are the result of one's salvation.

> Titus 1:16--They profess that they know God, but in works they deny him, being abominable, and disobedient, and unto every good work reprobate.

> Titus 2:7--In all things showing thyself a pattern of good works; in doctrine showing uncorruptness, gravity, sincerity.

> Titus 3:1--Put them in mind to be subject to principalities and powers, to obey magistrates, to be ready to every good work.

> Titus 3:5--Not by works of righteousness which we have done, but according to his mercy he saved us, by the washing of regeneration, and renewing of the Holy Spirit.

> Titus 3:8--This is a faithful saying, and these things I will that thou affirm constantly, that they who have believed God might be careful to maintain good works. These things are good and profitable unto men.

> Titus 3:14--And let ours also learn to maintain good works for necessary uses, that they be not unfruitful.

Genuine faith, by its very nature, contains within it the seeds of perseverance, determination, obedience, fidelity. Believers must continue to grow so these seeds will germinate and produce a hundredfold the fruit that God intends to be visible in their lives, thus glorifying Him.

> 1 Timothy 6:1--Let as many servants as are under the yoke count their own masters worthy of all honor, that the name of God and his doctrine be not blasphemed.

> Titus 2:9-10--Exhort servants to be obedient unto their own masters, and to please them well in all things, not answering again; Not purloining, but showing all good fidelity, that they may adorn the doctrine of God, our Savior, in all things.

A believing servant in any walk of life who fails to serve his master well blasphemes both God and His Word. When he serves well, however, he "adorns" or beautifies the doctrine of God.

The servant of God must never quit. He must see his assignment through to the very end. Prescription #15: KEEP ON KEEPING ON should be taken daily by anyone who wants to serve the Lord until the Lord returns. The enemy's greatest desire is to disrupt the on-going program of Jesus Christ and to cripple the church so it cannot boldly proclaim the Word of God. Heavy doses of this medicine can prevent a mentality that easily falls prey to discouragement and defeat. I'll pass on to you a poem that has meant much to me.

DON'T QUIT
WHEN THINGS GO WRONG, as they sometimes will,
When the road you're trudging seems all uphill,
When the funds are low and the debts are high,

And you want to smile, but you have to sigh,
When care is pressing you down a bit,
Rest, if you must--but don't you quit.

Life is strange with its twists and turns,
As everyone of us sometimes learns.
And many a failure turns about
When he might have won had he stuck it out;
Don't give up, though the pace seems slow--
You might succeed with another blow.

Often the goal is nearer than
It seems to a faint and faltering man,
Often the struggler has given up
When he might have captured the victor's cup.
And he learned too late, when the night slipped down,
How close he was to the golden crown.

Success is failure turned inside out--
The silver tint of the clouds of doubt--
And you never can tell how close you are,
It may be near when it seems afar;
So stick to the fight when you're hardest hit--
It's when things seem worst that you mustn't quit.
AUTHOR UNKNOWN

When things seem grim, it might also help to remember that, as my dear friend Jack Wyrtzen says, "Praise God. We're on the victory side!"

ENDNOTES

1. Don Bubna, *Leadership* magazine article "Ten Reasons Not to Resign" (Carol Stream, IL: *Christianity Today*, 1983), p. 74.

2. William Steuart McBirnie, *The Search for the Twelve Apostles* (Wheaton, IL: Tyndale House Publishers, 1973) p. 291-292.

3. Charles F. Scheide, *The Building of a Full-Service Church* (Perth, NY: Perth Bible Church) p. 29.

4. Gerald W. Gillaspie, *The Restless Pastor* (Chicago, IL: Moody Press, 1974) p. 19.

16

Dealing With Disease

Although the goal of this book is to furnish preventative medicine, sometimes it's too late for prevention. The disease has already germinated and nothing short of strong curative measures will heal the body so the church can get on with serving the Lord. Unfortunately, curative medication is not usually pleasant. Like a shot of penicillin, it can carry a terrible sting. But when a shot is what is needed, a doctor cannot hesitate to administer it. Neither can a church hesitate to take strong action because the alternative is often much worse: a split in the unity of the body. Paul administered large doses of "penicillin" when necessary, as demonstrated by his letter to the churches of Galatia which had become infected with Judaistic legalism:

> Galatians 1:6-9--I marvel that ye are so soon re-
> moved from him that called you into the grace of
> Christ unto another gospel, Which is not another;
> but there are some that trouble you, and would
> pervert the gospel of Christ. But though we, or an
> angel from heaven, preach any other gospel unto
> you than that you have received, let him be accursed.
> As we said before, so say I now again, If any man
> preach any other gospel unto you than that ye have

received, let him be accursed.

Accursed! That is strong language indeed. The Galatian epistle was written to a group of churches located in the center of what is now Asia Minor. The Scofield Reference Bible states:

> The original inhabitants (of Galatia) were Phrygians, with a religion of nature worship. The Galatians were noted for their impetuosity, fickleness, and love for new and curious things. Paul visited Galatia on both his first missionary journey (Acts 13:51; 14:8, 20, Iconium, Lystra and Derbe being situated in southern Galatia), and on his third (Acts 18:23), although of his labor in founding these churches there is no record. On his second missionary journey the apostle was forbidden by the Holy Spirit to preach there (Acts 16:6).[1]

Believers there were facing a double threat involving both purity of doctrine and purity of behavior. Certain individuals were, in Paul's words, attempting to "pervert the Gospel of Christ: (Gal. 1:7; 5:10). They falsely taught that faith in the crosswork of Christ was insufficient for salvation. They held that works were also necessary and promoted keeping various Jewish holidays and following certain Jewish practices, such as circumcision. These false teachers, known as "Judaizers," enticed these non-Jewish Galatians into practicing a system that mixed law and grace because it considered one's salvation and subsequent sanctification the result of faith plus the keeping of the Jewish Law.

This teaching infuriated Paul. In the strongest language possible he repudiated them and their message. The Galatians had heard and had responded to the true Gospel when Paul and his entourage had visited there. Now they were being tempted to accept "another gospel, which is not another" (Gal. 1:6-7). The word "gospel" means "good news." It certainly would not be good news if men had to work to secure their salvation and then had to work to keep it. In Acts 15:10, Peter told the church council in Jerusalem that to live according to the Law was too heavy a yoke for even the Jews to bear. Why require the Gentiles to live that way? History records that before A.D. 70, the Jewish rabbis had added 341 rules for daily living. What a load! Who could carry it?

R$_x$:
Note
the Disease:
Administer the
Medication

Paul said that even if an angel from heaven were to preach a gospel other than that of pure grace, "let him be accursed" (Gal. 1:8). He repeats himself in verse nine, emphasizing that anyone who perverts the Gospel of Christ is worthy of God's eternal condemnation. The Phillips translation handles this passage well:

> I say unto you that if I, or an angel from heaven, were to preach to you any other gospel than the one you have heard, may he be damned! You have heard me say it before, and now I put it down in black and white--may anybody who preaches any other gospel than the one you have already heard be a damned soul! (Gal. 1:8-9). [2]

Why was Paul so direct in his confrontation and so firm in his condemnation? Because, as he says in 2 Timothy 2:17, false teaching leads to gangrene, which left untreated can result in death. As we noted earlier, it is better to lose the leg than to lose the whole body. Problems in the church today must be dealt with head-on, and as the saying goes, let the chips fall where they may.

DEALING WITH FALSE TEACHERS
This subject was dealt with earlier from a preventative point

of view. But if it is too late for preventative measures, then aggressive combative measures must be taken. The leadership must confront false teachers head on, "charging them that they teach no other doctrine" (1 Tim.1:3). They must be rebuked sharply and their mouths must be stopped (2 Tim.2:24-25; Titus 1:9-13, 2:15). Anyone in danger of being swallowed up in false teaching must be counseled against fellowshipping with people who propagate it. Paul's wording is eminently clear:

1 Timothy 1:4	-- "Neither give heed to"
1 Timothy 4:7	-- "Refuse"
1 Timothy 6:3-5	-- "Withdraw thyself"
2 Timothy 2:16	-- "Shun"
2 Timothy 2:23	-- "Avoid"
and Titus 3:9	

False teaching can only be combatted effectively with sound doctrine. Perhaps the wisest counsel to give Christians who are in danger of falling prey to false teaching is "to study to show thyself approved unto God, a workman that needeth not to be ashamed, rightly dividing the word of truth" (2 Tim. 2:15). W. W. Rugh, one of the founders of the school known today as Philadelphia College of Bible, identified the school's primary purpose as the teaching of the truth. Said Rugh, "If we teach the truth, error will correct itself."

DEALING WITH ERRING LEADERS

What do you do when a leader sins? Sin in the life of any believer carries with it all sorts of negative consequences, but they are magnified when leaders are involved. A leader's sins will likely affect the entire congregation, as well as the ministry of the church. As a result, the situation must be dealt with swiftly and biblically. If the sin is public, it demands public rebuke (1 Tim. 5:19-21). Certain sins may result in removal from office and permanent disqualification from serving again in a leadership role.

This may seem like a high price to pay for transgression, but God has high standards for those whom He has entrusted with the care of His sheep. In the book of Hosea (4:9) He comments not only upon the sins of His people, Israel, but upon the sins of Israel's leaders. The text basically says: "Like people, like priest." Whatever the leaders are is what the congregation will become.

Isaiah 9:14-16 is another passage that reveals God's attitude toward leadership. Here God says He will punish Israel's leaders for making the people sin because they failed to lead them into holy patterns. In the New Testament the Lord Jesus makes an extremely revealing comment about leadership. He looks at the leaders of Israel and says:

> They are blind leaders of the blind. And if the blind lead the blind, both shall fall into the ditch (Matt 15:14).

Most people will follow the examples set for them, whether good or bad. That is why God places such a premium on leadership and why the standard for spiritual leaders is so extremely high. Good leaders are doubly blessed in serving Jesus; bad ones are doubly chastised for abdicating their responsibility, because "to whom much is given, much shall be required" (Lu. 12:48).

Church leaders must always maintain the integrity of character that qualified them for leadership in the first place. When a breakdown occurs, a church must be willing to follow the leadership discipline procedures outlined in 1 Timothy 5:19-21. It must gather the facts, judge without partiality and rebuke publicly when necessary. Over the years I have come to believe that such action is not taken often enough and as a result our churches are suffering. Spiritually speaking, they are far less than what they could and should be.

DEALING WITH LEGALISM AND TRADITIONALISM
When Paul writes to Titus he addresses the subject of leader-

ship and why, in that context, it is so important to teach God's Word. He writes:

> Titus 1:10-14--For there are many unruly and vain talkers and deceivers, specially they of the circumcision, Whose mouths must be stopped, who subvert whole houses, teaching things which they ought not, for filthy lucre's sake...Wherefore, rebuke them sharply, that they may be sound in the faith, Not giving heed to Jewish fables, and commandments of men, that turn from the truth.

Warren Wiersbe comments: "Wherever Christ sows the good seed (believers), Satan follows with counterfeit seed and with false teachers."[3] This was the situation on the Island of Crete where Titus was ministering. Titus was faced with a group of individuals who were contradicting and rejecting the teachings of Paul while proffering "Jewish fables and the commandments of men." The "Jewish fables" apparently involved legalistic practices, and the "commandments of men" referred to time-honored traditions. Both, says Paul, turn men away from the truth and pollute their minds and consciences. Such is the nature of erroneous teaching. As Paul observes:

> Unto the pure all things are pure, but unto them that are defiled and unbelieving is nothing pure; but even their mind and conscience is defiled (Titus 1:15).

Legalism and traditionalism were also problems facing Timothy in Ephesus (see 1 Tim. 1:4-11). How does a church deal with people who force extra-biblical and/or unbiblical practices upon others? Very directly:

Stop Their Mouths	**Rebuke Them Sharply**
(Titus 1:11)	(Titus 1:13)
They must be silenced as effectively as if a gag were put in their mouths, preventing them from speaking at all.	They must receive a cuttingly sharp rebuke, but in a manner that is restorative in nature, not vindictive.

Legalistic and traditionalistic practices constitute a false doctrine that will spread like an infection through the body of Christ. Such teaching must never gain a foothold in the church. That is why Paul charges Titus to make sure that only sound doctrine is being fed to his flock. That charge applies to every pastor today as well. The truth must never be compromised. Paul makes it clear that decisive corrective action is the only wise and effective course to follow when a church has this type of problem.

DEALING WITH TROUBLEMAKERS

Every church whether in Paul's day or today, seems to have its share of troublemakers. Some are harmless. Others, however, can destroy a ministry. These latter types must be dealt with sternly or division will erupt in the church and bring shame to the cause of Christ.

In Titus 3:10-11 Paul specifies how to discharge this responsibility:

> A man that is an heretic, after the first and second admonition, reject, knowing that he that is such is subverted, being condemned of himself.

The issue here is one's conduct. Again Paul employs the positive/negative approach in telling Titus how to promote proper conduct in the life of believers.

> (the positive)
> By Continually Affirming
> Those Things That Are
> Profitable

Titus 3:8--These things will that thou affirm constantly, that they who have believed in God might be careful to maintain good works. These things are good and profitable unto men.

> (the negative)
> By Avoiding
> Those Things That Are
> Unprofitable

Titus 3:9--But avoid foolish questions, and genealogies, and contentions and strivings about the law; for they are unprofitable and vain.

Paul then provides instructions on how to deal with those who fail to follow such procedures and who become, in effect, troublemakers. He calls them "heretics," a term that is based on a root word that means "choice." It suggests a person who causes choices or divisions, in an unfavorable sense. In Galatians 5:20 Paul lists heresy (the forming of parties, divisions) as a work of the flesh. It was a characteristic of the carnal church in Corinth (1 Cor. 11:19). The problem Paul addresses here is that of individuals who cause division within the assembly. And his instruction to Titus is quite explicit: admonish such a person once; admonish him a second time; but if a third time is needed "reject" him -- have nothing to do with him.

Warren Wiersbe places these instructions in a 20th century setting. A heretic, he says, is "one who makes a choice, a person who causes divisions." Then he writes:

This is a self-willed person who thinks he is right, and who goes from person to person in the church forcing people to make a choice. "Are you for me or for the pastor?" This is a work of the flesh (see Gal. 5:20). Such a person should be admonished at least twice, and then rejected.

How do we apply this in a local church? Let me suggest one way. If a church member goes about trying to get a following, and then gets angry and leaves the church, let him go. If he comes back (maybe the other churches don't want him either), and if he shows a repentant attitude, receive him back. If he repeats this behavior (and they usually do), receive him back the second time. But if he does it a third time, do not receive him back into the fellowship of the church (Titus 3:10). Why not? "Such a man is warped in character, keeps on sinning, and has condemned himself " (3:11, literal translation). If more churches would follow this principle, we would have fewer "church tramps" who cause problems in various churches.[4]

Wiersbe's excellent illustration is based upon Paul's diagnosis of the "heretic" as one who is identified (in 3:11) as being (1) subverted (warped, perverted, turned inside out), (2) sinful, and (3) self-condemned. Rejection of and separation from this sort of individual is the proper biblical course to follow.

It is not easy to maintain purity within a church. The enemy is very subtle and very clever. He will creep in quietly and begin working to infect and destroy the body. Problems do not simply go away. If you put off dealing with them today you will have to face them again tomorrow, and by then they may be worse. They must be confronted swiftly and directly, even if it means becoming unpopular until the Lord vindicates you. When Jude wrote the little epistle that bears his name, he said:

> Beloved, when I gave all diligence to write unto you of the common salvation, it was needful for me to write unto you, and exhort you that ye should <u>earnestly contend for the faith</u> which was once delivered unto the saints (Jude 3).

Then he explains the reason for his exhortation:

> For there are certain men crept in unawares, who were before of old ordained to this condemnation, ungodly men, turning the grace of our God into lasciviousness, and denying the only Lord God, and our Lord Jesus Christ (Jude 4).

Jude, the Lord's own brother, was faced with people who would distort the truth and live lives of moral degradation. Christians, he said, must "earnestly contend for the faith which was once delivered to the saints." Paul did just that, even when it was difficult and unpopular.

Every local church should pray that God will grant believers the courage that marked Paul's life and infuse His church with a willingness to tackle the problems that the Lord permits to come its way. Life is never without problems, but Christians should always bear in mind that earnestly contending for the faith produces maturity and faithfulness, which are of great value in God's sight. If the church carries out its responsibilities as God intends it to, there will be more believers who will be able to say, as Paul did at the end of his life on earth:

> I have fought a good fight, I have finished my course, I have kept the faith; henceforth there is laid up for me a crown of righteousness, which the Lord, the righteous judge, shall give me at that

day; and not to me only, but unto all them that
love his appearing (2 Tim. 4:7-8).

ENDNOTES

1. C. I. Scofield (E. S. English, rev.) *The New Scofield
Reference Bible* (New York: Oxford University Press)
p. 1264.

2. J. B. Phillips, *Letters to Young Churches* (New York: The
Macmillan Co., 1947) p. 93.

3. Warren W. Wiersbe, *Whole Bible Study Course - Orig. by
D. B. Eastep* (Covington, KY: Calvary Baptist Church
Book Room, n.d.) notes from Titus 1.

4. Warren W. Wiersbe, *Be Faithful* (Wheaton, IL: Victor
Books) p. 119-120.

Postscript

This postscript, at least my comments in it, will be brief. I trust that they do not appear to be too self-serving. As I have re-read the pages that have preceded these final words, I believe that I have been able to achieve the goal I set out to accomplish: <u>to identify the problems</u> that were faced by Paul's pastoral proteges, Timothy and Titus (as revealed on the pages of the Pastoral Epistles), and then to prescribe the needed care. Those prescriptions, if taken, would go a considerable distance in helping today's church <u>to successfully avoid the problems noted</u>, and in doing so, come that much closer to being the healthy, reproductive church our Lord desires.

That the "prescriptions" offered really work can be attested to by personal experience. The testimonies of observation that follow will underscore that attestation. That is not to say that I have personally experienced every problem that has been identified, for I haven't. I have, however, faced enough of them, either first hand or second hand, to know that our Lord has not left us without aid in the administration of a local church. No... He has provided for our use, PRESCRIPTIONS THAT COUNT. He wants us to succeed in the mission to which He has assigned us, and all the medications, therapies, and surgical techniques necessary to reach that end have been included in our "medical manual," the Word of God.

If this volume proves to be of service to even one church, I will be very pleased. Should it be of service to more than one, that pleasure will increase proportionately. May God bless all into whose hands these pages fall, and may their utilization of the prescriptions offered be a significant factor in the accomplishment of our Lord's congregational will, and in the building of his church.

TESTIMONIES OF OBSERVATION

The comments that follow are from a number of individuals who have observed the author's ministry over an extended period of time. They have also taken the time to review the original manuscript of *Prescriptions That Count*, and to speak to various portions of it. The author would like to thank them for their gracious willingness to be included in this postscript, and to support the thesis that the "PRESCRIPTIONS THAT COUNT" really do.

REV. WILLIAM R. BOULET
Senior Pastor
Grace Bible Church - Dunmore, Pa.
Former Student - Word of Life Bible Institute
Former Staff Member - Perth Bible Church (N.Y.)

There are many books written about how to solve problems in the local church once you have them. How much better to prevent them before they happen.

Chuck Scheide has seen both sides. He has seen God build effective ministries by applying the principles in his book as well as taking established churches at various levels of dysfunction. He speaks from years of experience when he encourages us as readers to use God's Preventative Medication for Church Problems, i.e. the Prescriptions That Count. These prescriptions have been applied and proven true in the crucible of Chuck's pastoral ministries. As a former student, co-worker and now peer, I have learned much from Dr. Scheide's ministry. He has a love of the church which exudes from the pages of this book. If you love the church as he does, you'll love this book.

The greatest personal recommendation I can give is as a disciple of Chuck's. Some of the fruit of his life is seen in my ministry, for which I'll ever be thankful.

RENALD SHOWERS, Th. D.
Bible Conference Speaker, Author
Faculty: Institute of Biblical Studies (Friends of Israel)
       Formerly: Phila. College of Bible
                 Moody Bible Institute

My first in-depth acquaintance with Charles Scheide was in 1976 when I had the privilege of ministering at the church of which he was senior pastor in Perth, New York. Immediately, I was impressed with the fact that through this man's leadership God had built a local church with approximately 1,000 in attendance in a village not much larger. I soon discovered that here was a pastor who had a zeal for evangelism, a heart for teaching solid doctrine, an effective program of training the saints to do the work of the ministry and an unswerving commitment to the authority of the Scriptures and the centrality of the local church in God's ministry for the present age. In the years since 1976 I have continued to be impressed with the commitment of this pastor.

In light of the trends today, I am convinced that the emphases in this book by Dr. Scheide are desperately needed. For example, there are local churches, leaders and many Christians who permit circumstances, expediency, personal or family desires and society to dictate actions and values contrary to the Word of God. Although they claim the Scriptures as their authority, in practice they do not allow it that God-intended function. (See Chap. 1)

In addition, it is difficult to find churches where solid, sound doctrine is taught. Increasingly one hears the statement, "Doctrine is not important," and many Christians are ignorant of the great truths of biblical Christianity -- all in spite of God's incredible emphasis upon the importance of correct doctrine in His Word. (See Chap. 2)

Further, many Christians are so "me" oriented that they don't understand the times in light of God's program for history. They need to be confronted with the questions, "In light of the urgency of the times, what should I be doing with my life, and what should be my priorities?" (See Chap. 11)

DR. JOHN R. MASTER, Th. D.
Faculty, Philadelphia College of Bible
Previously: Dallas Seminary
           Word of Life Bible Institute
           Baptist Bible College & Seminary

For over twenty years I have had the privilege of knowing pastor Charles Scheide. He is a man of God whose zeal for the ministry is contagious and stimulating. I have seen him live the truths he preaches from the Word of God -- a message soundly grounded in the Scripture. (See Chapters 1-2)

In his book *The Prescriptions That Count*, Pastor Scheide seeks to articulate in a simple and direct way biblical principles he has utilized in his own ministries - ministries that have enjoyed both a sound preaching of the Word and numerical growth. He does not attempt to provide an exegetical biblical theology, but an outline of truth from the Word which will have a positive impact on any church ministry.

Pastor Scheide's section on handling money properly is especially important in light of Luke 16:10. Greater spiritual riches will not be entrusted to us if we do not first demonstrate an ability entrusted to us if we do not first demonstrate an ability to handle well the material riches God has already entrusted to us. (See Chap. 13)

This book may not contain the "secret' to Pastor Scheide's ministry, which after all is the Holy Spirit, but it will provide a helpful guide to a similar God blessed ministry.

STANLEY R. PONZ, D. Min.
Senior Pastor, Perth Bible Church
Former President - Texas Bible College

I doubt seriously if a pastor could enjoy his ministry more than I. Oh, it's not without its occasional challenges and testings, but the foundation is strong and sure.

You see I have the privilege of serving as senior pastor in a church, which for all practical purposes, was built up by Pastor Scheide. Though 15 years have passed since the Lord has moved Chuck on, the ministry is strong. Why?

Perhaps for three significant reasons out of many possibilities this ministry stands today as a growing, vibrant fellowship of saints.

First, Pastor Scheide, if cut, would bleed the importance of the local church. The growing group of new believers were grounded in the beginning of what a local church is, how it is to function, and why it is crucial to understand its importance. This has helped to prevent "the gates of hell" from impeding the church's efforts for God. (See Chap. 3)

Second, the staff and leadership, with whom I serve, are the results of proper future planning by implementing quality discipleship. By obeying the mandate of the Great Commission and using the strategy of II Tim. 2:2, Perth Bible Church was able to be self-perpetuating even when the church was without a senior pastor. Chuck took a good group of men and women through basic Bible doctrines in home meeting. (See Chap. 4)

Third, there has been a family atmosphere here. This was one of the single most qualities which the Lord used to draw my wife and I here over the past ten years to speak and now serve as pastor. There is a spiritual/social atmosphere where folks are treated very much like family members. People who have practical needs or who are hurting are responded to as a family. Different ones serve the "body" in their area of spiritual influence. (See Chap. 9)

There is a uniqueness about this New England church - the size and growth in a rural setting, the warmth of friendliness, the reproduction of future leaders, and the responsibility each person has to one another.

Do I feel intimidated by walking in the shadow of a former pastor the Lord used to walk tall in this church? Not on your life - I relish the privilege and responsibility to be used as another bricklayer in the household of God!

DR. ELWOOD McQUAID
Executive Director - The Friends of Israel
Author, Former Pastor and Missionary

Charles Scheide writes from a wealth of experience as the pastor of local churches with all the pluses and problems common among Christian congregations today. He is, by observation and reputation, a servant of the Lord whose ministry has exemplified the commitment and competence Scripture requires of Christian leaders.

A refreshing aspect of *The Prescriptions That Count* is found in the fact that the book is developed from a biblical rather than a psychological frame of reference. After having been exposed to so many

269

pseudotheological treatments, which seem designed to accommodate rather than correct deficiencies, it is good to read a straightforward application of Scripture that cuts to the heart of the problems faced by pastors and churches in this chaotic decade.

Granted, many of the remedies prescribed by the author are strong medicine. But the appeal offered is based on sound biblical principles. In his concluding chapter, for example, Pastor Scheide prescribes discipline rather than delay in addressing serious offences. Following the biblical standard, "heretics" (defined as "people causing divisions") who refuse correction are to be expelled from the fellowship. Such corrective prevention deals evenhandedly with every member of the body, from leaders to laymen. (See Chap. 16)

Negatives are constantly tempered by constructive and positive elements. Pursuing righteousness, godliness, faith, love, patience, and meekness instills the balance and practical perspective that will enable churches and individuals to become effective emissaries of Christ. (See Chap. 12)

Pastor Scheide has brought these elements together in a comprehensive, readable fashion that will bring new life and meaning to the Pastoral Epistles.

P. JOHN MARCUCCI, JR. D.D.S.
Dentist, S.S. Teacher
Church Member, Choir Director

Today's society seems to wait until a problem occurs and then responds in a way that seems right in their own eyes. The world of Christianity is unfortunately no different; yet in God's perfect plan this should not be the rule. In fact, He gives the plan for a successful individual and corporate Christian life.

The medical community has recognized for many years that "an ounce of prevention is worth a pound of cure," and the same can certainly be claimed in the Christian life. (See intro.)

I was a part of Dr. Scheide's ministry for ten years and knew of his ministry for ten years prior to my direct involvement. I have worked in the youth ministries and the music departments of several churches over the years and visited churches both large and small throughout. I can tell you that nowhere is the Word of God taught more clearly and without comprise than from the pulpit of Dr. Charles Scheide. (See Chap. 1 &

Chap. 2)

He prepares diligently so he can bring a working understanding of God's Word to his people. This dogma for scriptural accuracy is evident in this work *The Prescriptions That Count*. This book relies on Scripture to bring a clear picture of God's purpose and program for the Church. No church is immune to problems; but if the leadership and the people are trained according to the Word of God, and have this foundation which is unfailing, and are willing to act upon these principles; no circumstance, no problem, no event apart from the coming of our Lord could prevent a local congregation from claiming II Timothy 4:7. (See Chap 15)

My prayer is that this book will be used by many as an added tool to build up the Church of Christ until He comes.

PAUL BUBAR
Executive Director - Overseas Division
Word of Life Fellowship

I have known Chuck Scheide for almost three decades. The man is obsessed with the ministry of the local church and all that Christ intended it to be. In the churches he has pastored, he was and is constantly raising the vision of the people, motivating them, teaching them and putting them to work carrying out the task given to the church. He is both a practical man and yet, a visionary.

This book is definitely not written by a lofty theorist. It is written authoritatively by a man who has built large churches by giving everything he had available to him. As you read this book, know that Chuck Scheide has not only based his premise on the Word of God, but he has experienced this himself.

When Chuck addresses the problem of "INGROWNITIS" (Chapter 10), he writes from experience and conviction. I know. I have seen him live out this chapter for twenty-seven years. Without question, he practices what he preaches. Within my broad circle of acquaintances, I would nominate Chuck Scheide as one of the top five missions-oriented pastors in North America. Every church he has pastored has quickly become a missionary church that began by reaching out locally and very soon thereafter on a global basis. I can tell you, without hesitation, that what he proposes in this chapter truly works. I have witnessed it happening. It could happen in your church too.

271

CHRISTINE (SCHEIDE) TONIELLI
Daughter

What you have in your hands is a view of the pastoral epistles as seen by a pastor. That means you will not just be shown the mountains or the valleys of the terrain but the entire panorama... because your guide is not merely a tourist. He is a resident. He did not move there for the property values and he did not move out when the earth shifted and his foundation began to sink. Instead, he tore things up and made it stronger than ever. He had to start from scratch a few times, and I suppose that some of his patch jobs didn't always do the trick... but his work rarely strayed from the blueprints and it was always done with loving care.

This view of I, II Timothy and Titus is also seen through eyes of a rare breed of man who was better at being a pastor than at anything else in his life, sometimes to his own chagrin. Though occasionally plagued by his own limitations, he has been an exceptional husband, father and man. The simplicity of his success is found in his belief that in being the best possible pastor and man of God he would become a better father and husband. And he was right. By example and precept he taught his children the value of a life of service, the importance of sacrifice and cost of vision.

Please take this hearty endorsement for what it's worth from a child who has shared her father with thousands of people and still finds him one in a million.

SELECTIVE BIBLIOGRAPHY

Aldrich, Joseph, *Lifestyle Evangelism* (Portland, OR: Multnomah Press, 1981).

Anderson, Robert C., *The Effective Pastor* (Chicago, IL: Moody Press, 1985).

Arn, Drs. Win and Charles, *The Master's Plan for Making Disciples* (Pasadena, CA: Church Growth Press, 1982).

Barclay, William, *The Letters to Timothy, Titus and Philemon* (Philadelphia, PA: Westminister Press, 1977).

Bixby, Howard L., *The Elder Issue* (Cherry Hill, NJ: Association of Baptists for World Evangelism, 1983).

Bounds, E. M.., *Purpose in Prayer* (Chicago, IL: Moody Press, n.d.).

Chafer, L.S. & Walvoord, John F., (Grand Rapids, MI: Zondervan, rev. 1974).

Criswell, W.A., *The Criswell Study Bible* (Nashville, TN: Thomas Nelson Pub. 1979).

_____ *Criswell's Guidebook for Pastors* (Nashville, TN: Broadman Press, 1980).

_____ *The Baptism, Filling & Spiritual Gifts of the Holy Spirit* (Grand Rapids, MI: Zondervan, 1973).

_____ *Why I Preach That The Bible Is Literally True* (Nashville, TN: Broadman Press, 1969).

DeHaan, Richard W., *Your Church and You* (Grand Rapids, MI: Radio Bible Class, 1974).

Dollar, Truman, *How to Carry Out God's Stewardship Plan* (Nashville, TN: Thomas Nelson Pub. 1974).

Egner, David, *The Gender Benders* (Grand Rapids, MI: Radio Bible Class, 1981).

Engstrom, Ted W., *The Making of a Christian Leader* (Grand Rapids, MI: Zondervan, 1976).

Epp, Theodore H., *Brief Outlines of Things to Come* (Chicago, IL: Moody Press, 1952).

Erdman, Charles R., *The Pastoral Epistles of Paul* (Philadelphia, PA: The Westminister Press, 1925).

Fairbairn, Patrick, *Commentary on the Pastoral Epistles* (Grand
      Rapids, MI: Zondervan, 1956).

Fickett, Harold L., *A Layman's Guide to Baptist Beliefs* (Grand
      Rapids, MI: Zondervan, 1965).

Flynn, Leslie B., *19 Gifts of the Spirit,* (Wheaton, IL: Victor
      Books, 1985).

Gangel, Kenneth O., *You and Your Spiritual Gifts* (Chicago, IL:
      Moody Press, 1975).

Gerber, Vergil, *A Manual for Evangelism/Church Growth*
      (South Pasadena, CA: William Carey Library, 1973).

Getz, Gene A., *Building Up One Another* (Wheaton, IL: Victor
      Books, 1976).

_____*Sharpening the Focus of the Church* (Chicago, IL:
      Moody Press, 1974).

Gillaspie, Gerald W., *The Restless Pastor* (Chicago, IL: Moody
      Press, 1974).

Good, Kenneth H., *Why Every Christian Should Be a Member
      of a Local New Testament Church* (Elyria, OH: Baptist
      Mission of North America, rev. 1987).

Gurganus, W. Eugene, *Investing for Eternity* (Cherry Hill, NJ:
      Association of Baptists for World Evangelism, n.d.)

Haggai, John, *Lead On!* (Waco, TX: Word Books, 1986).

Hiscox, Edward T., *The New Directory for Baptist Churches*
      (Valley Forge, PA: Judson Press, 1894).

House, H. Wayne, The Role of Women in Ministry Today
      (Nashville, TN: Thomas Nelson, Inc., 1990).

Ironside, H.A., *In the Heavenlies* (New York, NY: Loizeaux
      Brothers, 1946).

Jackson, Paul R., *The Doctrine and Administration of the
      Church* (Des Plaines, IL: Regular Baptist Press, 1968).

Kelly, J.N.D., *The Pastoral Epistles* (Peabody, MA:
      Hendrickson, 1987).

Kent, Homer, A. Jr., *The Pastoral Epistles* (Chicago, IL:
      Moody Press, 1982 rev.).

King, Geoffrey R., *Let Us Pray* (Fort Washington, PA: Christian Literature Crusade, n.d.).

King, Guy H., A Leader Led (London, ENG: Marshall, Morgan & Scott, Ltd., 1951).

_____, To My Son (London, ENG: Marshall, Morgan & Scott, Ltd., 1944).

Lewis, Norm, Faith Promise for World Witness ((Lincoln, NE: Back to the Bible, 1973-1974).

Lutzer, Erwin W., *Pastor to Pastor* (Chicago, IL: Moody Press, 1987).

McBirnie, Wm. S., *The Search for the Twelve Apostles* (Wheaton, IL: Tyndale House Publishers, 1973).

McDonald, Bruce W., *Bridge Evangelism* (Cherry Hill, NJ: Association of Baptists for World Evangelism, 1984).

McGavran, Donald, *Understanding Church Growth* (Grand Rapids, MI: Wm. B. Eerdmans Pub. Co., 1970).

Miller, C. John, *Outgrowing the Ingrown Church* (Grand Rapids, MI: Zondervan, 1986).

Pawson, J. David, *Leadership Is Male* (Nashville, TN: Oliver Nelson Pub., 1988, 1990).

Pentecost, J. Dwight, Things to Come (Findley, OH: Dunham Pub., 1958).

Peterson, Jim, *Evangelism as a Lifestyle* (Colorado Springs, CO: Navpress, 1980).

Phillips, J.B., *Letters to Young Churches* (New York, NY: The Macmillan Co., 1947).

Pippert, Rebecca Manley, *Out of the Saltshaker and into the World* (Downer's Grove, IL: Intervarsity Press, 1979).

Robinson, Haddon W., *Jesus' Blueprint for Prayer* (Grand Rapids, MI: Radio Bible Class, 1989).

Ryrie, Charles C., *What You Should Know About Inerrancy* (Chicago, IL: Moody Bible Institute, 1981).

_____, *Balancing the Christian Life* (Chicago, IL: 1969).

_____, *A Survey of Bible Doctrine* (Chicago, IL: Moody Press, 1982).

_____, *Pattern for Christian Youth* (Chicago, IL: Moody Press, 1966).

_____, *Ryrie's Concise Guide to the Bible* (San Bernadino, CA, Here's Life Pub., 1983).

_____, *The Place of Women in the Church* (New York, NY: Macmillan, 1958).

_____, *The Final Countdown* (Wheaton, IL: Victor Books, 1982).

_____, *The Holy Spirit* (Chicago, IL: Moody Press, 1965).

Radmacher, Earl D. *What the Church Is All About* (Chicago, IL: Moody Press, 1978).

Saucy, Robert L., *The Church In God's Program* (Chicago, IL: Moody Press, 1972).

Scheide, Charles F., *The Building of a Full-Service Church* (Perth, NY: Perth Bible Church, 1978).

_____, *Leadership and Church Growth* (Perth, NY: Perth Bible Church, 1979).

Scroggie, W. Graham, *Is the Bible the Word of God?* (Chicago, IL: Moody Press, 1922).

Shelley, Bruce L. *The Church: God's People* (Wheaton, IL: Victor Books, 1978).

Slavin, George H., *Call Unto Me* (Southfield, MI: Highland Park Baptist Church, n.d.).

_____, *Basic Bible Studies* (Southfield, MI: Highland Park Baptist Church, n.d.).

Stock, Eugene, *Practical Truths from the Pastoral Epistles* (Grand Rapids, MI: Kregal Publications, 1983 - a reprint of a 1914 volume pub. by R. Scott).

Strauss, Lehman, *God's Plan for the Future* (Grand Rapids, MI: Zondervan, 1965).

Towns, Elmer, *What the Faith Is All About* (Wheaton, IL: Tyndale House Pub., 1983).

_____, *Winning the Winnable* (Lynchburg, VA: Church Growth Institute, 1987).

Wagner, Charles U., *The Pastor, His Life and Work* (Schaumburg, IL: Regular Baptist Press, 1988).

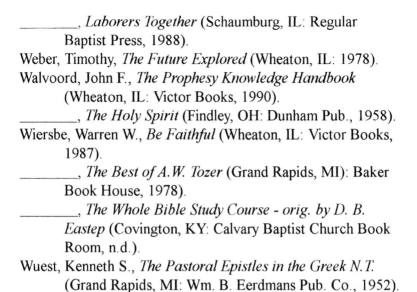

_____, *Laborers Together* (Schaumburg, IL: Regular Baptist Press, 1988).

Weber, Timothy, *The Future Explored* (Wheaton, IL: 1978).

Walvoord, John F., *The Prophesy Knowledge Handbook* (Wheaton, IL: Victor Books, 1990).

_____, *The Holy Spirit* (Findley, OH: Dunham Pub., 1958).

Wiersbe, Warren W., *Be Faithful* (Wheaton, IL: Victor Books, 1987).

_____, *The Best of A.W. Tozer* (Grand Rapids, MI): Baker Book House, 1978).

_____, *The Whole Bible Study Course - orig. by D. B. Eastep* (Covington, KY: Calvary Baptist Church Book Room, n.d.).

Wuest, Kenneth S., *The Pastoral Epistles in the Greek N.T.* (Grand Rapids, MI: Wm. B. Eerdmans Pub. Co., 1952).

(Author's note: Not all the books listed above are quoted on the preceding pages. All, however, have contributed either directly or indirectly to my efforts, and would provide additional information relative to the material covered.)

1 & 2 Timothy, Titus

Titus

Commentaries
by Charles F. Scheide, D. Min.

Author's Note

For many years Word of Life through its Local Church Ministries division, has produced a very effective Bible Study tool known as the WORD OF LIFE QUIET TIME DIARY. It's stated purpose: "To meet the needs of spiritual growth in the life of the Christian in such a way that they learn the art of conducting their own personal investigation into the Bible." It has been my privilege to serve as one of the Quiet Time writers in recent years, and three of the books that were assigned to me are the three books that are the focus of our study in THE PRESRIPTIONS THAT COUNT: 1 Timothy, 2 Timothy, and Titus. These studies have been included in this reprint of PRESCRIPTIONS to enhance the student's comprehension of the text. May they prove to be spiritually beneficial.

2

Introduction to 1 Timothy

1 Timothy is one of three books (the others: 2 Timothy & Titus) written by the Apostle Paul to two younger men, Timothy and Titus, who were serving in pastoral-like roles to tell them how to "behave" themselves "in the house of God – the Church of the living God" (1 Timothy 3:15). As a result of their purpose and content these three books have come to be known as the Pastoral Epistles.

To understand 1 Timothy effectively some background on all three of the books, and all three of the men involved should prove to be helpful. As he writes these books Paul is approaching the end of his life and ministry; Timothy and Titus, both a generation younger than the Apostle, were anticipating many years of ministry still ahead. Both of them had been greatly influenced by Paul, beginning first with their salvation. He addresses each of them as his "own son" in the faith, using the Greek word "teknon," which means "born one," rather than "huis," which means "an adult son." Paul also attaches the qualifier "in the faith" in his address to Timothy, and "after the common faith" to Titus, leading to the conclusion that he is their spiritual father.

Timothy was born of mixed parentage, with a Greek father and a Jewish mother (Acts 16:1). Following his salvation, which apparently took place his hometown of Lystra under Paul's ministry, he soon became one of Paul's most trusted aides, ministering with him in such places as Philippi, Thessalonica, Berea, Corinth and Ephesus. It was at Ephesus where Timothy was left on his own, becoming the "senior pastor" of the Ephesian church. It was there he received this first of the Pastoral Epistles. The relationship between Paul and Timothy was very special and could be legitimately described as "father-son-like" in nature. Of all Paul's letters his second epistle to Timothy, his "own son in the faith," is his most personal (apart from his unusual letter to Philemon).

Titus was a Greek believer converted from heathenism and may have been the younger brother of Luke. As 2 Corinthians 2:13 points out, he was a member of Paul's ministering team. Both of these trusted young men were ministering in exceedingly difficult places when Paul wrote to them. For Timothy it was in Ephesus, where stood the famous Temple of Diana where all sorts of violent acts took place in the name of worship. It was a city famous for sorcery, superstition and sexual debauchery. Paul had ministered there for three years and his ministry had borne much fruit. Yet he warned that after his departure, "shall grievous wolves enter in…not sparing the flock" (Acts 20:29). It is to this work and to this condition that Timothy was called.Titus fared no better. His assignment: Crete. The people there, by their own admission, were "liars, evil beasts, lazy gluttons" (Titus 1:11,13).

As for Paul himself, little needs to be said. This is the great champion of the Christian faith, who at one time was a "blasphemer, and a persecutor" of those who claimed the name of Christ (1 Tim. 1:13).

Then on the Damascus Road (Acts 9) he became a believer, and the change in his life became a pattern for others to follow (1 Tim. 1:16).

While these three books were written to individuals, Paul identifies himself as "an apostle of Christ Jesus." Surely neither Timothy nor Titus needed such substantiation, but what they did need was the weight of Paul's title behind them as they discharged their duties. On their own merit they could have been challenged. So Paul gives them a hammer – the hammer of his apostleship. And in the days prior to the canonization of the Scripture, this hammer gave these young men authority they would not otherwise have had.

Three themes seem to resonate throughout all three books: (1) Church Organization; (2) Sound Doctrine; and (3) Consistent Christian Living. While all three books touch on all three themes, each book has its particular emphasis, and those themes follow the order of the way in which they have been placed in most Bibles (though not written in that order).

1 Timothy emphasizes Church Organization; 2 Timothy, Sound Doctrine; Titus, Consistent Christian Living. Charles Erdman, in writing of these three books early in the 20th century, offered this summation of the three themes in this manner: "Church government is not an end in itself; it is of value only as it secures sound doctrine: and doctrine is of value only as it issues in life."

1 Timothy 1:1-11

Paul introduces himself: he's an apostle of Christ Jesus. He is writing to Timothy, his "son in the faith" (v. 1). He refers to Christ in three tenses: He is (1) "our Savior" – the past, looking back to redemption; (2) "our Lord" – the present, responsibility; (3) "our hope" – the future, His return.

To Timothy ("he who honors God") he extends the usual "Grace and Peace" salutation, and adds "mercy" (v. 2). Grace: favor extended where wrath is deserved; Mercy: shows our unworthiness and God's compassion; Peace: harmony with God.

He identifies his reason for writing. Timothy has been left in Ephesus to rebuke false doctrine (v. 3), not a pleasant task for an apparently timid individual like Timothy. Paul exhorts him to "hang in there" ("abide still"), and challenge those who were teaching false doctrine. These false teachers, "Judaizers," who mixed law and grace taught that the work of Christ on the cross was only partial payment for sin. Works and law keeping needed to be added.

Paul then introduces a basic Gospel principle: love; a love that comes from (1) a pure heart, (2) a good conscience (cf. v. 19), and (3) a sincere faith, characteristics not found in the Judaizers. They were marked by "vain jangling" (purposeless talk) (vv. 5-6), and did not understand the purpose of the Law (v. 7). It was not to save people, but to show their need of salvation. It is "good" when used lawfully (v. 8). Paul then lists the sinners who are condemned and convicted by the law (vv. 9-10) (compare the 10 commandments).

"Sound doctrine" (v. 10) means "healthy teaching," teaching that promotes spiritual health. The Greek word translated "sound" gives us our English word "hygiene." Such teaching is vital, for false teaching will eat as does a canker / gangrene (2 Tim. 2:17). Only sound doctrine can successfully combat false teaching.

LifeStep

Paul's instructions to Timothy are appropriate today. False teaching must not be permitted to flourish. It must be rebuked, but to do so we must teach sound doctrine. Let us be sure that we know what we believe.

1 Timothy 1:12-20

Paul's tone changes here in verse 12. The emphasis will be on praise and thanksgiving, an attitude prompted by his mentioning his call to the gospel ministry (see v. 11). He thanks God for: (1) <u>Enablement,</u> strength to fulfill his calling; (2) <u>Trust,</u> God counted him faithful; (3) <u>Calling,</u> He put him into the ministry (v. 12). He then reviews his past, "a blasphemer...persecutor...injurious..." Nevertheless, he received mercy, and that mercy erupts in praise. Paul was not excusing his past, he was rejoicing in God's mercy.

Paul then lists the three motivating forces in his life: <u>grace,</u> providing salvation; <u>faith,</u> appropriating it; and <u>love,</u> applying it (v. 14). He then offers the first of five "faithful sayings" found only in the Pastorals. (see 3:1; 4:9; 2 Timothy2:11; Titus 3:8). Probably "prophetic sayings" by N.T. prophets prior to the completion of Scripture, they helped form an early statement of faith. Here: "Christ Jesus came in to the world to save sinners" (cf. Luke 19:10), v. 15. Paul refers to himself as "the chief of sinners," an indication that he never got over God's grace. His life is then a pattern for others: turn to Christ and experience salvation. Others could do the same (v. 16). This review of God's grace prompts a doxology on the part of this blasphemer turned apostle (v. 17).

Paul then returns to the charge he had begun in v. 3. He uses military language: "War a good warfare"(v. 18), a war to be waged on two fronts: doctrinal and moral, and to be fought using two offensive weapons: <u>faith</u> and <u>a good conscience</u> (v. 19). Paul mentions two men whose words and conduct were blasphemous, and were judged by excommunication, the purpose of which was intended to be remedial ("that they may learn not to blaspheme" v. 20) and not punitive.

LifeStep

Paul's salvation provides a pattern for all who follow: turn to Christ and be saved, and follow that salvation up with praise and thanksgiving. Why not take time to offer that praise today?

1 Timothy 2:1-8

Paul now moves from "sound doctrine;" to prayer. These two, the ministry of the Word and the ministry of prayer, are the two main pastoral responsibilities (see Acts 6:4). The words "first of all" (v. 1) emphasize prayer's place of high priority in the church. Four ingredients are to be included: (1) "Supplications," asking for needs; (2) "Prayers," suggesting worship and adoration; (3) "Intercessions," requests on behalf of others; and (4) "Giving of thanks," appreciation for who He is and what He has done.

In verses 3-8 we see the Aims of Prayer: (1) To maintain peace in society. Through prayer "for Kings and for all that are in authority" God overrules and protects His church making possible "a quiet and peaceable life" (v. 2); (2) To please God. It is good and acceptable in His sight (v.3). If we pray only to have needs met we have a low view of God; (3) The salvation of the lost (vv. 4-7). Christ died for all and wants all to be saved, cf. 2 Peter 3:9.

Proper prayer also meets some basic conditions. It is offered to the Father through the only "mediator" possible, the Lord Jesus Christ (v. 5). He is the only acceptable "go between," between God and men, for He is both, and understands both sides (Heb. 4:14-16). His willingness to be a "ransom" (payment) for man made salvation possible (v. 6).

Praying in the local church is to be: (1) "without wrath" – should exist in love within the church family; (2) "lifting up holy hands" – not so much a external position, but an internal one based on a pure, cleansed life. Pilate washed his hands unsuccessfully attempting to disassociate himself from Christ's death; (3) "without doubting" – the positive side of which is faith. Believe that God hears and answers.

LifeStep

If chapter one caused us to check our doctrinal content, then chapter two should cause us to check our prayer life. If it is less than it should be, why not plan now to make the necessary corrections?

1 Timothy 2:9-15

Paul here deals with the dress (vv. 9-10), behavior (vv. 11-12) and role (vv. 13-14) of women in the church. He deals with dress both positively and negatively. <u>Positively</u>: "They should make themselves attractive by their discreet, quiet and modest dress" (v. 9) and "good works" (v. 10). <u>Negatively</u>, extreme hairstyles and culturally acceptable attention – getting jewelry, would be inconsistent with the woman professing godliness (v. 10). Immodest or inappropriate dress would distract others from seeing her "good works," of a godly woman's true adornment.

With verse 11 Paul forcefully attacks the subject of the woman's behavior in the church, providing some boundaries not to be crossed. To do so demonstrates a low view of inspiration. While Paul's ministry included female co-workers (1 Cor. 11:5; Phil. 4:11, etc.), he makes it clear that their role is one of subordination to male leadership. A woman is not "to teach or usurp authority over the man" (v. 12). He supports his teaching <u>doctrinally</u> (Adam was created first and had precedence over Eve, 1 Cor. 11:8-9), and <u>observationally</u> (Satan finds the woman easier to deceive, verse 14 with 2 Cor. 11:3). To accept such a role of subordination demonstrates Christ-like humility, for Christ, though equal with the Father, subordinated His will to the Father's will in order to provide salvation (see John 14:7-11,28).

Verse 15 needs to be interpreted in its context, that of the Garden of Eden. At issue is not "soul" salvation, but "societal" salvation. Adam's "salvation" (or reversal of the curse) was to be found in the "sweat of his face," said "sweat" providing for his needs. Eve's "salvation" was to be found in childbirth, i.e., accepting God's ordained role of subjection to her husband and bearing children should they be so blessed. (Note: "they" in this verse refers to both husband and wife.)

LifeStep

Both men (as subsequent verses will show) and women have clearly defined roles in the local church. Let's be sure that whatever our gender, we willingly accept and carry out our God assigned roles.

1 Timothy 3:1-7

Verses 1-13 give the primary qualifications for local church leaders: those of pastor (vv. 1-7), and deacon (vv. 8-13). The title of pastor does not appear here. Instead we have the term, bishop. A number of N.T. passages make it clear that those two terms, as well as a third, elder, are used interchangeably. All refer to the same individual and provide a job description for the church's senior officer. As elder he provides authority; as bishop administrative oversight; as pastor, he feeds the congregation as a shepherd does his sheep (see Acts 20:17,28; 1 Peter 5:1-2.).

To be worthy of the title one must meet certain qualifications. This passage deals with those of the elder/pastor/bishop. A total of 16 are found here, and fall into three categories. (1) PERSONAL QUALIFICATIONS, 2-3. Some 13 are listed, beginning with being "blameless" (irreproachable), nothing in his life that would discredit his witness. It continues down through "not covetous," he consistently puts Christ and his church first in his life. (2) FAMILY QUALIFICATIONS, 4-5. He, not his wife, is the leader in his home. He is to be in control. After all, if he cannot rule his own house, how shall he take care of the house of God? (3) CHURCH QUALIFICATIONS, 6-7. He cannot be a novice. Leadership demands experience and wisdom; serious decisions must be made. A novice could be in danger of the sin of pride. Finally, he must have a "good report" of those outside the church. Non-Christians find nothing in church leaders that would hinder the cause of Christ. The bottom line: the men who serve as pastors must be men of unquestioned character.

LifeStep

Church leaders should take care that they measure up to their Biblical qualifications. Let us pray for them as they lead, lest they fall into "the condemnation" (v. 6) and "snare" (v. 7) of the devil.

1 Timothy 3:8-16

Here we have the qualifications of a Deacon, many similar to those of a pastor. Transliterated from the Greek word diakonos, and often translated as "minister" or "servant", it finds its best definition in the latter translation: servant. Collectively the term "deacons" is a reference to a class of helpers chosen to serve the church under leadership. They came into being in Acts 6. Selected to meet some people needs (then a dispute between two groups of widows), this responsibility continues today.

As with the Pastor, the qualification emphasis is on character (vv. 8-10,12). Here, too there is a need for provenness (v. 9), marital fidelity, and parental control (v. 12). The skill requirement in a pastor, "apt to teach, " is not repeated. In the middle of his list of qualifications are four for his wife (v. 11). Hers are similar to his. There must be a comparable level of spirituality on the part of ministry wives. The deacon who serves his office "well" will gain the esteem of those whom he serves, and provide him with credentials to function with "great boldness" (v. 13).

Paul goes on to describe the church and its ministry using word pictures. It is the household of God (v. 15) and "the pillar and ground of the truth" (v. 15), architectural language that stresses the church's responsibility of faithfully preserving, preaching and practicing the "truth" (i.e., the Word of God). Verse 15 is the book's key verse, summarizing the purpose behind Paul's writing: to give to Timothy instructions as to how to "do church."

Verse 16 is likely an early Christian hymn, beginning with "the mystery of godliness," God's hidden program to bring about godliness in the person of Christ into the world. It begins with His birth, and concludes with His glorious ascension.

LifeStep

The church is the "foundation" ("pillar and ground of the truth") in this world. The qualifications of its key workers must be of the highest quality. Let us pray that such is the case in all of our churches.

1 Timothy 4:1-8

Paul had warned the Ephesian elders (Acts 20:29-30) about the coming of false doctrine. Here he predicts its coming is imminent, in fact, already present. That prompts him to issue a stern warning. An "apostasy," a "falling away" from the true faith will take place (2 Thess. 2). It's cause: the satanic influence of demons (v. 1). The marks of these false teachers: <u>first</u>, they are hypocritical liars, with "seared" (without feeling) consciences; <u>second</u>, they teach a false piety/asceticism, forbidding marriage and certain foods. This asceticism reflects Gnostic teaching, that all matter is evil, and only that which is spirit is good. Abstinence in these areas would increase one's holiness. Paul deals with the food issue, not the marriage issue (Gen. 2:18 cares for that) v. 3.

Paul's answer to the danger of verses 1-3 is found in verses 4-6. "The Word of God and prayer" (v. 5). God has declared all foods clean (Gen. 1:29-31; Mark 7:14-23; 1 Cor. 10:23-26; Acts 10). Genesis 9:3 points out that God has provided man with meat and plant life for nourishment. Through prayer the believer thanks God and dedicates the food to His glory (1 Cor. 10:31). The pastor who is "nourished up in the words of faith and of good doctrine," and points out these truths to his people, is judged to be "a good minister" (v. 6).

In verses 7-8 Paul instructs Timothy to "refuse profane and old wives fables." False teaching will always prove detrimental (contrast with "sound doctrine," 1:10). Perhaps concerned that Timothy was leaning toward an ascetic lifestyle, Paul exhorts him to emphasize spiritual discipline over physical discipline. This is not to ignore genuine healthy habits, but the fact is that "bodily exercise profits for little time but spiritual exercise (practicing godliness) is profitable for this life and the life to come" (paraphrase of v. 8).

LifeStep

The contrast between "sound doctrine" and "false teaching" is again the issue. If you have a pastor who fits the "good minister" definition of verse 6, why not take the time right now to lift him up in prayer?

1 Timothy 4:9-16

Paul once again resorts to a "faithful saying" (see 1:15) to drive home a truth. Some suggest he is referring back to verse 8. More likely he is looking forward to verse 10. The saying: " We trust in the living God, who is the Savior of all men, specially of those who believe." The bottom line: that Jesus Christ is the only Savior that has been provided for humanity, and His work at Calvary provided salvation for all (1 John 2:2). His work on the cross, however, is effective only for those who believe.

This truth prompted Paul to state that he was giving the ministry his best efforts. Offering self-plaudits was not common with Paul. To do so shows the seriousness with which he tackled his responsibilities, and provides a backdrop for his instructions to Timothy relative to his ministry. He begins: "Let no man despise thy youth" (v. 12). It may be that some older believers (Timothy was 30-35) were doing so. The best way to counter any attacks in this area would be to become an example to all who were watching; to demonstrate exemplary characteristics and conduct.

In verse 13 Paul emphasizes the public reading of the Word of God. It is to be "read;" then explained – "doctrine," a teaching ministry; and applied – "exhortation." Timothy's gifting, which had been recognized by the church (v. 14 with 2 Timothy 1:6), would stand him in good stead as he carried out his role – "neglect it not."

Paul than challenges Timothy to "meditate" on what had just been written. Putting Paul's instructions into action, and doing so wholeheartedly, will remove any opportunity for others to look down on him. Paul closes with a reminder: "Take heed unto thyself and unto the doctrine." Be sure to care for your own spiritual welfare while carrying out ministry responsibilities. Proper care will result in the "salvation" of one's ministry.

LifeStep

The value of one's ministry is directly related to one's character. Check out the characteristics that needed to be demonstrated in Timothy's life, and then evaluate yourself against them. How did you come out?

1 Timothy 5:1-8

In chapters 5 and 6 Paul details various categories of people to whom the church must minister. Age relationships are dealt with first, and instruction given to encourage the establishment of a family mentality within the church. Older men and women are to be treated like parents; younger men and women like brothers and sisters. Added caution was to be exercised in relationships with young women: treat them "with purity" (v. 2). Impropriety in ministering to young women was never to come into question.

Verse 3 begins an extended treatment of widows. Four classes are mentioned: (1) Real widows, 3,5,9,10; (2) Widows with relatives, 4,8,16; (3) Widows living in pleasure, 6,7; (4) Young widows, 11-16. The early church cared for widows (Acts 6:1-6; James 1:27), giving them "honor" (v. 3), a word meaning "to fix the value," and would include financial assistance. To guard fund distribution, some guidelines were put in place. A real widow (a "widow indeed") was truly destitute, without family, and no means of support. Having met the guidelines (vv. 5-10) they were to be church supported, with the church becoming her family. The first responsibility for widows with family, however, belonged to the family (v. 4). In fact, any believer who does not provide for his/her own is worse than an infidel (v. 8), for even pagans have a sense of family responsibility. Widows living in pleasure (v. 6), having chosen a decidedly unchristian path placed themselves outside the Church's responsibility.

Paul instructs Timothy to pass this information on as a command to church families (v. 7), for only as they accept their family responsibilities can they be considered "blameless."

LifeStep

Family relationships bring family responsibilities. While the Church has a responsibility to care for widows, it is a secondary responsibility. Primary responsibility belongs to the family. Let us be faithful in this matter.

1 Timothy 5:9-16

Paul now goes on to enumerate the qualifications necessary for inclusion on the widow's support list. Being without family support was not reason enough. One's lifestyle and even age (minimum: 60) must be considered. Those qualifications begin in verse 5 and continue through verse 10. They number 10 in all. Included would be that of an unblemished married life (v. 10), and a good testimony earned by: (1) raising of children, if so blessed; (2) hospitality, "lodging strangers"; and (3) humility, having "washed the saints feet," a demonstration of her willingness to accept even menial tasks.

Younger widows (v. 9) were not to be included (vv. 11-16). Reason: they might pledge faithfulness to serve Christ and the Church early in their widowhood, and in time turn away and be consumed by a desire to be remarried. Result: they grow wanton ("feel the impulses of sexual desire") and grow cold spiritually. They stop serving others ("they learn to be idle" v. 13) and become "tattlers...and busy-bodies" (v. 13), bringing reproach upon the name of Christ and the witness of the Church.

Having offered his reason for refusing to enroll young widows, Paul then gives instruction. Young widows should (1) remarry, (2) bear children and (3) guide the household. In carrying out these duties she will "give none occasion (no base of operations) to the adversary to speak reproachfully (v. 14)," as some had already done (v. 15). Their unacceptable behavior was because they lacked the wisdom of age and experience, leading them to fall prey to their own sexual desires (v. 11).

Paul then summarizes his instructions concerning widows. Responsibility for care falls first on the family. In meeting their obligations, the church will be free to care for the genuinely destitute (v. 16).

LifeStep

In Galatians 6:7 Paul writes: "Whatever a man soweth, that shall he also reap." Widows who sow a godly lifestyle will reap positive consequences in their declining years. Observing their godly lifestyle, let us give them proper "honor."

Paul now deals with two issues relative to church leaders: (1) How they are to be paid, and (2) How to treat them when they sin. Elders who "rule well" – lit. "having taken the lead well" – are "worthy of double honor" (same word used to financially care for widows, 5:3). The qualifying word is "well," and if that is the case "double pay," or at the very least, "ample" or "generous" pay would be proper. "The ox that treads out the corn" is not muzzled, nor should the one be who "labors" in the word and doctrine (v. 17)." According to Christ, says Paul, he is worthy of his reward.

When leaders sin: (1) Get the facts. Accusations must be supported by two or three witnesses, verse 19. (2) Give the matter honest, non-partial appraisal, verse 21. (3) Rebuke publicly if proven guilty. Such a procedure if followed would deter others from falling into the same sin, verse 20.

Verses 22, 24-25 address the issue of prematurely laying on of hands. In time an individual's true colors will emerge. Hasty action could lead to the placing of unworthy men in places of leadership, whether in the 1st or 21st century.

In verse 23 Paul inserts a personal bit of medical advice to Timothy that some have erroneously used to support the use of alcohol. Such a position is not supportable. Timothy had stomach problems that were being exacerbated by drinking polluted and unsafe water. His advice: "Drink no longer water (only), but use a little wine." He was offering Timothy a water purification method – the placing of a little wine in a much larger portion of water, a common procedure in that day. Timothy's ascetic leanings, or perhaps an abstinence based on Nazaretic teachings he may have received from his mother (2 Timothy 1:5; 3:15), may have made him hesitate to use such a procedure. Paul encourages him to do so.

LifeStep

Leaders must understand that sin in one's life merits public rebuke. Church members must remember that hasty action in selecting leadership can cause great damage. Pray now for your church leaders.

1 Timothy 6:1-8

In biblical times slaves made up 25-50% of the population. Many found Christ. Those with unbelieving masters, who often considered them on a par with cattle, might be prone to develop a pious superiority because of their new found freedom in Christ, leading them to provide less than optimum service. Paul cautions against this, for such an attitude would blaspheme both God and His Word (v. 1). Slaves with believing masters, perhaps tempted to take advantage of their spiritual oneness were to understand that such behavior would be unacceptable. They are to serve them well ("do them service") because of their faith in Christ (v. 2). See also Ephesians 6:5ff; Colossians 3:22ff.

Verses 3-5 contain teaching similar to 1:3-7. They warn about false teachers who "consent not to wholesome words, " especially that which centers around the foundational doctrine of Christ, and that which pertains to "godliness." Paul describes them as "proud," ignorant, sick ("doting" – mental sickness), and argumentative (v. 4). In verse 5 he makes it clear their behavior is evil and disruptive and has no place in the Body of Christ. Possessing "corrupt minds and destitute of the truth," and "supposing that gain is godliness," they use religion to further their goals. The believer has no business keeping their company (v. 5).

Conversely, "godliness with contentment is great gain," because "we brought (absolutely) nothing into this world (when we were born), and it is certain we can carry (absolutely) nothing out (when we die)" (Job 1:21;Eccl. 1:15). The point: Possessions are external; contentment is internal. Money is material; godliness is spiritual. Contentment and godliness will go with us when we depart. All else will be left behind (vv. 6-7). Therefore, having food and raiment let us be content (v. 8).

LifeStep

Ministry and material gain are not partners. Our service for the Lord is never to be motivated as if they are. Let us serve Him in faithfulness, not regarding the cost, leaving our care completely in His hands.

1 Timothy 6:9-16

Paul moves from the positive ("godliness with contentment") to the negative (greed). In verse 9 his warning is not to those already rich, but those "whose will it is to be rich." Focused on gaining wealth, they are "foolish," they "fall," and then "drown." Paul warns them (v. 10) with a much-misquoted phrase that really reads: " The love of money is a root (there are other roots) of all kinds of evil." Such a mind-set will find its possessors "pierced through with many sorrows."

Verses 11-16 are parenthetic. Paul will return in verse 17 to the subject of riches – not to those who desire it, but to those who have it. In this parenthesis he repeats by way of instruction to Timothy much of what he has already written. He calls him a "man of God," i.e. a mature Christian, surely a great encouragement to Timothy as he endeavored to carry out his charge which is three fold. (1) FLEE: pride, covetousness, false teaching-v. 10. Sometimes the wisest thing a believer can do is run (cf. 2 Tim. 2:22). But fleeing is not enough. (2) FOLLOW: righteousness, godliness, faith, love, patience, meekness. –Six virtues to be in evidence in a man of God. (3) FIGHT: "the good fight of faith," (a picture taken from the Olympics where the contestant keeps on until attaining the prize or goal). "Fight" is a word meaning "to contend for a prize." Eternal life is found in a relationship with Jesus Christ (1 John 5:11-13), and is both a present possession and future promise. Paul then challenges Timothy to keep this three-fold commitment until Christ appears (v. 14).

Verses 15-16 are a doxology to the "King of Kings and Lord of Lords," a title Paul uses nowhere else. He focuses on His sovereignty and His immortality, an immortality that is unique, for unlike ours which has no end, His never had a beginning.

LifeStep

The challenge to Timothy is one that every servant of Jesus Christ is to accept personally. Take a good look at it, and check yourself out. How are you doing?

In verses 17-19 Paul returns to the subject of riches, this time addressing not those who wish to be rich (vv. 9-10), but those who are. He instructs as to how to use wealth for the glory of God. (1) <u>BE HUMBLE</u> ("not high-minded") – recognizing that what one has is a gift from God. Focus on the Giver, not the gift. (2) <u>BE APPRECIATIVE</u> – it has been given to be richly enjoyed. (3) <u>BE USEFUL</u> – it has been given for but enjoyment and employment. Be generous and willing to share. (4) <u>BE VISIONARY</u> – or forward looking. Invest that which has given in that which is eternal, "laying...a good foundation against the time to come." This is what Christ calls "treasures in heaven" (Matt. 6:20).

Paul closes the letter by challenging Timothy to remember his calling, and to avoid the "profane and vain babblings" of false teachers. He was to "keep (guard, see v. 14) that which is committed (entrusted) to his trust (lit. 'deposit')." Paul is using a banking term, referring to that which has been placed on deposit, and which when demanded, is to be returned in its entirety. What had been deposited with Timothy was the gospel message, which had earlier been committed to Paul (1:11), and which Timothy will later pass on to others (2 Tim. 2:2).

Paul's admonition of avoidance was a warning to Timothy not to get involved with those of the Gnostic cult who claimed to have "special spiritual knowledge" from visions and other experiences. They failed to give Christ His rightful place in their teachings, and taught that salvation was possible through knowledge. Phillips calls their "babblings" a "godless mixture of contradictory notions," and they "have erred concerning the faith," says Paul. With that he offers his closing salvation: "Grace be with you."

LifeStep

The Gospel message came from God to Paul, and then to Timothy. He passed it on to others. Now it is our turn. May we be found faithful.

Introduction– II Timothy

II Timothy is one of three books known as the Pastoral Epistles, the other two being I Timothy and Titus. They were written by the older Apostle Paul (in his 60's) to two younger men, Timothy and Titus (probably in their 30's). These young men were serving in pastoral-like roles, Timothy in Ephesus and Titus in Crete, to tell them how to "behave" themselves "in the house of God... the Church of the Living God" (1 Tim. 3:15).

Helpful to the understanding of the books individually is to take them collectively. Three themes seem to resonate throughout all three: (1) Church Organization; (2) Sound Doctrine and (3) Consistent Christian Living. While all three books touch on all three themes, each book has its particular emphasis, and those three themes follow the order in which they have been placed in most Bibles (thought not written in that order). I Timothy emphasizes Church Organization; II Timothy, Sound Doctrine; and Titus, Consistent Christian Living. Charles Erdman, in writing of these three books early in the 20th century, offered this summation of these three themes this way: "Church government is not an end in itself; it is of value only as it secures sound doctrine; and doctrine is of value only as it issues in life." The point is this: you Organize (that's I Timothy) so that you can each Sound Doctrine (that's II Timothy), and you teach Sound Doctrine so that Consistent Christian Living (that's Titus) can result.

As Paul writes, Timothy is serving as his representative to the church in Ephesus. His background is that during Paul's first missionary journey (Act 13-14), he and Barnabas preached the gospel in the cities of Lystra and Derbe (Acts 14:1-20), and Timothy, who had a Greek father and Jewish mother, responded to the message, leading Paul to address him as "my son in the faith" – my own "born-one in the faith" (I Tim. 1:2; II Tim. 1:2). The book of Acts, as well as Paul's own letters, makes it clear that Timothy was a capable, trustworthy individual. He could be sent ahead or left behind to carry on the Apostle's work (19:22; 20:4). As to personality, there is some indication that he was somewhat timid in nature (II Tim 1:6-7); easily discouraged or frightened (I Cor. 16:10-11; Ii Tim. 1:8); and prone to sickness (I Tim. 5:23). And yet, all that being said, there is no question that Paul placed great trust in him. His recommendation to the Philippian church makes that crystal clear: "I have no one else like him" (Phil. 2:20).

As to II Timothy itself, it is written from prison where Paul is awaiting execution.

It is the last known writing we have from the great Apostle's pen, and in effect it is his "last will and testament," the most personal of all his letters (with the possible exception of the short letter written to Philemon). It is believed by many that Paul was arrested and placed in prison when Nero began his campaign of persecution shortly after Rome burned down in A.D. 64. Nero blamed the Christians for starting the fire (after all, had they not predicted the world would come to an end in a great fire?), and executed many of them in extremely cruel fashion, including Peter, who, according to one of the early church fathers, Origin, was crucified upside down. As Paul authors this second letter to his son-in-the-faith Timothy, he was very much aware of his apparently soon to come death (by beheading).

This letter, as well as the other Pastoral Epistles, but even more so, is marked by the open sharing of feelings and thoughts. The major emphases of the book would include: (1) Encouragement to be faithful... Timothy was somewhat timid and Paul, reminded of his "tears" (1:4), used this letter to challenge him to "hang in there." Paul was well aware that the Christian life is not played out on a ball field, but lived out on a battlefield, and that one of the essential characteristics of a faithful servant of Jesus Christ would be endurance in the midst of difficulties. (2) To turn over leadership to Timothy... generations come and go, and knowing his time was short Paul wanted to be sure that leadership for the next generation was in place. Jack Wyrtzen, founder of Word of Life Fellowship, often remarked, "It is responsibility of each generation to reach its generation for Christ." (3) Paul's final and definitive testimony...a reminder to Timothy that he (Paul) had finished well, and an underlying, not-so-gentle hint that he (Timothy) too, should desire a similar finish.

Major theological emphases would include: (1) The coming apostasy of the last days, detailed in chapter 3. Paul warns Timothy that there will be difficult days ahead for believers, and so he passes on instruction as to how Christians are to behave and respond. Jesus had predicted such times would come (John 15:18-25; 16:33; 17:15-18), and Paul himself had written earlier of those coming days (I Thess. 3:1-8), and warned the Ephesian elders of them (Acts 10:29). (2) The importance, value and application of Scripture, scattered throughout the book, including 1:13; 2:2, 15; 3:14-17; 4:2-4. Paul was encouraging Timothy not only to pass on the truths of Scripture to the generations that follow, but also to pass on the basis of those truths, the inspired (God-breathed) Word of God. It is, as many conservative local church constitutions state: "The final authority (the supreme standard) for all faith (what we believe) and practice (how we behave)."

II Timothy 1:1-7

Paul, as in his earlier letter to Timothy, introduces himself as "an apostle of Jesus Christ," a title unnecessary if this letter was for Timothy's eyes only, for Timothy certainly knew Paul's position. But, as in his other "pastorals," Paul was providing Timothy with the credentials necessary to carry out his task of leading the church of Ephesus. While some might choose to downplay the words of their young pastor, they could hardly do the same with the words of one who was clearly recognized as "one sent from God," with a message to deliver. Adding the words "by the will of God," Paul makes it clear that he understood his apostleship was an assignment from God.

This letter, with the possible exception of Philemon, is the most personal of all that Paul wrote. Written from a Roman dungeon, it is often looked upon as Paul's "last will and testament," and was the final book from his pen. He addresses Timothy as his "dearly beloved son" (or: his own born-one), and in that designation makes it clear that he and Timothy had a very special relationship, that of father and son "in the faith" (see I Tim 1:2). The relationship engendered both deep concern as well as thanksgiving in Paul's heart for his young protégé (vv. 3,4)

Concerned that Timothy's apparently timid nature could curtail his ministry (see "tears," v.4), Paul reminded him of <u>his faith</u> (found first in his mother and grandmother, v. 5) and of <u>his gifting</u> (v. 6). That gifting was the enabling resource that Timothy was to use to carry out his ministry; it was already present, not something to be added to his character, and was to be "rekindled." Extending the thought of gifting Paul challenges Timothy to remember that neither he nor Paul ("us" in v. 7) had been given "the spirit of fear, but of <u>power</u>...<u>love</u>, and a <u>sound mind</u> (v. 7), three vital ingredients for effective Christian service.

LifeStep
Timothy had Paul's letters; we have much more, the entire Word of God. He was gifted; so are we. Let us see to it that we use what we have been given (and it is not "fear") to carry out the ministry tasks to which we've been assigned.

II Timothy 1:8-12

Aware that Timothy's timidity could cause enough shame for him to back away from an effective ministry, as well as from Paul (as a prisoner) himself, the apostle encourages his young follower to be a "partaker of the afflictions of the gospel." (v. 8). Suffering is part of the believer's calling and when it comes, should be accepted as part of God's will. Furthermore, when it comes it will be accompanied by the "power of God," always available for encouragement and strength.

V. 8, which ends with "God," is followed by the work of God in salvation, ("hath saved...and called us"). He does so "not according to our works, but according to his own purpose and grace." That purpose, once hidden, is now revealed through Paul. God did not eliminate death through the cross, but He did disarm it. For the believer, its sting is gone (cp. I Cor. 15:55-57), and Christ has brought "life and immortality" (v. 10)...the condition of never dying to light (they were in the shadows in the O.T.).

The believer is called to holiness (v. 9; I Pet. 1:15-16). Writing to persecuted believers, Peter advocated holy living... lives consecrated to God, and lives befitting our true identity and position in Christ (see I Pet. 2:10-11). Paul's challenge to Timothy is similar, using himself as an example. He had suffered many things for the cause of Gospel, (vv. 11-12), but was never ashamed. Why? Because: "I know whom I have believed (a continuing attitude of belief with trust), and am persuaded that He is able to keep that which I have committed unto Him (his very being) v.12...and that which God committed to both he and Timothy, v. 14: "God had committed the Gospel to Paul (I Tim 1:11); he was passing it on to Timothy (I Tim. 6:20; II Tim 4:7), who was to pass it on to faithful men...(and) others also (II Tim 2:2).

LifeStep
The believer has a choice when suffering comes. To back away in shame from his commitment to Christ hoping to avoid pain; or to accept it as part of God's purpose in his life and meet it head on with the provided power of God. May the latter mark our lives even as it did Paul's.

II Timothy 1:13-18

In v.12, we found Paul using himself as one who steadfastly remained faithful to his commitment. In vv. 13-14 Timothy is exhorted to maintain a similar commitment. He is to "hold fast the form of sound words. "Form" can mean "example" or "pattern" (see 1 Tim. 1:16). Paul both preached and lived the Gospel, establishing a pattern for others to follow (see 1 Cor. 11:1). "Sound" comes from a Greek word that gives us our English word "hygiene," meaning "healthy." "Words" means "teaching" (in Titus 1:9 it is "sound doctrine," also 1 Tim 1:10). Taken together the challenge is to provide "healthy teaching," for the opposite (cp. II Tim, 2:17) could result in crippling disease.

"That good thing that was committed unto thee (v. 14)," is a clear reference to the Gospel (I Tim. 6:20). Having received it Timothy was to "keep" it, and was reminded that only by the power of the Spirit could he do so. "Keep" means to "guard," and coupled with I Tim. 6:20 ("keep that which is committed to thy trust") means the Gospel has been placed on deposit with Timothy (a banking analogy). It is to be guarded and kept, and available for use on demand.

Remember, this letter is being written from a prison dungeon where Paul awaits trial and subsequent beheading. Circumstances are dire. Desertion has escalated. The "some" of I Timothy (1:6; 1:19; 5:15; 6:10; 6:21) have become the hyperbolic "all" of II Timothy (1:15; 4:16), many being led by two deserters named "Phygellus" and "Hermogenes." Yet even in troubled times God provides relief, and he does so here in the person of "Onesiphorus" ("one who brings profit or benefit." This godly man may have been a deacon in Ephesus when Paul was there, for v. 18 can be translated: "...and in how many things he fully played the deacon..." He came to Rome, searched hard for Paul, found him and served him without fear or shame (v. 16).

LifeStep
Onesiphorus: the unashamed servant of Jesus Christ, and of those who serve the Savior. Does that describe us? There's a thought to ponder. Let's put into practice those things that would make it so.

II Timothy 2:1-7

"Thou, therefore, my son (an expression of strong affection), be strong in the grace (undeserved divine help) that is in Christ Jesus (v.1)." With these words Paul both exhorts and challenges Timothy to be faithful to his calling, while at the same time drawing a contrast between that which he desires for his young "son-in-the-faith," and the defectors of the previous chapter (1:15). They had turned their backs upon Paul and the gospel ministry, but by depending on "the grace that is in Christ Jesus" and its accompanying power, and not upon his own, Timothy would not have to repeat their error nor experience their fate.

Then begins a series of pictures demonstrating the characteristics of a faithful servant of Jesus Christ. He is to first of all be faithful as a teacher (v. 2). That which he has heard he is to pass on to others. In fact, Timothy is to be part of an endless chain of passing on truth to succeeding generations (i.e., God to Paul to Timothy to faithful men to others also). This is the same procedure laid out by Christ in the Great Commission (Mt. 28:19-20), that of making disciples (discipleship).

In vv. 3-6 Paul gives three additional illustrations of faithfulness to demonstrate to Timothy the seriousness of his task. The first is that of a soldier, and as such he is to (a) endure hardness; (b) not entangle himself with the affairs of this life (not that they are wrong – just don't get caught up in them); and (c) seek to please his commander, and for the believer that is Jesus Christ. The second illustration is that of an athlete. He is to "strive for masteries" (contend in the games), but to do so lawfully. To receive the victor's crown his life and ministry must follow biblical directives. The third illustration is that of a hardworking farmer. Only through strenuous, diligent effort, will a bountiful harvest result.

LifeStep
In the 7th verse of this passage Paul summarizes his 3 illustrations of vv. 3-6. He challenges Timothy to carefully consider what has just been said, and to apply it to his ministry. We would be well advised to do the same.

II Timothy 2:8-14

Here Paul directs the readers' thoughts, as well as ours, to Jesus Christ and His resurrection. "Of the seed of David" points to His humanity and the fulfillment of the promises God made to David (cp. II Sam. 7:16). "Raised from the dead" focuses attention on the deity of Christ, and the power of God demonstrated in the resurrection (cp. Rom. 1:1-4). To Paul, the paramount truth of the gospel (he called it "my gospel" – Rom. 2:16; 16:25; I Cor. 15:1), was the resurrection.

That gospel of his (v. 8) is what brought about his present distress (v. 9). He is chained like a common criminal, because he preached it. Yet "the Word of God is not bound" (v. 9). Even though in prison, he could still preach the Word. In fact, as many have pointed out, he often had a "captive audience," the Roman soldiers to whom he was chained. That being the case he was able to "endure all the things for the elect's sake," that salvation may result in these who believe, culminating in eternal glory, salvation's final state (v. 10).

In vv. 11-13 we have the longest of the 5 "faithful sayings" contained in the pastorals (I Tim. 1:15; 3:1; 4:9; II Tim. 2:11-13; Titus 3:8). Thought to be "prophetic sayings" by the N.T. prophets in the early church, they summarized their beliefs in a pre-canon age. The theme here is Christ's death and resurrection, and our union with Christ in those significant historical events (v. 11). "If we suffer (better: endure), we shall reign with Him," but, "if we deny (fail to endure) Him, He will deny us (the reign or reward that could have been)" (v.12). Then comes a contrast of God's faithfulness vs. man's unfaithfulness (v.13). The latter can never abrogate the former. For Christ to abandon His own would be contary to His nature (cp. John 10:27-30; Heb. 10:23; 13:5).

LifeStep
In the O.T. God promised a Redeemer. In the N.T. He fulfills that promise. Christ went to the cross, purchased salvation for the one who believes, and today lives to keep that salvation secure. Pause now to thank Him for His Faithfulness, and re-commit to Him, yours.

Paul's charge to Timothy continues: "Don't get caught up in fighting over words!" The result is "no profit" and "the subverting (turning upside down) of the hearers." Positively, however, (v.15) "study (be eager, zealous, diligent) to show (present oneself for service) thyself approved (accepted after testing) unto God, a workman that needeth not to be ashamed, rightly dividing (cutting straight) the word of truth." Proper preaching, says Paul, goes straight ahead, never veering left or right, always "correctly handling" the word, never twisting or changing the truth.

Having been attacked by false teachers, Timothy was warned to: (a) Stick to the essentials, don't argue over empty words and philosophies (v. 16), and (b) Rightly divide the word, failing to do so gives room to false teachers to promote false doctrines which unchecked eats like a gangrene (Gk. Gangraina), i.e., a malignant sore that eats away healthy tissue (v.17). These false teachers (two are named) "erred" (wandered away) "concerning the truth" (v. 18), probably teaching there was no bodily resurrection, that the resurrection of believers had already occurred. Early gnosticism emphasized a spiritual resurrection over a future bodily resurrection. Unchecked, this sort of "spiritualization" will destroy weaker believers, because the resurrection is central to the gospel, hence the need for proper exegesis.

"Nevertheless" (v.19)…in spite of the efforts of the false teachers…"the foundation of God standeth sure." Exchanging his negative tone for a note of encouragement, Paul…based on the tense of the verb…indicates that he saw the truth of God standing firm, not only in the past but also in the present (cp. Isa. 40:8). Armed with that truth, and knowing to whom we belong, the challenge is to live a life of purity.

LifeStep
When you hold in your hands the Word of God…HANDLE IT WITH GREAT CARE. To fail to do so is to court great danger. And pray for those whose job it is to preach it. The souls of their listeners may be dependent upon their rightly dividing the word of truth.

Vs. 20 employs the phrase "a great house." A reference to the church, "the household of God" (I Tim. 3:15), in which are two general types of vessels: those of honor and much value ("gold and silver"), and those of dishonor and little value ("wood and earth" – pottery). The emphasis is not on the usefulness of the vessels, for the latter are probably more useful than the former which are saved for special occasions, but the value or quality of the vessel. Wood and pottery will eventually chip and break and must be replaced (a picture of false teachers whose worthlessness is recognized and leads to removal). This is not true with gold or silver. Their value is retained.

The honored vessel is to purge himself from those dishonored (v. 21). Contamination must be avoided. The results of doing so: (1) he is "sanctified" – set apart for a holy purpose; (2) he is "meet" – profitable for the Master's use ("Master" – gr. Despot – strong term denoting God's total authority); and (3) "prepared (ready) for every good work." Having avoided contamination, the honored vessel is to maintain his value by staying clean. This is a two-step process. Negatively – "Flee:" avoid, shun "youthful lusts" (more than simply sexual, but also pride, ego, power, love of money, etc.) Positively – "Follow": pursue after, righteousness, faith, charity, peace (see also I Tim. 6:11). Both steps are vital. To fail in either will render one's ministry valueless.

Paul then cautions Timothy to avoid "foolish and unlearned (stupid) questions (arguments)...they gender (breed) strifes (quarrels)." He had given similar instructions earlier (I Tim. 1:4,7; 4:7; 6:20; II Tim. 2:16). He then calls Timothy the "servant (doulos) of the Lord," and as such he has no will of his own. He is to be governed by his Master in every respect. The chapter's latter verses (23-26) explain how to deal with problems in God's house so that strife and contention are avoided.

LifeStep
If usefulness to God is our goal, circumspect behavior is required. Let us apply Paul's instruction to Timothy personally. Let us also "Flee," "Follow," and "Avoid."

II Timothy 3:1-7

Here we see the necessity of chapter two's exhortation. The theme is "the last days" (v.1), and the character of men in those days. Those "last days" began with the life and ministry of Christ (Heb. 1:2), and will continue until Christ returns. They will be difficult, days marked by "apostasy" (a falling away – the act of professed Christians who deliberately reject revealed truth as to the Deity of Christ and the efficaciousness of His crosswork). As Christ's return draws closer man's evil characteristics (vv.2-5,18 noted) will intensify (see v. 13). Civilized behavior will completely break down.

Numbered among those characteristics are "lovers of their own selves" and "covetous," the "twin sins" from which all the others flow. That such is the case can be seen in such characteristics of "unthankful," "unholy," "highminded (conceited), and "lovers of pleasure more than lovers of God." "Without natural affection" and "disobedient to parents" suggest the breaking up of society as God intended it to be. Striking one's father was as bad as murder in Roman law; abusing a parent in Greek culture caused disinheritance; and honoring parents was the 5th of the Jews 10 commandments. Today's divorce statistics show how rapidly we are moving away from God's standards, and how rapidly we seem to be moving to the end of the age. All of the age-end characteristics can be found on the pages of today's newspapers, further indication that Christ's return is drawing near.

Accompanying all of the above is "a form of godliness," but that is all that it is...a form...for the true power of godliness is denied. The apostate religionists of the last days go through the motions, and maintain their external forms, but they have not experienced the dynamic power of true Christianity that results in changed lives. From such, "turn away."

LifeStep
The dark days in which we live have only one remedy: the Gospel of Jesus Christ. Later Paul will tell Timothy: "Do the work of an evangelist." Good advice for us as well.

II Timothy 3:8-12

Paul uses Jannes and Jambres (not mentioned in the O.T., but found in Jewish tradition opposing Moses) as examples of men in the past who resisted God's truth. They were "men of corrupt minds," similar to the apostates of Paul's day (and ours) who cannot understand truth (cp. Rom. 1:21,22; Eph. 4:17,18; I Tim 6:5), and "reprobate concerning the faith" (v.8). Like Jannes and Jambres, this new group of truth-deniers will not get very far for "their folly shall be manifest unto all" (v.9). It will be exposed (Num. 32:23). Truth always triumphs in the end.

Vs. 10 begins a new section of what can be considered Paul's final advice to Timothy. To encourage him to "hang in there," he gives a strong word of personal testimony. He begins with "But thou...", demonstrating the difference between Timothy and the men Paul just referenced and continues: "hast fully known (you've observed)"...and notes that which that his observation revealed: a life-style (that of Paul's) worth emulating. It begins with "doctrine" (teaching), goes on to "manner of life"(conduct), "purpose" (chief aim), and "faith" (the gospel). To underscore that none of the above came easily he mentions some personal characteristics that are vital when persecution comes to those who desire to live godly lives (v. 12): "longsuffering, charity, patience (endurance)." He reminds Timothy that he had endured numerous persecutions, but out of them all the Lord delivered him (v.11; cp. Acts 14:19,20; Ps. 34:17).

Paul moves from his own experiences to a word of encouragement by noting that persecution, in some sense at least, is the lot of all non-compromising believers. Jesus said, "In the world ye shall have tribulation (John 16:33)." God does not always deliver His children from persecution but, as Paul has demonstrated, and as Scripture testifies, He promises to be with them as they go through it (Matt. 28:20b).

LifeStep
Endurance...a quality that Paul had, and one that will demonstrate the seriousness of our commitment to Christ. Let us be faithful to complete the tasks to which we've been assigned. Keep on keeping on!

II Timothy 3:13-17

V. 13 is a transitional verse linking Paul's charge to Timothy (v. 14ff), and the importance behind it to the offenders described earlier in the chapter. "Therefore, Timothy, remember what you've learned, and who taught you." (Your mother, grandmother and Paul). The ladies taught him the O.T. and pointed him to the Messiah. Paul comes along and provides the information that Christ indeed was the Messiah, and Timothy responded in faith.

Vv. 14-17 are the key verses in II Timothy, demonstrating the unparalleled value of the Scriptures. Its words bring about salvation (v.15), and equip for productive Christian living (v.17). Its effectiveness is because "all Scripture is given by inspiration of God" (one word in the Greek: God-breathed). Inspiration...the out-breathing of God...was the process that produced the product: the Word of God. And because it is God's Word, it is "profitable" (v.16). It takes the believer and guides all his footsteps, from start to finish. One writer (Guy King) describes those steps this way: (1) FORWARD STEPS – "doctrine," teaching. How to move ahead in the Christian life. (2) FALSE STEPS – "reproof." The pointing out of one's faults. (3) FALTERING STEPS – "correction." Learning not only how we have gone wrong, but how to get right. Cp. Ps. 119:9; John 7:17. (4) FIRST STEPS – "instruction." This is a word that would be used for the training of a child. And that training is to be "in righteousness." For all these purposes the holy Scriptures are both highly profitable and highly effective. By "faith" Timothy became "a child (teknon – born one) of God" (I Tim. 1:2). Now, by utilizing the Scriptures he has grown into a "man of God." The result is "good works" (v. 17).

LifeStep

The title "man of God" usually reserved for prophets in the O.T., can today belong to all believers. Let us demonstrate it as ours by our good works.

II Timothy 4:1-4

Be reminded as we work our way through this fourth and final chapter of the book that this is the last chapter we have from the pen of the Apostle Paul. As he begins to bring this letter to a close Paul's appeal to Timothy to "hang in there" comes into clear focus, and to support his appeal he reminds Timothy that Jesus will one day return in judgment (v.1), and he is answerable to the Lord as to how he carries out his ministry. This idea of judgment is a primary theme of the Apostle, especially as it relates to the life and ministry of believers (cp. 1 Cor. 3:11-17; 5:10).

The ministry Timothy is to have is spelled out in v. 2 where 5 exhortations are given, the final 4 of which flow quite naturally out of the first, which is: (1)"Preach the Word," for the Word is the foundation of any ministry. And it is to be done (2) with urgency: "instant in season, out of season..." Whether the time is convenient or inconvenient, or circumstances favorable or unfavorable...just do it! (3) Included should be reproof: to correct, convince – show them how they have done wrong. (4) Rebuke: show them how wrong they were to do wrong. Finally, (5) exhort – show them that they must right the wrong and not repeat it. There is an implication in this "Preach the Word" command: It is not preach about the Word, or even from the Word, but preach the Word, which implies knowledge, so study (remember 2:15) of the Word is vital. All of these exhortations are to be accompanied with "long-suffering" (great patience) and "doctrine" (careful instruction) v.2.

Why the command? Because "the time will come (v.3) when men will not want the Word; they will want to hear what makes them feel good, "having itching ears." Given time those "itching ears," that are satisfied with shallow religious entertainment, will soon become deaf ears, as they turn away from the truth to man-made fables (v.4).

LifeStep
"Preach the Word." The instruction is to Timothy but applies to us as well. May God give to each of us and our churches an unwavering commitment to do so. Anything else or less is sin.

II Timothy 4:5-8

Earlier (v.1) Timothy is told to "preach the word." Why? "…the time will come" when men will not want "sound doctrine" (v.3) or "truth," but will turn to "fables" (v.4). In the light of that Timothy is given 4 instructions in v.5: "Watch" - be sober in judgment; "endure afflictions" – the work of the ministry in not without its price; "do the work of an evangelist" – remember to evangelize the lost (a difficult, but still required, task for someone timid); "make full proof of thy ministry" – accomplish the purpose to which you've been called. Those instructions are valid not only for Timothy, but for all of God's children.

In vv.6-8 Paul makes it clear it is time for him to move on and pass the torch to others. His reflective words form perhaps the greatest "exit testimony" ever recorded. He has come to the end of his life with no regrets. He goes on (v.6) to illustrate in 2 ways his victorious view of death. First, "I am ready to be offered" (poured out like a drink offering). He considered his life and ministry an offering to God (Rom. 15:16; Phil 2:17). Second, "the time of my departure is at hand." It is time to set sail, take down the tent and move on (cp. II Pet. 1:14-15).

He then uses 3 illustrations (v.7) that demonstrate his finishing well. "I have fought a good fight," i.e., the act of a soldier (see 2:3-4); "I have finished my course," i.e., the goal of an athlete (see 2:5); "I have kept the faith," i.e., the responsibility of a steward of the gospel. Having done so (I Tim 1:11), Paul expects the same from Timothy (I Tim. 6:20, II Tim. 1:14).
"Henceforth," (v.8) a reward is waiting, the end result of a lifetime of faithful service to Christ, "the righteous judge," who when He returned, would bring with Him rewards for those who served God faithfully during their earthly sojourn (Mt.5:10-12).

LifeStep
To come to the end of one's life with no regrets, as Paul did, and to be able to verbalize the fact that the goal of finishing well has been accomplished… there could be no greater aspiration. May that be the goal of all who read these words.

II Timothy 4:9-15

Following his "exit" testimony (vv.6-8) Paul requests Timothy to: "come quickly to see me (v9)," and "come before winter" (v.21). Implied: when winter comes travel will be more difficult, so an early arrival would be preferable. "And when you come, Timothy, bring the cloak I left behind in Troas" (v.13), for it will provide some comfort in the cold surroundings of his prison cell.

Paul then begins to list some of his co-workers (he always recognized their importance and was grateful for their assistance). The first one mentioned, however, triggered unpleasant memories. Demas, who at one time had been one of Paul's trusted co-workers (cp. Col. 4:14; Philm.24), had deserted him for what the world had to offer (v.10), and apparently when he was most needed. Crescens was off to Galatia on ministry. Titus, to Dalmatia as Paul's emissary. "Only Luke is with me" (v.11), but for one afflicted with some physical problem as was Paul (II Cor. 12:7-9), who better to have as a companion than a medical doctor? And bring John Mark, the young man who had earlier deserted Paul had since proved himself (Col. 4:10), and is now "profitable" for the ministry (v.11). Tychichus is off to Ephesus (perhaps to replace Timothy should he join Paul).

Besides the cloak, Paul requests his "books" and "parchments." The "books" may have been some of Paul's own writings, and "parchments" Paul's personal copies of O.T. scriptures. In vv14-15 Paul refers to an Alexander who in some way did Paul "evil." Regardless of how it was done, Paul shows no bitterness or "get-even" attitude. He simply says it is the Lord's business and He will take care of it (cp. Ps. 62:12; Prov. 24:12; Rom. 12:9). At the same time Paul cautions Timothy to be on guard against him.

LifeStep
The ministry of one's co-workers can make or break the ministry being performed. Thank God for those who serve faithfully with you, and pray that like John Mark, you also will be "ministry-profitable."

II Timothy 4:16-22

In this passage the forgiving attitude of Christ is seen in Paul. Although many had abandoned him, he asked the Lord not to hold them accountable for their actions (v.16). He writes: "At my first answer (defense)"–the preliminary hearing prior to trial–"no man stood with me." No one appeared to serve as Defense Attorney, though that was a common practice. Furthermore, "all men forsook me." Those who could have testified for him were also absent. Yet Paul, in spite of their abandonment, like Christ (Lk. 23:34) and Stephen (Acts 7:60) before him, exhibits the grace of God he himself had experienced (I Tim.1:12-15).

Left alone, (but not alone – "the Lord stood with me," v.17), Paul conducted his own defense, and took the opportunity to preach the gospel... "that by me the preaching might be fully known." He left nothing out. Even as he said to the Ephesian elders in Acts 20:27, "I...declare unto you all the counsel of God," he used this opportunity to preach the complete gospel about which he had written (I Cor. 15:1-4). His defense was unusual; it said little about him, but much about the Lord, "that all the Gentiles might hear." The Lord again (see II Cor. 11:16-33), delivered him "out of the mouth of the lion," a metaphoric expression in Paul's day to express deliverance from extreme danger, and a biblical image Paul was familiar with (cp. Ps. 22:21; Dan. 6:22).

Paul extends final greetings (vv 19-22), naming 9 of his co-workers. Some were in Ephesus, some in Rome and two elsewhere. He includes greetings from some Roman believers Timothy would have known (v.21), as well as "all the brethren." Even though they had deserted him, he still sends their greetings to Timothy. His benediction (v.22) is two-fold. Personal to Timothy: "The Lord be with your spirit." Corporately to all believers: "Grace (a fitting way for Paul to conclude both his letter and ministry) be with you (all). Amen."

LifeStep
Grace... the watchword of Paul's life. He had experienced it, and he passed it along to others. May the forgiving Spirit that prevailed in him permeate our lives as well.

Introduction to Titus

The book of Titus, along with Paul's two letters to Timothy, make up that section of New Testament books known as The Pastoral Epistles. Separated from his two young protégés, the older mentor, Paul, provides them with written information, "how-to" books, if you will, to use in their respective ministries (Timothy in Ephesus; Titus on the Island of Crete). The key verse explaining that for all 3 books is found in I Tim. 3:15, where Paul says, in effect, since he cannot at the present time be with them, here is how they are "to behave" themselves "in the house of God... the church of the living God, the pillar and ground of the truth." It was a letter written shortly after I Timothy, approximately 63 A.D., during that period of time between Paul's two imprisonments.

Helpful to the understanding of the books individually is to take them collectively. Three themes seem to resonate throughout all three: (1) Church Organization; (2) Sound Doctrine and (3) Consistent Christian Living. While all three books touch on all three themes, each book has its particular emphasis, and those three themes follow the order in which they have been placed in most Bibles (thought not written in that order). I Timothy emphasizes Church Organization; II Timothy, Sound Doctrine; and Titus, Consistent Christian Living. Charles Erdman, in writing of these three books early in the 20th century, offered this summation of these three themes this way: "Church government is not an end in itself; it is of value only as it secures sound doctrine; and doctrine is of value only as it issues in life." The point is this: you Organize (that's I Timothy) so that you can each Sound Doctrine (that's II Timothy), and you teach Sound Doctrine so that Consistent Christian Living (that's Titus) can result.

As to Titus himself, our knowledge concerning him is somewhat limited (in comparison to Timothy, for example). We meet him first in Galatians where we learn that he was a Gentile (Gal. 2:3) who had been with Paul as early as, or even prior to the time when Barnabas went to Tarsus to bring Paul back to Antioch (Gal. 2:1; cp. Acts 11:25-30). Paul's reference to him as "my true son" or "mine own son after the faith" (Titus 1:4) is an indication that Titus had come to Christ through Paul's ministry. Some scholars have speculated that Titus may have been the younger brother of Luke, and to avoid charges of nepotism, Luke never mentioned him when he authored the Book of Acts.

That he was a very capable and gifted young man can be deduced from the assignments that Paul gave him.

He had been given the responsibility of reporting to Paul on the sad spiritual condition of the Corinthian church (II Cor. 2:12-13; 7:2-16). He then returned to Corinth to deliver Paul's second letter to that church, a letter designed to correct the problems there. He also represented Paul in the matter of the collection for the saints in Jerusalem (II Cor. 2:3-4; 13; 7:6-16; 8:16-24). In light of his success in these assignments it is no surprise that Paul left him on the Island of Crete to strengthen, organize, and correct the churches there. Paul offers a great compliment when he calls him his "partner and fellow-worker" (II Cor. 8:23).

As to the place of his assignment: Crete... we do know it was not an easy assignment as our studies will show. The people of Crete, by their own admission, were "liars, evil beasts, idle gluttons" (Titus 1:12). Paul confirmed that evaluation (Titus 1:13). Crete itself is a rather large island, approximately 160 miles long and 35 miles wide in the Mediterranean Sea, and located 100 miles southeast of Greece. As to when the church began we can only surmise. It could have been the result of a missionary journey that Paul took between his imprisonments, or it may go all the way back to the Day of Pentecost, some 30 years earlier (Acts 2:11 indicates Cretans were there). If the latter is the case, it is no wonder Paul placed him there to "set in order the things that are wanting," for a church with apparently minimal direction for such an extended period of time would have many things wanting.

The purpose(s) of the book can be summed up as follows:

> To remind Titus of his work of reorganizing the church and appointing elders.

> To warn him about false teachers.

> To encourage him in pastoring the different kinds of people in the church.

> To emphasize the true meaning of grace in the life of the Christian.

> To explain how to deal with church troublemakers.

(Expanding on the above: it is likely that the Cretan church suffered from two sources: (a) Visiting Judaizers, who mixed law and grace; and (b) Ignorant Christians who abused the grace of God, and turned their liberty into license.)

A major emphasis in the book is <u>CONSISTENT</u> <u>CHRISTIAN</u> <u>LIVING</u>. Paul wanted the Cretans to be both <u>hearers</u> and <u>doers</u> of the Word (James 1:22), hence there is a constant emphasis upon "good works" (1:16; 2:7,14; 3:1,5,8,14). Those "good works" ought to be the natural result of one's salvation, something Paul made very clear in Eph. 2:8,9 and 10. A key verse for the book would be Titus 3:8 – "...that they who have believed in God might be careful to maintain good works."

Titus 1:1-9

Paul introduces himself as a "servant of God" – (doulos – one born into slavery, whose will is swallowed up in the will of another – this should be true of all believers) – " and an apostle of Jesus Christ" – (apostolos – one sent with proper credentials to represent someone else), His commission: to further "the faith of God's elect leading to "godliness" (v. 1), a word introducing the theme of: "good works" (see 1:16; 2:7,14; 3:1,5,8,14). The addressee is Titus, though it is clear that like I and II Tim., the letter was to be widely read. He is referred to as Paul's "own son after the common faith," similar to Timothy (I Tim. 1:2), an indication both of these young men were products of Paul's ministry. Titus' assignment was two-fold: First, he was to preach the Word (v.3). Second (v.5) he was to organize the church and "set in order" (like setting a broken bone) the church's deficiencies. The state of disorganization may have been because of minimal apostolic instruction since its inception, which may have been a result of Pentecost some 30 years earlier (cp. Acts 2:11). Titus' task would involve dealing with false teachers (v. 9ff).

To correct the problems: "ordain elders in every city (v.5);" an ordination based on proper qualifications, some of which are listed in verses 6-9, and similar to I Tim. 3:1-7. Those qualifications fit into numerous categories, such as (1) General, vv. 6-7; (2) Family, v. 6; (3) Personal, vv 7-8a; (4) Mental, v.8b; and (5) Spiritual, vv. 8c-9 (H. Kent). Without biblically qualified leadership a church courts disaster, for leadership sets the pace and establishes the standards. The leader ("elder" in v.5, "bishop" in v. 7 – the terms are interchangeable, cp. Acts 20:17,28; I Peter 5:1-2) is "to hold fast the faithful word" so that by "sound doctrine" (healthy teaching) he can both exhort believers and rebuke opposers. "Good doctrine always results in good practice, and good practice is always based on good doctrine." (Ryrie).

LifeStep
A church's success, in God's eyes, is tied to its commitment to the Word of God. Here's a thought to ponder: Is your church's ministry Biblically-saturated, or simply Biblically-scented? It does make a difference

Titus 1:10-26

Having mentioned (v.9) the elder's responsibility to refute the false teachings of "gainsayers" (KJV), or opposers, leads Paul into a discussion of their characteristics and how to deal with them. They are just the opposite of the just described elder; "unruly" (demonstrated by a rebelliousness against both God's Word and God's messengers); "vain talkers" (their talk is useless, accomplishing nothing); and are intentionally "deceptive." This was especially true of those "of the circumcision" (cp. Gal. 2:12ff), mistaken Jewish believers in the Cretan congregation who taught that adherence to circumcision and Jewish ceremonial laws were necessary for salvation.

The description continues: they had an inordinate interest in money (v.11), and held to unscriptural "Jewish fables" (legalism), and "commandments of men" (traditionalism) (v.14). They were ascetics (practicing extreme self-denial for supposed spiritual value), labeling certain foods and practices as defiled, even that which God considered good (vv. 14-15; cp. I Tim.4:3-5, Acts 10:15). They did not understand that the blood of Christ sounded the death knell of legalism.

To effectively describe Cretan character Paul quotes a 6th century Cretan poet – philosopher named Epimenides. His description is unbelievably harsh (v. 12), but accurate (v.13). "To Cretanize" in Greek literature meant "to lie and cheat." To deal with such erroneous teaching Paul told Titus to do the following: (1) "Stop their mouths" – silence them, for in failing to do so, "whole (church) houses" would be subverted, or upset (v. 11), (2) "Rebuke them sharply." Rebuke – here it means to convict, convince, point out. The goal: "that they may be sound in the faith" (v.13). Correction and restoration are to be Titus' goals.

LifeStep
Never compromise the truth. False doctrine (unhealthy teaching) will lead to sickness in the Body of Christ. The emphasis must always be on "sound doctrine" (v. 9) and "sound faith" (v. 13).

Titus 2:1-10

Paul now moves to positive exhortation. Certainly error must be dealt with, but there must be balance: truth must be taught and exhortations given. Unless they are, negativity will permeate a ministry. So Paul instructs Titus to "speak thou the things which become sound (healthy) doctrine (v. 1)" – a phrase familiar in all 3 pastorals. Out of such teaching good works, such as faith, love and patience (v. 20) are produced. He then addresses 3 categories of church members:

The Aged Saints (or at least older, more mature) vv. 1-3. First the men, then the women. The point behind the instruction: both are to serve as spiritual examples to all. While the virtues noted should be possessed by all believers, they should to an eminent degree be manifested by those of advancing years. And to older women a very pointed assignment: pass on their insight as wives and mothers to the next generation of women. If those lessons are not taught and practiced, God's Word will be blasphemed.

The Younger Saints (vv. 4-8). They were to listen to the older saints, and pursue the character qualities that were to be already present in their parent's generation. As for Titus (vv.7-8), he is to set the pattern. One's action often speak louder than one's words, but both ("good works" – v.7, "sound speech" – v.8) are necessary.

Servants/Slaves (vv. 9-10) Upwards of 25% of the Roman Empire were slaves. Those who were believers, as with all other categories of believers, were to voluntarily submit to their masters in such a way that they beautified ("adorn the doctrine of God") their beliefs by their behavior. Paul's advice to slaves and masters, which he amplifies in other passages (see Eph. 6:5-9; Col. 3:22-4:1; I Tim. 6:1-2), would be good advice to employees and employers today.

LifeStep

There's a saying that matches today's passage: "Your talk talks, and your walk talks; but your walk talks louder than your talk talks." Read it again, and be sure to practice it. A consistent life gains a responsive audience.

Titus 2:11-3:3

In vv. 11-14 we have the first of two major doctrinal portions in the book. The second will follow a chapter later (3:4-7). These verses provide a perfect balance of doctrine with Christian living. They follow Paul's instruction (v.10) to "adorn the doctrine of God" with a lifestyle that pictures a transformed life. This passage begins with the incarnation ("the grace of God hath appeared," v.11), and then relates that doctrine to a life that: (a) negatively, denies "ungodliness and worldly lusts," and (b) positively, lives "soberly, righteously and godly" in the here and now: "this present age (v. 12). It continues by seeing in the return of Christ the incentive for Christ-honoring conduct (looking for that blessed hope…" v.13), and that ultimately expresses itself in personal holiness, i.e., purified "unto himself (Christ)…zealous of good works" (v.14). This passage, much like Eph. 2:8-10 teaches us that God's purpose in redeeming us is not only to save us from hell; He also wants to free us so that we can produce good works that glorify Him. Certainly these two appearances of the grace of God, the first of which (the incarnation) provided redemption, and the second of which (Christ's return) will result in rewards, should provide much motivation for <u>consistent</u> <u>Christian</u> <u>living</u> (a key theme in this book).

In the early verses of chapter 3 Paul addresses the Christian's obligation to earthly government (subjection to their authority), not a particularly positive trait among the Cretans (remember the description of them 1:12), so Paul reminds them to be good citizens ("ready to every good work," v.1). In doing so they would reflect positively on the power of the Gospel and bring glory to God. An additional motive for good works would be to remember that but for the grace of God (v.1:11) they would still be lost in their sins, no different than the pagans they lived with (v.3).

LifeStep

<u>Look back</u>: Christ came with redemption in mind; <u>Look ahead</u>: He will return with rewards in hand. <u>Look within</u>: Does your life demonstrate gratefulness for those two appearances of the grace of God?

Titus 3:4-15

This section begins with "But" --- a contrast is drawn between that which has gone before (v. 3 – a description of man's degenerative nature), <u>the worst</u> – versus – <u>the best</u>: God's "kindness and love" (v. 4). Here (vv. 4-7) we have the book's second major doctrinal portion. Paul writes that salvation is God's work, not the result of our own righteousness or works (v. 5), though good works result. The two agents of our new birth ("regeneration") are (1) <u>The Word of God</u> – pictured by "water for washing" – see John 15:3, Ps. 119:9; Eph. 5:26, and (2) <u>The Spirit of God</u> – John 3:5; I Pet. 1:23; James 1;18). The latter has been "shed" (poured out) upon on believers from Pentecost (Acts 2) on, and the Mediator of this wonderful outpouring is "Jesus Christ our Savior" (v.6).

Paul then moves from the overall doctrine of salvation to two of its aspects. The first is <u>justification</u> (God's declaration that the believer has been vindicated in His sight by the crosswork of Christ–cp. Rom. 3:24-25; 5:9), hence all charges have been dropped (Rom. 8:1,31-34). The second is <u>adoption</u>. Once justified, adoption takes place (Gal. 4:5) and the believers' lives are "hidden with Christ in God" (Col. 3:3), and they become heirs "according to the hope ("utmost confidence") of eternal life (v.7).
Verse 8 is transitional, with the "faithful saying" referring to the doctrinal statement of vv. 4-7. Titus is to keep on affirming "these things." Doing so is to result in continued "good works." Vv. 9-11 admonishes Titus to avoid anything that would cause unacceptable behavior in the assembly, and to cut off ("reject," v.10) divisive people after two warnings (cp. II Thess. 3; 14-15). In the remaining verses (12-15) greetings are given, and a challenge to "maintain good works." As in his other letters Paul closes with his favorite benediction: Grace be with you all.

LifeStep

The book's theme, Consistent Christian Living, carries the thought that when one places his faith in Christ, transformational results should be clearly observable. Stop and think now: How fervently can that be said about you? And if your answer is weak, make plans to correct it.

41